TEXTS AND STUDIES

CONTRIBUTIONS TO

BIBLICAL AND PATRISTIC LITERATURE

EDITED BY

J. ARMITAGE ROBINSON D.D.

HON. FELLOW OF CHRIST'S COLLEGE
DEAN OF WELLS

VOL. VIII.

No. 4.   THE SO-CALLED EGYPTIAN CHURCH
ORDER AND DERIVED DOCUMENTS

THE SO-CALLED
EGYPTIAN CHURCH ORDER
AND
DERIVED DOCUMENTS

BY

DOM R. HUGH CONNOLLY M.A.

Wipf & Stock
PUBLISHERS
Eugene, Oregon

Wipf and Stock Publishers
199 W 8th Ave, Suite 3
Eugene, OR 97401

The So-Called Egyptian Church Order and Derived Documents
By Connolly, R. Hugh
ISBN: 1-59244-901-8
Publication date 9/29/2004
Previously published by Cambridge, 1916

R · R · VIRO
HVGONI · EDMVNDO · FORD
ABBATI
GRATO · ANIMO

PREFACE

THE documents which come under consideration in this volume are, as its title may suggest, that closely related family of Church Orders in which the eighth book of the *Apostolic Constitutions* and the *Canons of Hippolytus* are the most conspicuous members. Although these documents, five in number, have now for some time past attracted widespread attention, yet but little agreement has been arrived at in regard to the question of their relative antiquity and the manner of their interconnexion. A fresh discussion of the problems involved calls therefore for no apology.

Since the publication, in 1891, of H. Achelis's *Canones Hippolyti* it is the *Canons of Hippolytus* that have stood in the foreground; and they have been widely accepted, especially in this country and in France, as the most ancient of these Church Orders, and indeed as the source from which all the others have been derived. But the late Dr F. X. Funk of Tübingen maintained that the earliest of the documents, and the source of the rest, was the eighth book of the *Apostolic Constitutions*; and his view still enjoys a considerable measure of acceptance in Germany. The present discussion deals afresh with the question of the relations of the whole group of documents. The main results arrived at are, (1) that neither the *Canons of Hippolytus* nor the *Apostolic Constitutions* bk. viii can be accorded the place of honour; (2) that the *Canons of Hippolytus* in particular are one of the latest members of the group; (3) that the so-called *Egyptian Church Order*, which has persistently been thrust into a subordinate position, is not merely the earliest of all, and the main source of each and all of the other Orders, but is in reality the work of Hippolytus, and dates accordingly from the early decades of the third century. The interest and importance of this last conclusion, if it be accepted (and I venture to believe that it will be), hardly needs to be emphasized.

I am now reassured to find that these conclusions are not wholly new. It was only after my own results had been finally drawn out, and after this essay had been submitted to the Editor of *Texts and Studies* (in the summer of 1915), that I read Professor E. Schwartz's tract *Ueber die pseudoapostolischen Kirchenordnungen*, published in 1910[1]. On reading it, I found that on all essential points my results coincided with those of Professor Schwartz. I have since inserted, in text or notes, the proper references to his tract. I may here add a word in explanation of the wholly different conception and scope of his work and mine. His tract is one of forty quarto pages; and much of it is devoted to matters which bear only indirectly on the subject of this essay. Only in the last fifteen pages, or thereabouts, and only on two points—vital points, however—does he enter in any formal way into the question of the relations subsisting between the different members of this group of documents; and even here his statement of the evidence is as condensed and summary as possible. His judgments upon other important but debated points are thrown out rather as *obiter dicta*, here and there, in the course of other discussions. I cannot regret that my own study of these documents was carried on independently and in ignorance of Schwartz's conclusions. Had I known of them, I might have been tempted to deal more summarily with several questions in regard to which, I now feel, it will be less unsatisfactory to have laboured the proof unnecessarily than to have set aside the opinions of others without stating the evidence sufficiently.

[1] In 'Schriften der wissenschaftlichen Gesellschaft in Strassburg,' no. 6.

There remains the agreeable task of thanking all those who have helped me, in different ways, with the writing and printing of this book. And my first acknowledgment must be to the Rev. George Horner. It is through Mr Horner's kindness that I have been able to make such free use of his translations in the *Statutes of the Apostles*, and especially of those from the Ethiopic texts which he has first made accessible. My indebtedness to this invaluable book will appear on almost every page. I can only hope that the use I have made of it may tend to emphasize its importance, or rather its indispensable character, for the study of these Church Orders. Mr Horner has also most kindly given me his permission, and obtained for me the permission of the publishers, to print in an Appendix a large part of his translation from the Ethiopic of the 'Egyptian Church Order'; and it is thus that I am enabled to carry out a suggestion of the Editor and give a continuous text of that document, by supplementing the fragments of the old Latin from the Ethiopic version.

To the Editor my very sincere thanks are due for much kind encouragement and good counsel. His watchful care and sure judgment have redeemed the book from many deformities; and throughout he has given me help of which I can here make but an inadequate, though a very grateful, acknowledgment. From my friend Mr Edmund Bishop, whose part it has ever been to inspire and help others at the sacrifice of himself, I have received here, as elsewhere, unfailing guidance and succour in my necessities. My present debt to him goes to swell a now long-standing account.

Despite the present adverse conditions, the University Press has executed the printing of the volume with a despatch and unimpaired efficiency for which I cannot be too grateful.

R. H. C.

DOWNSIDE ABBEY,
NEAR BATH.
Easter, 1916.

CONTENTS

	PAGE
INTRODUCTORY (ON THE DOCUMENTS)	1
(a) The 'Canons of Hippolytus'.	2
(b), (c) The 'Egyptian Church Order' (in Ethiopic, Coptic and Arabic)	2
(d) The 'Egyptian Church Order' (Verona Latin fragments) .	2
(e) The 'Testament of our Lord'	6
(f) The 'Constitutiones per Hippolytum,' or 'Epitome' of the 'Apostolic Constitutions' bk. viii	6
The 'Apostolic Constitutions' bk. viii.	8

CHAPTER I. THE BISHOP'S ORDINATION PRAYER 11

i. Ep. in relation to Eg. C. O. 21
    Notes on Mr Horner's text and variants . . . 22

ii. A. C. in relation to Eg. C. O. 26
    Funk's view 28
    The 'Lost Church Order' 33

iii. The relation of Test. to the other documents . . . 35

iv. The relation of Ep. to A. C. viii 37
    The hypothesis of Achelis 39
    The hypothesis of a 'first draft' 41
    The section on the Reader 46
    The Ordination Prayer for a Presbyter 50
    Summary of conclusions 53

		PAGE
CHAPTER II. EG. C. O. IN RELATION TO C. H.	. . . .	55
A. Schoolmasters	. .	63
B. Extempore prayer by the Bishop .	. . . .	64
C. A warning against instability	. . . . .	66
D. Fasting Communion, and the Easter Fast .	. . .	67
E. Care of the Holy Eucharist in communicating	. . .	77
F. Communion of the newly baptized	. . . .	83
G. Instruction. Hours of Prayer. Sign of the Cross	. .	94
H. Service of the Evening Lamp	. . . . .	111
J. Burial of the Dead (κέραμοι) .	. . . .	116
K. Prayer over Firstfruits .	. . . . . .	119
L. C. H. canon xxx .	. . . .	121
M. Baptismal features in C. H. .	. . . . .	129
N. Terminology, etc., in C. H. .	. . . . .	130
i. Eucharistic terminology .	. . . .	130
ii. Parts of the church .	. . . .	131
iii. Vestments .	. . . . . .	132
iv. Excommunication	. . . . .	132
Conclusions	. . . .	132
CHAPTER III. HIPPOLYTUS AND THE CHURCH ORDERS	. . .	135
Conclusions	. . . .	147
ADDITIONAL NOTES		
I. Some Ep. readings in the Bishop's Ordination Prayer	.	150
II. Two suggested interpolations in Eg. C. O. .	. .	155
III. C. H. and Pseudo-Athanasius *de Virginitate*	. .	156
IV. The custom of giving *Apophoreta*	. . .	158
V. Some parallels to Eg. C. O. from Hippolytus	. .	160
VI. Supplementary note on the *Testament of our Lord* .	.	169
APPENDIX A. COMPARATIVE TABLES OF A. C. VIII AND EP.	. .	170
APPENDIX B. A TEXT OF EG. C. O. .	. . . .	174
INDEX	. .	195

THE CHIEF MODERN WORKS QUOTED[1]

ACHELIS, H.; *Die Canones Hippolyti* (Texte und Untersuchungen VI: Leipzig, 1891).

ACHELIS, H.; *Hippolytus*, i, 2 (the ed. of H.'s works in the Royal Prussian Academy series 'Die griechischen christlichen Schriftsteller der ersten drei Jahrhunderte': Leipzig, 1897).

BARDENHEWER, O.; *Patrology* (English transl., from the 2nd German ed., by T. J. Shahan: Herder, 1908).

BARDENHEWER, O.; *Geschichte der altkirchlichen Literatur* (Freiburg im Breisgau, 1903).

BONWETSCH, G. N.; *Hippolytus*, i, 1 (see 'Achelis').

BONWETSCH, G. N.; *Drei Georgisch erhaltene Schriften von Hippolytus* (Der Segen Jacobs, Der Segen Moses, Die Erzählung von David und Goliath) (Texte und Untersuchungen, N. F. XI, 1 a: Leipzig, 1904).

BRIGHTMAN, F. E.; *Liturgies Eastern and Western* (Oxford, 1896).

COOPER, J., and MACLEAN, A. J.; *The Testament of our Lord translated into English with Introduction and Notes* (Edinburgh, T. & T. Clark, 1902).

FRERE, W. H.; 'Early Ordination Services,' in *The Journal of Theological Studies*, XVI 323 ff. (April, 1915).

FUNK, F. X.; *Die apostolischen Konstitutionen* (Rottenburg am Neckar, 1891).

FUNK, F. X.; *Das Testament unseres Herrn und die verwandten Schriften* (Mainz, 1901).

FUNK, F. X.; *Didascalia et Constitutiones Apostolorum* (Paderbornae, 1905).

[1] This list is not meant to be a bibliography; it merely supplies fuller titles of works sometimes quoted compendiously, or even by the formula '*op. cit.*'

HANEBERG, D. B.; *Canones S. Hippolyti* (Monachii, 1870).

HARNACK, A.; *Die Chronologie der altchristlichen Litteratur bis Eusebius*, ii (Leipzig, 1904).

HAULER, E.; *Didascaliae apostolorum fragmenta ueronensia latina; accedunt Canonum qui dicuntur Apostolorum et Aegyptiorum reliquiae* (Lipsiae, 1900).

HORNER, G.; *The Statutes of the Apostles, or Canones Ecclesiastici* (London, Williams and Norgate, 1904).

LUDOLF, I.; *Iobi Ludolfi (alias Leutholf dicti) ad suam Historiam Æthiopicam Commentarius* (Francofurti ad Moenum, 1691).

MACLEAN, A. J.; *The Ancient Church Orders* (Cambridge, 1910).

RAHMANI, I. E.; *Testamentum Domini nostri Iesu Christi* (Moguntiae, 1899).

RIEDEL, W.; *Die Kirchenrechtsquellen des Patriarchats Alexandrien* (Leipzig, 1900).

SCHWARTZ, E.; *Ueber die pseudoapostolischen Kirchenordnungen* (in 'Schriften der wissenschaftlichen Gesellschaft in Strassburg': Strassburg, 1910).

SCHWARTZ, E.; Review of Th. Schermann's *Weiherituale der römischen Kirche am Schlusse des ersten Jahrhunderts*, in *Oriens Christianus* (neue Serie, vierter Band, ii Heft, 347–354: 1915).

TURNER, C. H.; 'A primitive edition of the Apostolic Constitutions,' in *The Journal of Theological Studies* XIV 53 ff. (Oct., 1913).

TURNER, C. H.; 'The ordination prayer for a presbyter in the Church Order of Hippolytus,' *ibid.* XVI 542 ff. (July, 1915).

WORDSWORTH, J.; *The Ministry of Grace* (London, Longmans, Green and Co., 1901).

INTRODUCTORY

THE late Dr John Wordsworth, Bishop of Salisbury, in his well-known book *The Ministry of Grace*[1], devotes a section to a document which he designates 'The lost Church Order.' Of this 'lost' work he writes (p. 18):

'Next to the "Didaché" we must place a lost book of which we infer the existence from the common matter contained in a number of others, the earliest of which is the "Roman Church Order"... and the latest the "Testament of our Lord."'

On p. 21 ff. the Bishop describes 'the different existing Church Orders based on the lost book.' As it is with these existing Orders that the present study is to be concerned, and as it is necessary at the outset to specify them and give at least a general account of them, I venture for convenience to take Dr Wordsworth's description as a basis, or rather starting point, of my own remarks. But while for the occasion I follow his general arrangement and classification of the documents, I do not commit myself here in advance to any particular view as to the relation of the documents one to another; since to determine, if possible, this relation is precisely the object of the present study[2]. The documents, then, of which the Bishop speaks are the following:

[1] Messrs Longmans, Green, and Co., 1901.

[2] As regards titles for the various documents to be dealt with, there is in the case of some of them a somewhat confusing variety of names more or less current. I adopt those most likely to be readily understood in this country, explaining my reasons where I depart from this rule, and generally endeavouring to make it clear what is the actual composition about which I am speaking. In case some readers may miss allusions to such familiar titles as *The Syrian Octateuch* and *The Egyptian Heptateuch*, it may be as well to explain that as the works so denoted are mere collections containing, amongst other pieces, some of the documents here treated of, and later than any of them, they do not fall within the scope of the present essay and will not hereafter be mentioned in it.

(a) The 'Roman Church Order.' This is the name given by Dr Wordsworth to the document generally known as the 'Canons of Hippolytus.' The latter designation is based on the title which the work bears in the Arabic version in which it has been published[1], viz. *Canones ecclesiae cum praeceptis quae scripsit Hippolytus summus episcopus Romae, secundum mandata apostolorum*, etc.

(b) and (c) The 'Egyptian Church Order.' This exists in two forms: (b) that preserved in an Ethiopic translation, and sometimes called in this country the 'Ethiopic Church Order'[2]; and (c) that form of the document which is extant in Coptic and Arabic translations. The main difference between (b) and (c) is that the latter omits certain prayers contained in the former, notably the text of the eucharistic anaphora and the prayers for ordination of a bishop, a presbyter and a deacon. All three versions have now been published in a single volume and translated into English by the Rev. G. Horner[3].

(d) The 'Verona Latin Fragments.'[4] Amongst other matter these fragments contain in an ancient Latin version considerable portions of the same document as that mentioned under (b) and (c) above. And it follows, that if the name 'Egyptian Church Order' has anything to commend it as a description of the Ethiopic, Coptic and Arabic versions, it must be allowed to be

[1] *Canones S. Hippolyti*...edidit D. B. Haneberg; Monachii, 1870. The general character of this document will appear from what follows. A German translation, from earlier and better (Arabic) MSS, is given by Wilhelm Riedel in *Die Kirchenrechtsquellen des Patriarchats Alexandrien* (Leipzig, 1900), pp. 200–230.

[2] Portions of this were first edited in Ethiopic with a Latin translation by Job Ludolf: *Iobi Ludolfi ad suam Historiam Æthiopicam Commentarius* (Frankfort, 1691), pp. 323–328.

[3] *The Statutes of the Apostles*: London, 1904. The Coptic text edited by Mr Horner is that in the Sahidic dialect. The text translated by H. Tattam in 1848 (in *The Apostolical Constitutions or Canons of the Apostles in Coptic*) is in the Bohairic dialect. This Bohairic version was made from the Sahidic so late as the nineteenth century; Mr Horner says of it: 'but so recent and therefore corrupt is the text, that many inaccuracies occur, and often where the version appears to differ from the Sahidic no such variation really exists' (*op. cit.* Introd. p. ix). In the following pages therefore whenever the 'Coptic' is mentioned the reference will be to the Sahidic, unless otherwise stated.

[4] Edited by E. Hauler in *Didascaliae apostolorum fragmenta veronensia latina*: Leipzig, 1900.

applicable to the Latin version also. It is to be remembered, however, that the name 'Egyptian Church Order' is no real title of the document which it denotes, but only one amongst other modern makeshifts for a title; it was invented and bestowed upon the document by Achelis, as he says, 'merely to give it a name, which so far it lacks.'¹ Had it not been for the circumstance that the document first became known to the modern world in Ethiopic and Coptic translations, it is questionable whether it would have occurred to anyone to describe it as specifically 'Egyptian.' The original language of the work, as also of the 'Canons of Hippolytus,' was Greek; and now that we have parts of it in a Latin version as well there is the less reason for making Egypt the place of its origin on the mere ground that it was translated into Coptic and Ethiopic.

As it has reached us the 'Egyptian Church Order' has no title of its own. It forms part of a collection, in which it has been incorporated with other documents, of independent origin, which purport to be directly apostolic; and—a point to be noted—it does not occupy the first place in the collection. In all four versions—Ethiopic, Coptic, Arabic, Latin—it stands immediately after that curious little work known variously as the 'Ecclesiastical Canons' and the 'Apostolic Church Order,' in which each enactment is ascribed explicitly to one of the apostles with the formula 'John said,' 'Matthew said,' etc. Now the 'Egyptian Church Order' itself makes no pretence throughout its text of having been composed by the apostles, or even of containing any definite enactments of theirs²; and thus it is reasonable to suppose that its title, when it had one, did not make this claim either; and we should beware of concluding it to be a pseudo-apostolic composition from the mere fact that it is bound up with other documents which have that character. I shall continue to refer to it as the 'Egyptian Church Order' simply for want of a better current name, and without for the present expressing any opinion as to its place of origin.

As the lack of a separate title to this document in the collections in which it is embodied is apt not only to obscure

---
¹ *Die Canones Hippolyti*, p. 26.
² On this point see further p. 23 and p. 146 ff.

its distinctive and independent character but even to make it difficult to locate in the printed editions, I add here an indication of its whereabouts in the editions of Horner and Hauler.

The Ethiopic version: Horner, p. 138, l. 11—p. 162, l. 19, and p. 178, l. 22—p. 186, l. 8. The intermediate pages contain a collection of prayers and prescriptions for baptism which do not belong to the 'Egyptian Church Order' but have somehow got inserted into the Ethiopic text. They are not found in the Coptic, Arabic, or Latin.

The Arabic version: Horner, p. 244, l. 26—p. 266, l. 11.

The Coptic (Sahidic) version: Horner, p. 306, l. 17—p. 332, l. 8.

The Latin version: Hauler, p. 101, l. 31 ('Ea quidem,' et seqq.), to the end of the Fragments (p. 121).

The introductory passage with which the Latin opens (Hauler, p. 101), and which evidently belongs to the beginning of the document, has in the Ethiopic been thrust into the middle (Horner, p. 162, l. 1–19), just before the interpolated passages on baptism[1]. In the Coptic and Arabic the passage has been omitted altogether.

Although as they stand (*b*), (*c*) and (*d*) present considerable textual divergences, these are not to be thought of as the outcome of any deliberate process of redaction, but (apart from certain omissions by (*c*), noted above) are due in the main to circumstances of transmission—copying, translation, minor editorial retouching, and the like. The four versions give us what is essentially one and the same document; and to treat the Ethiopic, Coptic and Latin versions as in any sense separate and independent redactions of some earlier form of the document is to introduce an unnecessary element of confusion into a problem already sufficiently complex[2].

The Latin supports the Ethiopic against the Coptic and Arabic in containing the eucharistic and ordination prayers. From this

---

[1] A passage answering to this introduction, or preface, is found in the 'Apostolic Constitutions' (of which below) bk. viii, chap. 3; and its position there supports the evidence of the Latin version of the 'Egyptian Church Order.'

[2] Dr A. J. Maclean, Bishop of Moray, in his book *The Ancient Church Orders* (Cambridge, 1910), appears to make each of these three versions—just in the same way as documents like the 'Canons of Hippolytus' and the 'Testament of our Lord'—rest separately on a 'Lost Church Order' (see, for example, p. 144 ff.). The effects of this are at times a little puzzling.

INTRODUCTORY 5

and other evidence it is seen that the Ethiopic, though possibly
only a translation of an Arabic translation of a Coptic translation of the original Greek, yet rests ultimately upon a Greek
text other than that represented by the Coptic and Arabic
versions which have come down to us[1]. As a textual witness,
therefore, the Ethiopic is of independent value; indeed the
indications go to shew that it represents an earlier and better
(Greek) textual tradition than do our present Coptic and Arabic
translations, better even, in some respects, than does the Latin.
As Mr Brightman says, the Ethiopic is 'not derived from
the present form of the sahidic, but lies nearer to the form
which must have been the common source of the ethiopic, the
sahidic and *A.C.* viii,'[2] and—we may now add—of the Latin
version also and of the 'Testament of our Lord' (see p. 6). The
chief drawback in the case of the Ethiopic is the difficulty of being
sure, after a process of perhaps three successive translations, how
far any modern version of it (such as Mr Horner's English one)
may represent the meaning and form of the Greek text from which
the process started. If we might judge by the Latin and Coptic
versions, which doubtless were made directly from Greek texts, it
would appear that the Ethiopic, where reproducing the same
matter, more often differs from the other texts merely by giving
a blurred and confused version of the original *sense* than by
suggesting any substantial *variant* in the underlying Greek. In
other words, the Ethiopic, while representing a good textual
tradition, suffers much from obscurity contracted, largely, in the
course of successive translations. In any attempt to recover the
exact meaning of the original Greek the Latin, which has the
appearance of being a very literal version, may be regarded

---

[1] I am here assuming for the moment that the omissions in the Coptic and
Arabic go back to a Greek text or texts; but of course it may be that the omissions
took place during, or after, the process of translation from Greek into Coptic.
There is, however, sufficient evidence for the independence of the Ethiopic version
even apart from the question of the ordination and other prayers. The Arabic was
probably translated from Coptic.

[2] *Liturgies Eastern and Western*, vol. I p. xxii. The Ethiopic preserves several
considerable passages not found in any of the other versions, yet proved to be
genuine, or at least early, by their occurrence, in various forms, in others of the
documents we are dealing with (see below, p. 36, note 1).

generally as the most useful help, provided that the Ethiopic be in substantial agreement. A special virtue of the Coptic is that it often uses Greek words, many of which are no doubt preserved from the original.

When this 'Egyptian Church Order' is compared with the 'Canons of Hippolytus,'[1] it is found that the divergence here cannot be explained as the result of any normal process of 'textual transmission.' Though the two documents have the bulk of their subject-matter in common, yet the difference in treatment, presentation, arrangement, is such that it must be due ultimately to real and deliberate re-editing, or redaction. Thus, in regard to the relation of these two documents to each other there are two main possibilities: (1) one may be immediately or remotely (through one or more intervening redactions) based on the other; or (2) the two may be descended collaterally from a common source.

(e) The 'Testament of our Lord.'[2] Though much of the material found in the two foregoing documents, (a) and (bcd), is embodied in this work also, yet the 'Testament' is something more than a mere redaction, or adaptation, of either of those other texts, or of their possible source. It is strongly marked by the individuality of its compiler, who used, indeed, matter which is found in the other two documents, but made it his own in such a way as to produce a distinct and rather more extensive treatise.

(f) The 'Constitutiones per Hippolytum.' 'This book,' says Dr Wordsworth (op. cit. p. 33), 'is usually considered to be the first draft of the central and latter part of the eighth book of the "Apostolic Constitutions," to which it answers from ch. 4 [of "A. C." viii] onwards, but without the Antiochene Liturgy in ch. 5–15 and the daily and other services in ch. 35–41.' The document, however, as I think will appear later on, is in reality merely an excerpt from the 'Apostolic Constitutions' bk. viii made by a later hand. I shall accordingly refer to it in the

---

[1] See (a) at p. 2 above.

[2] The 'Testament' has been published in a Syriac version, in which it is preserved, by Mgr Ignatius Ephraim Rahmani, Uniat Syrian Patriarch of Antioch (*Testamentum domini nostri Iesu Christi*: Mainz, 1899). An English translation is given in Cooper and Maclean's *Testament of our Lord* (T. and T. Clark, 1902).

following pages as the 'Epitome,' after Funk's designation 'Epitome Constitutionum Apostolorum VIII.' But in adopting the name 'Epitome' I must say in advance that it is an inexact description of the document in question. Though derived from the 'Apostolic Constitutions' bk. viii, it is so not by 'epitomization' in the ordinary sense of condensation and abbreviation, but by mere textual excerption of the charismatical matter of bk. viii (or that dealing with the ordination and functions of the various grades in the Christian ministry), with omission of matter pertaining to divine worship. Only in the prayers for ordination of a bishop and a presbyter and in the direction as to the appointment of a reader does the 'Epitome' contain what may conceivably be regarded as a *condensed form* of the corresponding 'Ap. Const.' text. These three passages will be considered in detail in the investigation which follows.

As regards the name 'Constitutiones per Hippolytum,' Dr Wordsworth says (p. 33) that it is 'perhaps due to its [the document's] association with the Hippolytean Περὶ χαρισμάτων ("A. C." viii 1–2).' But it is to be observed that the name in question is given to the *whole* document only by modern writers. In the Greek MSS the book is divided into five parts, of which the first (identical with 'Apost. Const.' viii 1–2) is entitled Διδασκαλία τῶν ἁγίων ἀποστόλων περὶ χαρισμάτων, and only the second Διατάξεις τῶν ἁγίων ἀποστόλων περὶ χειροτονιῶν διὰ Ἱππολύτου[1]. Thus the name of Hippolytus is not, in the work itself, brought into connexion with the 'Teaching' περὶ χαρισμάτων—which two Greek words formed the title (or part of the title) of a work known to have been composed by Hippolytus. The question how the name of Hippolytus came to be connected with the 'Epitome' at all, as also with the 'Canons of Hippolytus,' will be considered later (see p. 135 ff. below).

Had Dr Wordsworth taken the view that the 'Constitutiones per Hippolytum' are an 'epitome' of, or rather an excerpt from, the 'Apostolic Constitutions' bk. viii, he would doubtless have set down the latter instead of the former as his sixth document (*f*); but regarding 'Const. per H.' as a first draft of 'Apost. Const.,' he did not deem it necessary to enumerate the latter

[1] See Funk, *Didascalia et Constitutiones Apostolorum*, II p. xi.

among the works which he derived—immediately, it would seem—from the 'Lost Church Order.'

The 'Apostolic Constitutions' is such a well-known work that it hardly needs introduction. On the other hand, the views current regarding it are so divergent that it is difficult to speak about it at all without getting upon debated ground. This is true at least of bk. viii, with which alone we are to be concerned. It is, however, pretty generally recognized that the document was compiled in the latter half, and somewhere about the seventh decade, of the fourth century; also that the compiler was Pseudo-Ignatius, or the person who interpolated the seven genuine epistles of St Ignatius of Antioch and forged six others. Of this writer's fondness for working up earlier documents to the ecclesiastical standard of his own time we have ample illustration in the 'Apostolic Constitutions.' His first six books are based upon the third-century *Didascalia*, which he has freely altered by omissions, additions and readjustments to suit his own ideas and taste. In bk. vii the ancient *Didache* receives similar treatment; and there is some further matter in that book (vii) of which the source has not been identified. Funk's method of editing these documents makes clear at a glance what the redactor has taken over from the *Didascalia* and the *Didache* and what he has added of his own. With the writer's work (if it be in reality his) on the Ignatian epistles and with the first seven books of his 'Apostolic Constitutions' we are not concerned—unless it be to mark and remember the extraordinary record of literary forgery (or should we call it merely 'dramatic fiction'[1]?) which they present. The literary and historical connexion of the 'Apostolic Constitutions' with the cycle of documents represented by (*a*)—(*f*) above is confined to its eighth book; and hence it is bk. viii alone that will fall under discussion in the following pages.

If the documents (*b*), (*c*) and (*d*) are regarded (as they must be) merely as different textual witnesses to one and the same work, and in no sense independent redactions or recensions thereof, there remain five allied documents the relative priority of which

---

[1] So Dr A. J. Maclean, Bishop of Moray, *The Ancient Church Orders*, p. 5. Achelis, however, speaks of the compiler as 'the great Syrian forger' (*Die Canones Hippolyti*, p. 272), and 'the Syrian forger' (*ib.* p. 274).

and the precise lines of their interconnexion have formed the subject of widely different opinions. The five documents are, in the order in which Dr Wordsworth takes them:

The 'Canons of Hippolytus' = (*a*) above.
The 'Egyptian Church Order' = (*b*), (*c*), (*d*) above.
The 'Testament of our Lord' = (*e*) above.
The 'Constitutiones per Hippolytum,' or 'Epitome' of the 'Apost. Const.' bk. viii = (*f*) above.
The 'Apostolic Constitutions' bk. viii.

If for the moment we leave aside the 'Testament of our Lord,' which has only comparatively recently made its appearance, there are (or have been until quite lately) three leading views as to the interrelation of the remaining four documents.

Dr Hans Achelis makes the genesis of these documents to be as follows:

1. 'Canons of Hippolytus' (early 3rd century).
2. 'Egyptian Church Order.'
3. An earlier form of 'Apost. Const.' viii, from which 'Const. per Hipp.' is an excerpt[1].
4. 'Apostolic Constitutions' bk. viii, in its present form.

But Dr F. X. Funk steadily maintained that the order of derivation was precisely the reverse of this[2]. He placed the 'Apostolic Constitutions' bk. viii first and the 'Canons of Hippolytus' last in a direct line, thus:

1. 'Apostolic Constitutions' viii (beginning of fifth century).
2. 'Epitome' of 'A. C.' viii[3].   3. 'Egyptian Church Order.'
4. 'Canons of Hippolytus.'

[1] Achelis thought it necessary to postulate such an earlier form of 'A. C.' viii mainly in order to account for two passages in 'Const. per H.' (= 'Ep.') which agree with 'Egypt. C. O.' more closely than do the relative texts of 'A. C.' viii, viz. the ordination prayer for a bishop and the direction as to the institution of a reader. 'Const. per H.' is, then, according to him, an excerpt from 'A. C.' viii, though from an earlier form of that book than the one that has reached us. Thus on his view 'Const. per H.' is not itself a first edition, or first draft, of 'A. C.' viii, but only a portion of a lost first edition. On this see his *Die Canones Hippolyti*, pp. 3–4, 27, 242–3; and especially 271, where he says that the group of MSS containing 'Const. per H.' 'present an excerpt, but one from an older form of text of *Const. Apost.* viii.' His position on this matter is not always quite clearly stated.

[2] For a concise statement of Funk's views see his latest considerable work *Didasc. et Const. Apostolorum*, vol. II (1905), p. xiii.

[3] Funk thought that 'Ep.' formed a real step between 'A. C.' viii and

Funk's view has been accepted substantially by such authorities as Harnack[1] and Bardenhewer[2].

The third view which calls for notice is that of Dr John Wordsworth. He held, if I understand him rightly, that all and several of the above four documents, and likewise the 'Testament of our Lord,' were derived immediately from a lost document—the 'Lost Church Order.' This is, in the main, the view of Dr Maclean in his *Ancient Church Orders*[3] (see pp. 142-144); but he thinks it probable that some of the existing orders may not have been *directly* based on the lost original (pp. 146-7), and he shares Achelis's view that 'Const. per H.' (= 'Epitome') is an abbreviation of an earlier text of 'Apost. Const.' viii (*ib.* p. 154). Dr Wordsworth's hypothesis of a lost source for all our documents seems also to underlie an interesting article recently contributed to the *Journal of Theological Studies*[4] by Dr W. H. Frere.

The purpose of what now follows is to suggest a reconsideration of these opinions, with a view to determining whether any one of them can be accepted as it stands, or whether there may not be elements of truth and error in them all. The essay, however, has a limited scope. A comparative study of the whole contents of the various documents would call for an elaborate work of several hundreds of pages. This I am not prepared to undertake. My present plan is to take only certain passages and submit them to examination, in the hope that some clear indications will emerge as to the manner of interdependence of the documents as wholes.

'Eg. C. O.'; but he had to suppose that in certain places, where it lacks some matter common to 'A. C.' and 'Eg. C. O.,' it is defective: see *op. cit.* II p. xx: 'Epitome in duobus locis, ubi lacunam habet, e Constitutionibus apostolorum supplenda est.'

[1] *Chronologie* vol. II (1904), pp. 507, 512.

[2] *Patrology* (English trans. 1908), pp. 354-356. Cf. *Gesch. d. altkirch. Lit.* (1903) II 543.

[3] In the series of 'Cambridge Liturgical Handbooks,' 1910.

[4] Vol. XVI p. 323 ff. (April, 1915), under the title 'Early Ordination Services.' He says (p. 369): 'It is quite possible that (except in the case of mere versions) no one of the existing documents is derived directly from any other. A number of documents representing different stages and filiations must have disappeared.'

CHAPTER I

THE BISHOP'S ORDINATION PRAYER

THE first and chief of the passages which I select for examination is the prayer for the ordination, or consecration, of a bishop. This occurs in all the documents which embody, in some form, that 'common' matter which the late Bishop of Salisbury traced to a 'Lost Church Order.' In referring to these documents I shall henceforth employ the following abbreviations:

C. H. = 'Canons of Hippolytus.'
Eg. C. O. = 'Egyptian Church Order.'
A. C. = 'Apostolic Constitutions.'
Ep. = 'Epitome,' otherwise 'Constitutiones per Hippolytum.'
Test. = 'Testament of our Lord.'

I begin by giving a synopsis of the bishop's ordination prayer in six columns, in such a way as to shew at a glance what is and what is not contained in each of the texts. As already stated, the Coptic and Arabic versions of Eg. C. O. have not the ordination prayers, which therefore are represented only by the Ethiopic and Latin versions. For the Ethiopic I use Mr Horner's translation (*Statutes of the Apostles*, p. 138). It needs to be pointed out, however, that in his text Mr Horner prints a late, because a complete, manuscript, which requires to be controlled by some earlier and better copies, the readings of which are recorded in the Collations at the end of his book[1]. The chief points in this prayer at which the text calls for correction are indicated at pp. 22 ff. below. For the Latin I use, of course, Hauler's edition (p. 103); for C. H., the revision of Haneberg's Latin translation made for

[*Continued on p.* 20.

---

[1] See his Introduction, pp. xxxvi-xxxvii. The ms actually printed is called a.; the earliest and best mss are b., e., and v. (the ms used by Ludolf).

THE SO-CALLED EGYPTIAN CHURCH ORDER

	Eg. C. O. (Eth.)	Eg. C. O. (Lat.)	C. H.
(1)			
(2)			
(3)	See (11) below	See (11) below	See (11) below
(4)			
(5)	God, the Father of our Lord Jesus Christ,	Deus et pater domini nostri Iesu Christi,	O Deus, pater domini nostri Iesu Christi,
(6)			
(7)	Father of mercies and God of comforts,	pater misericordiarum et Deus totius consolationis,	pater misericordiarum et Deus totius consolationis,
(8)	who dwelt with the lofty	qui in excelsis habitas	qui habitat in altis
(9)			
(10)	and (yet) sees the humble,	et humilia respicis,	et humilia respicit,
(11)	and who knew all before it came to pass:	qui cognoscis omnia, antequam nascantur,	qui novit omnia, antequam fiant;
(12)			
(13)	thou gavest an ordinance to the church,	tu, qui dedisti terminos in ecclesia	tu, qui constituisti fines ecclesiae,
(14)	by the word of thy grace;	per verbum gratiae tuae,	
(15)			

THE BISHOP'S ORDINATION PRAYER 13

Ep.	A. C.	Test.
	Ὁ ὤν, δέσποτα κύριε ὁ θεὸς ὁ παντοκράτωρ, ὁ μόνος ἀγέννητος καὶ ἀβασίλευτος, ὁ ἀεὶ ὢν καὶ πρὸ τῶν αἰώνων ὑπάρχων, ὁ πάντη ἀνενδεὴς καὶ πάσης αἰτίας καὶ γενέσεως κρείττων, ὁ μόνος ἀληθινός, ὁ μόνος σοφός, ὁ ὢν μόνος ὕψιστος, ὁ τῇ φύσει ἀόρατος, οὗ ἡ γνῶσις ἄναρχος, ὁ μόνος ἀγαθὸς καὶ ἀσύγκριτος,	O God, who hast done all things in power, and hast established them, and hast founded the inhabited world in reason, and hast adorned the crown of all things which were made by thee; who hast given to them to keep thy commandments in fear; who hast bestowed upon us the understanding of the truth, and hast made known unto us that good Spirit of thine; who didst send thy beloved Son, the only Saviour, without spot, for our salvation;
See (11) below	ὁ τὰ πάντα εἰδὼς πρὶν γενέσεως αὐτῶν, ὁ τῶν κρυπτῶν γνώστης, ὁ ἀπρόσιτος, ὁ ἀδέσποτος·	See (11) below
Ὁ θεὸς καὶ πατὴρ τοῦ κυρίου ἡμῶν Ἰησοῦ Χριστοῦ,	ὁ θεὸς καὶ πατὴρ τοῦ μονογενοῦς υἱοῦ σου τοῦ θεοῦ καὶ σωτῆρος ἡμῶν, ὁ δημιουργὸς τῶν ὅλων δι' αὐτοῦ, ὁ προνοητής, ὁ κηδεμών,	O God and Father of our Lord Jesus Christ,
ὁ πατὴρ τῶν οἰκτιρμῶν καὶ θεὸς πάσης παρακλήσεως, ὁ ἐν ὑψηλοῖς κατοικῶν	ὁ πατὴρ τῶν οἰκτιρμῶν καὶ θεὸς πάσης παρακλήσεως, ὁ ἐν ὑψηλοῖς κατοικῶν	Father of mercies and God of all comfort, who in the pure heights dost dwell eternally, who art high and adorable, dreadful and great;
καὶ τὰ ταπεινὰ ἐφορῶν,	καὶ τὰ ταπεινὰ ἐφορῶν·	who seest all things,
ὁ γινώσκων τὰ πάντα πρὶν γενέσεως αὐτῶν·	See (3) above	who knowest all things before they are, with whom all things were before they were [made];
σὺ ὁ δοὺς ὅρους ἐκκλησίας	σὺ ὁ δοὺς ὅρους ἐκκλησίας	who gavest illumination to the church
διὰ λόγου χάριτός σου,	διὰ τῆς ἐνσάρκου παρουσίας τοῦ Χριστοῦ σου ὑπὸ μάρτυρι τῷ παρακλήτῳ διὰ τῶν σῶν ἀποστόλων καὶ ἡμῶν τῶν χάριτι σῇ παρεστώτων ἐπισκόπων,	by the grace of thy only-begotten Son,

	Eg. C. O. (Eth.)	Eg. C. O. (Lat.)	C. H.
(16)	thou who foreordainedst	praedestinans	cuius imperio fit
(17)	originally	ex principio	ut ex Adamo perseveret
(18)	a family of righteous men;	genus iustorum	genus iustum
(19)			
(20)			
(21)	from Abraham	(? ab) Abraham,	ratione huius episcopi, qui est magnus Abraham[1];
(22)			
(23)			
(24)	thou ordainedst judges and priests;	principes et sacerdotes constituens	qui praelaturas et principatus constituit;
(25)			
(26)			
(27)	and thou didst not leave thy sanctuary without ministers;	et sanctum tuum sine ministerio non derelinquens,	
(28)	and ever since the creation of the world	ex initio saeculi	
(29)			
(30)	thou hast desired to be glorified in the (place) which thou chosest.	bene tibi placuit in his, quos elegisti, *praedicari*[2]:	
(31)			
(32)	*Cf.* (51) *below*	*Cf.* (51) *below*	respice super N., servum tuum,

[1] Riedel (p. 201), with a better sense, 'through that Bishop who is the Mighty One of Abraham.'

[2] Probably read '⟨laud⟩ari.'

THE BISHOP'S ORDINATION PRAYER 15

Ep.	A. C.	Test.
ὁ προορίσας τε	ὁ προορίσας	having foreordained
ἀπ' ἀρχῆς	ἐξ ἀρχῆς	from the beginning
γένος δίκαιον		those who delight in just things, and do those things that are holy, to dwell in thy habitations;
	ἱερεῖς εἰς ἐπιστασίαν λαοῦ σου, Ἄβελ ἐν πρώτοις, Σὴθ καὶ Ἐνὼς καὶ Ἐνὼχ καὶ Νῶε καὶ Μελχισεδὲκ καὶ Ἰώβ·	
ἐξ Ἀβραάμ,	ὁ ἀναδείξας Ἀβραὰμ	who didst choose Abraham, who pleased thee by his faith [cf. Heb. xi 8], and didst translate holy Enoch [cf. Heb. xi 5] to the treasure-house of life;
ἄρχοντάς τε καὶ ἱερεῖς καταστήσας,	καὶ τοὺς λοιποὺς πατριάρχας σὺν τοῖς πιστοῖς σου θεράπουσιν Μωϋσεῖ καὶ Ἀαρὼν καὶ Ἐλεαζάρῳ καὶ Φινεές, ὁ ἐξ αὐτῶν προχειρισάμενος ἄρχοντας καὶ ἱερεῖς ἐν τῇ σκηνῇ τοῦ μαρτυρίου, ὁ τὸν Σαμουὴλ ἐκλεξάμενος εἰς ἱερέα καὶ προφήτην,	who hast ordered princes and priests in thine upper sanctuary;
		O Lord, who didst call [them] to praise and glorify the name of thee and of thy Only-begotten in the place of thy glory; O Lord God, who before the foundation of the world
τό τε ἁγιασμά σου μὴ καταλιπὼν ἀλειτούργητον,	ὁ τὸ ἁγίασμά σου ἀλειτούργητον μὴ ἐγκαταλιπών,	didst not leave thine upper sanctuary without a ministry,
ὁ ἀπὸ καταβολῆς κόσμου		and also since the foundation of the world hast adorned and glorified thy sanctuaries [on earth] with faithful princes and priests [cf. (24) above], after the pattern of thine [own] heaven;
εὐδοκήσας ἐν οἷς ᾑρετίσω δοξασθῆναι,	ὁ εὐδοκήσας ἐν οἷς ᾑρετίσω δοξασθῆναι·	thou, Lord, even now [cf. (33) below] also art well pleased to be praised,
		and hast vouchsafed that there should be princes for thy people:
Cf. (51) below	Cf. (51) below	Cf. (51) below

Eg. C. O. (Eth.)	Eg. C. O. (Lat.)	C. H.
(33) And now	nunc	
(34)		
(35) pour out from thee the might	effunde eam virtutem, quae a te est,	tribuens virtutem tuam
(36) of the Holy Spirit,	principalis spiritus,	et spiritum efficacem;
(37) which thou gavest (38) to thy beloved Son Jesus Christ,	quem dedisti dilecto filio tuo Iesu Christo,	quem tribuisti sanctis apostolis [see (40)] per dominum nostrum Iesum Christum filium tuum unicum;
(39) which thou grantest (40) to us[1] the holy apostles, (41)	quod donavit sanctis apostolis,	See (38) above
(42) thy helpers in thy church (43) (working) with the plough of thy cross (44) and in the place (45) of thy holiness— (46)	qui constituerunt ecclesiam per singula loca, sanctificationem tuam,	illis, qui fundaverunt ecclesiam in omni loco
(47) to thee be glory and praise unceasingly to thy name. (48)	in gloriam et laudem indeficientem nomini tuo.	ad honorem et gloriam nominis tui sancti.
(49) Give, (thou) knower of the heart, (Father,)[2] (50) and send the Holy Spirit[3] (51) upon thy servant (52) whom thou hast chosen for the pontificate, (53)	Da, cordis cognitor pater, super hunc servum tuum, quem elegisti ad episcopatum,	Quia tu cognovisti cor uniuscuiusque, concede illi [see (32) above], ut ipse sine peccato videat[4] populum tuum,

[1] See below, p. 23.   [2] See below, p. 25.
[3] See on this p. 25 below.   [4] Riedel 'pascat.'

THE BISHOP'S ORDINATION PRAYER 17

Ep.	A. C.	Test.
καὶ νῦν ἐπίχεε τὴν παρὰ σοῦ δύναμιν	αὐτὸς καὶ νῦν μεσιτείᾳ τοῦ Χριστοῦ σου δι' ἡμῶν ἐπίχεε τὴν δύναμιν	Cf. (30) above cause to shine forth and pour out understanding, and the grace which is from
τοῦ ἡγεμονικοῦ πνεύματος, ὅπερ [see (38)] διὰ τοῦ ἠγαπημένου σου παιδὸς Ἰησοῦ Χριστοῦ δεδώρησαι [see (39)]	τοῦ ἡγεμονικοῦ σου πνεύματος, ὅπερ διακονεῖται τῷ ἠγαπημένῳ σου παιδὶ Ἰησοῦ Χριστῷ,	thy princely Spirit, which thou didst deliver to thy beloved Son Jesus Christ;
See (38) above τοῖς ἁγίοις σου ἀποστόλοις,	ὅπερ ἐδωρήσατο γνώμῃ σου τοῖς ἁγίοις ἀποστόλοις σου τοῦ αἰωνίου θεοῦ·	give wisdom, O God, [give] reasoning, strength, power, unity of spirit to do all things by thy cooperation [lit. 'work'].
οἳ καθίδρυσαν τὴν ἐκκλησίαν		Give the Spirit which is thine, O holy God; send to thy holy and pure church,
κατὰ τόπον ἁγιάσματός σου		and to every place which singeth to thee 'Holy,' Him who was given to thy Holy One [cf. (36)—(38) above];
εἰς δόξαν καὶ αἶνον ἀδιάλειπτον τοῦ ὀνόματός σου.	δὸς [see (49)] ἐν τῷ ὀνόματί σου,	and grant, O Lord, that this thy servant may please thee for doxology, and for laud without ceasing, O God, for fitting hymns of praise, and for suitable time, for acceptable prayers, for faithful asking, for an upright mind, for a meek heart, for the working of life and of meekness and of truth, for the knowledge of uprightness.
καρδιογνῶστα πάντων, δὸς	καρδιογνῶστα θεέ,	O Father, who knowest the hearts, [grant]
ἐπὶ τὸν δοῦλόν σου τοῦτον, ὃν ἐξελέξω εἰς ἐπισκοπήν	ἐπὶ τὸν δοῦλόν σου τόνδε, ὃν ἐξελέξω εἰς ἐπίσκοπον,	to this thy servant whom thou hast chosen for the episcopate,

C.   2

Eg. C. O. (Eth.)	Eg. C. O. (Lat.)	C. H.
(54) that he may feed thy flock	pascere gregem sanctam tuam	ut mereatur pascere gregem tuum magnum sacrum.
(55) and minister as priest to thee without blame, serving thee	et primatum sacerdotii tibi exhibere, sine repraehensione servientem	
(56)		
		Effice etiam, ut mores eius sint superiores omni populo sine ulla declinatione. Effice etiam, ut propter praestantiam illi ab omnibus invideatur, et accipe orationes eius
(57) by day and night,	noctu et die,	See (64) below
(58)	incessanter	
(59) supplicating to see thy face worthily;	repropitiari vultum tuum	
(60)		
(61) that he may offer thine oblation	et offerre dona	et oblationes eius, quae tibi offeret
(62) in thy holy Church	sancta(e) ecclesiae tuae,	
(63)		
(64) See (57) above	See (57) above	die noctuque,
(65) See (81) below	See (81) below	et sint tibi odor suavis.
(66)		Tribue etiam illi, o domine,
(67) in the Holy Spirit of the priesthood,	spiritu[1] primatus sacerdotii	episcopatum et spiritum clementem
(68) having authority to forgive sin	habere potestatem dimittere peccata	et potestatem ad remittenda peccata;
(69) according to thy commandment,	secundum mandatum tuum,	
(70) (and) give the ordination of thy ordinance,	dare sortes secundum praeceptum tuum,	
(71)		et tribue illi facultatem
(72) and loose all bonds of iniquity,	solvere etiam omnem colligationem	ad dissolvenda omnia vincula iniquitatis daemonum,
(73)		et ad sanandos omnes morbos, et contere Satanam sub pedibus eius velociter [Rom. xvi 20],
(74) according to the authority which thou gavest to thine apostles;	secundum potestatem, quam dedisti apostolis,	
(75) and that he may please thee with gentleness and purity of heart,	placere autem tibi in mansuetudine et mundo corde,	
(76)		

[1] The MS has 'spm'

THE BISHOP'S ORDINATION PRAYER

Ep.	*A. C.*	*Text.*
σου τὴν ἁγίαν,	ποιμαίνειν τὴν ἁγίαν σου ποίμνην	to feed thy holy flock,
καὶ ἀρχιερατεύειν σοι ἀμέμπτως, λειτουργοῦντα	καὶ ἀρχιερατεύειν σοι, ἀμέμπτως λειτουργοῦντα	and to stand at the head of the priesthood without fault, ministering to thee
νυκτὸς καὶ ἡμέρας, ἀδιαλείπτως τε ἱλάσκεσθαι τῷ προσώπῳ σου	νυκτὸς καὶ ἡμέρας καὶ ἐξιλασκόμενόν σου τὸ πρόσωπον, ἐπισυναγαγεῖν τὸν ἀριθμὸν τῶν σωζομένων	day and night; grant that thy face may be seen by him;
καὶ προσφέρειν σοι τὰ δῶρα	καὶ προσφέρειν σοι τὰ δῶρα	vouchsafe, O Lord, that he may offer to thee the offerings
τῆς ἁγίας σου ἐκκλησίας	τῆς ἁγίας σου ἐκκλησίας.	of thy holy Church carefully with all fear;
See (57) above See (81) below	See (57) above See (81) below	See (57) above See (81) below
	δὸς αὐτῷ, δέσποτα παντοκράτορ, διὰ τοῦ Χριστοῦ σου	bestow upon him that he may have
καὶ τῷ πνεύματι τῷ ἀρχιερατικῷ	τὴν μετουσίαν τοῦ ἁγίου πνεύματος,	thy powerful spirit
ἔχειν ἐξουσίαν ἀφιέναι ἁμαρτίας	ὥστε ἔχειν ἐξουσίαν ἀφιέναι ἁμαρτίας	
κατὰ τὴν ἐντολήν σου,	κατὰ τὴν ἐντολήν σου,	
διδόναι κλήρους κατὰ τὸ πρόσταγμά σου,	διδόναι κλήρους κατὰ τὸ πρόσταγμά σου,	
λύειν τε πάντα σύνδεσμον	λύειν δὲ πάντα σύνδεσμον	to loose all bonds,
κατὰ τὴν ἐξουσίαν ἣν ἔδωκας τοῖς ἀποστόλοις,	κατὰ τὴν ἐξουσίαν ἣν ἔδωκας τοῖς ἀποστόλοις,	as thou didst bestow on thy apostles,
εὐαρεστεῖν τε σοὶ ἐν πραότητι καὶ καθαρᾷ καρδίᾳ,	εὐαρεστεῖν δέ σοι ἐν πραότητι καὶ καθαρᾷ καρδίᾳ,	to please thee in meekness;
	ἀτρέπτως, ἀμέμπτως, ἀνεγκλήτως	

THE SO-CALLED EGYPTIAN CHURCH ORDER

	Eg. C. O. (Eth.)	*Eg. C. O. (Lat.)*	*C. H.*
(77)			
(78) (79)	offering to thee	offerentem tibi	
(80)			
(81)	a sweet savour,	odorem suavitatis	See (65) *above*
(82)	through thy Son Jesus Christ, through whom to thee be glory and might and honour, to the Father and the Son and the Holy Spirit in thy holy church now and always and for ever and ever. Amen.	per puerum tuum Iesum Christum, per quem tibi gloria et potentia et honor, patri et filio cum spiritu sancto, et nunc et in saecula saeculorum. Amen.	per dominum nostrum Iesum Christum, per quem tibi gloria cum ipso et spiritu sancto in saecula saeculorum. Amen.

Continued from p. 11.]

Achelis by H. Vielhaber (*Die Canones Hippolyti*, p. 42)[1]; for Ep. and A. C., Funk's edition (in *Didasc. et Const. Apost.*) vol. II p. 78 and vol. I p. 474 respectively[2]; for Test., Cooper and Maclean's translation, p. 65.

With this synopsis before us we may begin to study the relations subsisting between the different documents, in so far as they may be indicated by the parallel texts of the bishop's ordination prayer. There are reasons which make it desirable to begin by considering the Ep. text in its relation to the text of Eg. C. O.

[1] After canon XIX Achelis alters the order of the text considerably; but this does not affect the bishop's prayer, which falls in can. iii. I have thought it more satisfactory to employ a version made directly from the Arabic than to venture upon an English translation of Riedel's German. This latter, however, is constantly kept in view; and I shall make it my aim to base no argument on any text of the Latin of which the point, for which it is cited, is not substantially borne out by Riedel's version.

[2] Whenever these two documents are cited in the following pages the references given are to Funk's edition, which has now superseded all others.

THE BISHOP'S ORDINATION PRAYER

Ep.	A. C.	Test.
		fill him full of love, knowledge, understanding, discipline, perfectness, strength, and a pure heart [cf. (75)], when he prayeth for the people, and when he mourneth for those who commit folly and draweth them to [receive] help;
προσφέροντά σοι	προσφέροντά σοι	when he offereth to thee praises and thanksgivings and prayers
	καθαρὰν καὶ ἀναίμακτον θυσίαν, ἣν διὰ Χριστοῦ διετάξω, τὸ μυστήριον τῆς καινῆς διαθήκης,	
ὀσμὴν εὐωδίας	εἰς ὀσμὴν εὐωδίας	for a sweet-smelling savour
διὰ τοῦ παιδός σου Ἰησοῦ Χριστοῦ, τοῦ κυρίου ἡμῶν, μεθ' οὗ σοι δόξα, κράτος, τιμὴ σὺν ἁγίῳ πνεύματι νῦν καὶ ἀεὶ καὶ εἰς τοὺς αἰῶνας τῶν αἰώνων· ἀμήν.	διὰ τοῦ ἁγίου παιδός σου Ἰησοῦ Χριστοῦ τοῦ θεοῦ καὶ σωτῆρος ἡμῶν, δι' οὗ σοι δόξα, τιμὴ καὶ σέβας ἐν ἁγίῳ πνεύματι νῦν καὶ ἀεὶ καὶ εἰς τοὺς αἰῶνας τῶν αἰώνων....Ἀμήν.	through thy beloved Son, our Lord Jesus Christ, by whom to thee praise and honour and might, with the Holy Ghost, both before the worlds, and also now, and at all times, and for ever and ever without end. Amen.

i. Ep. in relation to Eg. C. O.

If we compare Ep. with the Latin version of Eg. C. O., we are forced to recognize that the prayers in these two columns are identical; and further, that the Latin is nothing else than a literal translation of the Greek text in Ep. The only differences which do not readily admit of explanation as mere accidental 'variae lectiones' are those at nos. (37)–(39), (49), (54), and (82)—the doxology. On these passages some observations will be offered later, in the Additional Notes (see pp. 150–154).

As regards the correspondence between the Latin and the Ethiopic, it is equally clear that these two versions give essentially the same prayer. But it has already been observed that the text of the Ethiopic which Mr Horner prints and translates follows an inferior manuscript and needs to be controlled by his collation of some earlier and better copies[1].

---

[1] See p. 11 above, and note 1 there.

Notes on Mr Horner's text and variants.

The following notice of the chief variants of Mr Horner's other MSS will, when the variants are considered in conjunction with the evidence supplied by the parallel documents, serve to indicate more clearly the true relation of the Ethiopic to the Latin version of the bishop's prayer and, consequently, to the Greek text found in Ep.

1. At no. (5) of the synopsis all the MSS, apparently (Mr Horner says, 'L [= Ludolf's text] etc.'), except that in the text, add 'and our Saviour' after 'our Lord.' This can hardly represent an original Greek reading, since the additional words occur in none of the parallel documents (except A. C.), which all follow the scriptural form of the phrase (2 Cor. i 3); yet the addition probably got into the Ethiopic text at a fairly early stage of its history, and it may be only by an accident of omission that the one inferior MS in the text has got back to the reading of the original Greek.

2. At nos. (33)–(36) the meaning of nearly all the remaining MSS appears to be as follows: 'And now pour out from thee the might of the Spirit, the judge.'[1] Ludolf translates the last expression 'virtutem Spiritus principalis'; and it is evident that 'of the judge' stands for $\dot{\eta}\gamma\epsilon\mu o\nu\iota\kappa o\hat{v}$ (Ps. l 14), which we find in A. C. and Ep. The same word is represented in Hauler's Latin by 'principalis,' in Test. by 'princely,' and in C. H. by 'efficacem.' It is evident then that the reading 'of the judge,' though it does not appear in the text, must be original.

Instead of 'pour out *from thee*' one MS (v.) has 'which is upon thee.' Here the presence of the relative points to the $\tau\dot{\eta}\nu\ \pi\alpha\rho\dot{\alpha}\ \sigma o\hat{v}\ \delta\dot{v}\nu\alpha\mu\iota\nu$ of Ep., of which the Latin 'eam virtutem quae a te est' is a literal rendering. It may be noticed that all the MSS except that followed in the text agree with the other Church

---

[1] Or, possibly: 'And now pour out from thee the might of the judge, the Spirit.' As I do not understand Ethiopic, I cannot be quite sure here in what order the variants in Mr Horner's English collation are to be substituted in the translation so as to get a continuous version of any one of the MSS collated. The collation of the passage is as follows: 'line 2, from thee] which is upon thee, L. v.; which is without thee and from thee, d.   3, might] + of the judge, L. etc.   Holy om. L. etc.'

Orders in omitting 'holy' before 'Spirit': that epithet can, of course, have no place beside the true reading 'of the judge' (= ἡγεμονικοῦ).

3. At no. (40) the pronoun 'us' has no support in any of the other MSS, or in the parallel documents; and thus we are enabled to eliminate an appearance of apostolic pretence attaching to Eg. C. O. in the text[1].

In nos. (40)–(42) the printed text reads: 'to us the holy apostles, thy helpers in thy church.' We have already disposed of the pronoun 'us.' For the rest, all the remaining MSS read here: 'to thy holy apostles of the church.' Thus 'thy helpers' has only the authority of the text MS. Again the other MSS are supported by the Latin, Ep. and C. H. in reading 'the church' instead of 'thy church'; but in reading 'the holy apostles' instead of 'thy holy apostles' the text seems superior, since it is not our Lord that is addressed here, or elsewhere, in the prayer. The Latin and C. H.—at no. (40)—have 'the'; but Ep. and A. C. have 'thy.' The case is obviously one in which variants might easily arise.

At no. (44) again the better MSS read 'in each place' for 'in the place' (text); and in this they are supported by the Latin ('per singula loca'), by C. H. ('in omni loco') and by Ep. (κατὰ τόπον).

At no. (43) all the Ethiopic MSS (including the one followed in the text) have a very singular clause which is not found in the Latin nor in any of the parallel documents, viz. 'with the plough of thy cross.' Before this reading is considered it will be well to attempt a reconstruction, on the basis of the evidence cited above, of the whole context in which it stands—nos. (33)–(45)—and to place opposite to this the text of the Latin version.

(α) And now pour out the might that is upon thee of the princely spirit	nunc effunde eam virtutem, quae a te est, principalis spiritus,
(β) which thou gavest to thy beloved Son Jesus Christ,	quem dedisti dilecto filio tuo Iesu Christo,
(γ) which thou grante⟨d⟩st to the holy apostles	quod donavit sanctis apostolis,
(δ) of the church	qui constituerunt ecclesiam
(ε) with the plough of thy cross,	
(ζ) and in each place of thy holiness.	per singula loca, sanctificationem tuam.

[1] Dr Frere (J.T.S. April, 1915, p. 337) has failed to note Mr Horner's collation at this point.

As far as (γ) inclusive the two texts are in verbal agreement, except that at (γ) the Ethiopic has (against the sense of the context) the second person ('grantest') instead of the third ('donavit').

At (δ), (ε) the Ethiopic would seem to have lost a verb—unless, indeed, this is represented by '*the helpers of* thy church,' found in Horner's text MS—for the Latin 'qui constituerunt ecclesiam' has the support of C. H. ('qui fundaverunt ecclesiam') as well as of Ep. (οἳ καθίδρυσαν τὴν ἐκκλησίαν). Mr Horner supplies the verb after 'church,' thus: '(working) with the plough of thy cross.' But Ludolf supplies differently; he translates, at (δ), 'ut' instead of 'of,' and puts 'the church' in the accusative, thus: 'ut ecclesiam (colerent) aratro crucis tuae.' This, if justifiable, is perhaps preferable, in view of the Latin, C. H. and Ep., to Mr Horner's expedient; but I do not feel at all sure that the Ethiopic here admits of a true emendation on the basis of those other texts, and I am far from satisfied that *any* of our texts represents the original Eg. C. O. reading of the prayer at this point. The Ethiopic may be corrupt, but in the words 'with the plough of thy [? the] cross' it may still preserve the remains of an original reading. The idea contained in these words is not only a striking but also a very early one, and one which, it might be thought, could hardly have been inserted in such a context as this by an Ethiopic editor or translator[1].

---

[1] The plough as a symbol of the cross is met with in a well-known passage of Justin Martyr (1 *Apol.* c. 55; *P. Gr.* VI 412 B): γῇ δὲ οὐκ ἀροῦται ἄνευ αὐτοῦ (sc. a figure of the cross). Compare also Minucius Felix (*Octavius*, c. 29): 'et cum erigitur iugum, crucis signum est.' This, of course, is only one of many symbols of the cross which early Christians saw in natural objects or the implements and uses of daily life. Another such symbol was found in the outstretching of the hands in prayer: so Justin *ib.*; and Tertul. *Apol.* c. 30: 'Sic itaque nos ad Deum expansos ungulae fodiant, cruces suspendant...paratus est ad omne supplicium ipse habitus orantis Christiani'; and again Minucius Felix (*loc. cit.*): 'et cum homo porrectis manibus Deum pura mente veneratur.' This method of praying with hands outstretched was no doubt connected in thought with our Lord's extension on the cross (as in two of the recently discovered *Odes of Solomon*—27 and 42). Dr Wordsworth (*op. cit.* p. 28) with probability explains the σημεῖον ἐκπετάσεως ἐν οὐρανῷ of the *Didache* as an allusion to the crucifixion. Now all these ideas about the cross, while they were widely diffused in the early Church, were evidently closely connected and formed a single class. When therefore we find in the eucharistic prayer of Eg. C. O. the words 'spreading out his hands for suffering' (Eth.; Horner p. 140), 'extendit manus cum pateretur' (Hauler

THE BISHOP'S ORDINATION PRAYER

4. At nos. (49)–(51) we have in Mr Horner's text: 'Give, (thou) knower of the heart, and *send the Holy Spirit* upon thy servant.' The italicized words are not found in the Latin, Ep., C. H., A. C. or Test.; and all other MSS of the Ethiopic except that which supplies the text have 'and give upon thy servant.' After 'heart' Ludolf adds the vocative 'Father.' Ludolf's rendering is: 'Da, ô gnare cordium, Pater.' This is also the reading of Hauler's Latin: 'Da, cordis cognitor pater.' Test. too has 'O Father, who knowest the hearts.' But Ep. has δὸς καρδιογνῶστα πάντων. As the present passage is clearly a reminiscence of Acts i 24, σὺ κύριε καρδιογνῶστα πάντων ἀνάδειξον ὃν ἐξελέξω κτλ. (the election of Matthias), it seems probable that the πάντων of Ep. is a later accommodation to the wording of the scripture passage; for it is more likely that a scribe or editor would restore the biblical phrase than that he would alter it if already in his text. This being so, it is odd that C. H. alone[1] is in agreement with Ep. at this point, reading: 'Quia tu cognovisti cor *uniuscuiusque*, concede.'

As regards the reading of the Ethiopic, 'Father' is not in Horner's text. Now as the word is in Ludolf's text[2] as well as in his translation, and as Mr Horner regularly records not only the readings of Ludolf's MS (v.) but also those of his printed text, it is puzzling to find that here he fails to record any variant to his own text, which omits the word[3]. Considering, then, that Ludolf's text is supported by the Latin version and by Test., it seems probable that the reading 'Father' after 'heart' stands in other (if not in all other) MSS of the Ethiopic as well as in v. (Ludolf's MS), and is in fact the true reading; and so the omission of the word from Mr Horner's text, translation and collation appears to be merely accidental.

5. At no. (55) for 'serving thee' (text) Ludolf's MS reads 'serving,' absolutely, as also the Latin, Ep. and A. C.

p. 106), it is tempting to regard them as merely a recurrence of the same set of ideas that is represented in the Ethiopic text of the bishop's prayer by the expression 'with the plough of thy cross.'

[1] A. C. has altered 'Father' to θεέ.
[2] This I have ascertained to be the case.
[3] Again I have ascertained that the word is absent from Horner's Eth. text as well as from his translation.

6. At no. (57) Ludolf's MS again agrees with the Latin, Ep. and A. C. in the order 'night and day,' for 'day and night' (text). The latter order is found in C. H.—at no. (64)—and Test.

These notes, though not exhaustive, may serve to indicate a probability that the already close agreement between the Ethiopic and Latin texts of Eg. C. O. would, generally speaking, be found to be more and more close the more material we possessed for establishing the original text of either version. But even as things stand at present we are in a position to assert that Ep. and the Ethiopic and Latin texts of Eg. C. O. give one and the same prayer for the ordination of a bishop.

It follows, that of the two documents Eg. C. O. and Ep. the later one (whichever be the later) has taken over the text of this prayer as it stood in the earlier. The question, which is the earlier and which the later document, will be considered in due course (see p. 45 below). The answer to that question can make no difference to the evident fact that both have this particular prayer in the same form and that, consequently, both here differ from, or agree with, the remaining documents (C. H., A. C. and Test.) in the same respects. Ep., then, gives us a text of that original Greek which underlay the Latin and (ultimately) the Ethiopic version *of this particular ordination prayer*[1]. I shall accordingly treat Ep. as merely a third textual witness for that form of the prayer which is found in Eg. C. O. in Ethiopic and Latin; and in all discussions which turn on this prayer it is to be understood, unless otherwise stated, that the Ep. witness is included under the reference 'Eg. C. O.'.

ii. A. C. in relation to Eg. C. O.

A careful examination of the synoptic table of the bishop's ordination prayer which has been given above will, I think, establish the essential truth of the following proposition: that, as regards the text of that prayer, *no two of the other documents*

---

[1] The reader is particularly desired to remember that the identity of Eg. C. O. and Ep. here asserted extends only to the text of this prayer. This identity was recognized by Hauler, who, in editing the Verona Fragments, printed the Greek text of the prayer from Ep. opposite the Latin (*op. cit.* pp. 102–105); also by Achelis, *Die Canones Hippolyti*, p. 243.

anywhere agree together without also agreeing with Eg. C. O. This means, in the present case, that A. C. is in agreement with C. H. or Test. only in so far as either or both of these documents agree with Eg. C. O.

But if we examine the synopsis a little more closely, we find further that A. C. has a quantity of matter in common with Eg. C. O. that is absent from C. H.[1], or from Test.[2], or from both C. H. and Test.[3]. Now it is evident that matter not found in C. H. or Test. could not have been transmitted through these documents from A. C. to Eg. C. O. or from Eg. C. O. to A. C.—*nemo dat quod non habet.* And hence we can conclude with certainty that *neither C. H. nor Test. can have stood between A. C. and Eg. C. O. in a direct line of derivation*, whether A. C. be placed first or third in the line. And it is clear, moreover, that this conclusion is valid not merely for the bishop's ordination prayer, but for the documents as wholes: if A. C. and Eg. C. O. have *anywhere* matter in common that is not shared by C. H. or Test., then C. H. or Test. cannot have stood between A. C. and Eg. C. O.

It follows, either that A. C. and Eg. C. O. are directly related, in the sense that one was derived immediately from the other[4],

---

[1] As at nos. (14), (27), (30), (33), (45), (52), (55), (59), (62), (69), (70), (74), (75), (78).
[2] As at nos. (39), (40), (68), (69), (70).   [3] As at nos. (69), (70).
[4] Here, of course, we have to remember that Funk derived Eg. C. O. from A. C. *through* Ep. His reason for this was that the bishop's ordination prayer and the passage on the appointment of a reader in Ep. agree with Eg. C. O. against A. C. He thought the Ep. form of the bishop's prayer was shortened from the A. C. form, and that this shorter form became the basis of that in Eg. C. O. But we have now seen that the Ep. form is not only nearer to the Eg. C. O. form than to that of A.C., but is identical with it. Hence, to say that Eg. C. O. was here derived from A. C., or to say that Ep. was so derived, is the same thing. If it should appear that this Ep.-Eg. C. O. form was *not* derived from A. C., but *vice versa*, then Funk's theory will have broken down—*so far as this prayer is concerned*. This question as to the relation between the A. C. and the Ep.-Eg. C. O. forms of the prayer is dealt with in what immediately follows. Funk's other point—as regards the reader—will be considered later (see p. 46 ff.). As regards the expression 'derived immediately from,' used above in the text, it may occur to some reader that I am here overlooking the possibility that some lost document may have stood between A.C. and Eg. C. O. But a moment's reflexion will shew that the alternative in question is in no way affected if we suppose any number of lost intermediaries between those two documents. The alternative supposes that a certain amount of matter has passed over from one of the documents to the other: how the passage was made is now a matter of indifference.

28   THE SO-CALLED EGYPTIAN CHURCH ORDER

or that both are descended, if not immediately at least collaterally, from a lost document. We have then to enquire whether

    a. A. C. is based immediately on Eg. C. O.; or
    b. Eg. C. O. is based immediately on A. C.; or
    c. both are descended from some lost document.

Of these hypotheses *a*. is substantially[1] that of Achelis; *b*. is that of Funk[2]; and *c*. was (apparently) that of Dr Wordsworth. It will be convenient to deal first with *b*.

Funk's view.

A glance at the synopsis of the bishop's prayer will shew that A. C. has, distributed throughout the prayer, a considerable number of pieces not found in any of the parallel texts. We must now examine this matter peculiar to A. C. with a view to determining whether (in accordance with Funk's view, that A. C. is the ultimate source of all the other documents) it is part of the original text of the prayer and has been omitted in the other Orders, or whether it be not perhaps of the nature of interpolation into an earlier form of the prayer, due to the compiler of A. C. As the author of A. C. is known to have very distinctive characteristics of style, language and ideas, and as we have ample material of his upon which to draw, a comparison of the peculiar passages in the prayer with other parts of his work—where he is not, so far as we know, merely transcribing from some earlier document—bids fair to provide some definite result.

    1. I begin with the opening passage, contained in nos. (1), (4)[3], part of (5), and (6) of the synoptic table. This passage must be placed beside one which occurs in the liturgy of A. C. viii, namely, at the beginning of the 'Thanksgiving' or 'Preface.'

---

[1] I say 'substantially,' because Achelis holds that A. C. viii has undergone some alteration from its original form—that in which it was first compiled on the basis of Eg. C. O. (see above, p. 9, note 1).

[2] As explained in note 4, p. 27. See also p. 9, and note 3 there.

[3] No. (3) occurs in the other texts, but at a later point, viz. at no. (11).

THE BISHOP'S ORDINATION PRAYER   29

Ordination prayer
(A. C. viii 4; Funk I p. 474.)

(a) Ὁ ὤν δέσποτα κύριε ὁ θεὸς ὁ παντοκράτωρ,
(b) ὁ μόνος ἀγέννητος
(c) See (l) below
(d) καὶ ἀβασίλευτος,
(e) ὁ ἀεὶ ὤν καὶ πρὸ τῶν αἰώνων ὑπάρχων,
(f) See (n) below
(g) ὁ πάντῃ ἀνενδεὴς
(h)
(i) καὶ πάσης αἰτίας καὶ γενέσεως κρείττων,
(j) ὁ μόνος ἀληθινός, ὁ μόνος σοφός, ὁ ὤν μόνος ὕψιστος,
(k) ὁ τῇ φύσει ἀόρατος¹,
(l) οὗ ἡ γνῶσις ἄναρχος,...
(m) Cp. (b), (j), (k) above

(n) ὁ ἀπρόσιτος, ὁ ἀδέσποτος...

Preface of liturgy
(A. C. viii; Funk I p. 496.)

Ἄξιον ὡς ἀληθῶς... ἀνυμνεῖν σε τὸν ὄντως ὄντα θεὸν τὸν πρὸ γενητῶν ὄντα,...
τὸν μόνον ἀγέννητον
καὶ ἄναρχον
καὶ ἀβασίλευτον
Cp. (a) above (τὸν πρὸ γενητῶν ὄντα)

καὶ ἀδέσποτον,
τὸν ἀνενδεῆ,
τὸν παντὸς ἀγαθοῦ χορηγόν,
τὸν πάσης αἰτίας καὶ γενέσεως κρείττονα....
Cp. (m) below

Cp. (m) below
σὺ γὰρ εἶ ἡ ἄναρχος γνῶσις,
ἡ ἀΐδιος ὅρασις, ἡ ἀγέννητος ἀκοή, ἡ ἀδίδακτος σοφία, ὁ πρῶτος τῇ φύσει καὶ μόνος τῷ εἶναι...
See (f) above

Further striking parallels to the opening passage of the prayer of A. C. are found in the prayer over the catechumens in viii 16 (Funk I p. 480 l. 10 ff.):

Ordination prayer
(a) ὁ ὤν δέσποτα κύριε ὁ θεὸς ὁ παντοκράτωρ, ὁ μόνος ἀγέννητος...
(b) See (d) below
(c) ὁ μόνος ἀληθινός,...
(d) ὁ ἀπρόσιτος,...
(e) ὁ θεὸς καὶ πατὴρ τοῦ μονογενοῦς υἱοῦ σου.

Prayer for catechumens
ὁ θεὸς ὁ παντοκράτωρ, ὁ ἀγέννητος
καὶ ἀπρόσιτος,
ὁ μόνος ἀληθινὸς θεός,
See (b) above
ὁ θεὸς καὶ πατὴρ τοῦ Χριστοῦ σου τοῦ μονογενοῦς υἱοῦ σου.

Again, with (5)ᵇ and (6) of the prayer—ὁ θεὸς καὶ πατὴρ τοῦ² μονογενοῦς υἱοῦ σου τοῦ θεοῦ καὶ σωτῆρος ἡμῶν, ὁ δημιουργὸς τῶν ὅλων δι' αὐτοῦ, ὁ προνοητής, ὁ κηδεμών—compare A. C. viii 37 (Funk I p. 544 ll. 18–19) ὁ τῶν ὅλων ποιητὴς διὰ Χριστοῦ καὶ κηδεμών; and A. C. viii 40 (Funk I p. 548 l. 23) κύριε παντοκράτορ, δημιουργὲ

¹ The expression ὁ τῇ φύσει ἀόρατος is found in A. C. viii 15 (Funk I p. 520 l. 14). In A. C. vii 35 (Funk I p. 432 ll. 10–15) we have the following coincidences with the language of the prayer above: ἀόρατος τῇ φύσει...οὗ ἀνενδεὴς ἡ ζωή,... ἀπρόσιτος ἡ κατοικία,...ἄναρχος ἡ γνῶσις.
² Thus far A. C. agrees with Eg. C. O. and the other texts.

τῶν ὅλων καὶ προνοητά, διὰ τοῦ μονογενοῦς σου παιδὸς Ἰησοῦ Χριστοῦ. The manner in which προνοητής and κηδεμών are introduced in these passages, additional as it is to an otherwise close agreement in sense and expression, will probably be recognized as in the highest degree distinctive.

2. At no. (15)—a passage peculiar to A. C.[1]—we find the expression ὑπὸ μάρτυρι τῷ παρακλήτῳ. This conception of the Holy Spirit as 'witness' is one that runs through the *Apostolic Constitutions*:

(α) In the Invocation of the liturgy (viii 12 ; Funk I p. 510 l. 11) the Holy Spirit is called τὸν μάρτυρα τῶν παθημάτων τοῦ κυρίου Ἰησοῦ[2].

(β) In the prescriptions regarding baptism in A. C. iii 17 (Funk I p. 211 l. 22) we read: τοῦ πατρὸς ἡ μνήμη ὡς αἰτίου καὶ ἀποστολέως, τοῦ πνεύματος ἡ συμπαράληψις ὡς μάρτυρος. This comes as an interpolation into the *Didascalia*, and is therefore due to the compiler of A. C. himself.

(γ) In A. C. v 7 (Funk I p. 263 l. 10) we find: καὶ μαρτυρίᾳ πνεύματος, ὅς ἐστι παράκλητος. This is in connexion with our Lord's command to baptize, and is another interpolation into the *Didascalia*.

(δ) In A. C. vii 22 (Funk I p. 406 ll. 3–6)—again in connexion with the command to baptize—we read: εἰς τὸ ὄνομα...τοῦ ἀποστείλαντος πατρός, τοῦ ἐλθόντος Χριστοῦ, τοῦ μαρτυρήσαντος παρακλήτου. This is an interpolation into the *Didache*.

(ε) Once more, in A. C. viii 46 (Funk I p. 558 ll. 7–8) it is said that those who disturb the established orders of the Christian ministry λυποῦσι δὲ καὶ τὸ πνεῦμα τὸ ἅγιον ἀκυροῦντες αὐτοῦ τὴν μαρτυρίαν.

3. The next piece to be considered is that which constitutes most of nos. (20), (21) and (23). This introduces a number of Old Testament names, and the whole passage, except the single word 'Abraham,' is peculiar to A. C.[3]. With it is to be compared

---

[1] I am, of course, dealing here exclusively with matter peculiar to the A. C. text of the prayer.

[2] This is based on 1 Pet. v 1; but there the 'witness' is St Peter himself: ὁ συνπρεσβύτερος καὶ μάρτυς τῶν τοῦ Χριστοῦ παθημάτων.

[3] The presence of 'Enoch' in Test. at (22) seems to be independent of any influence of A. C. and to be immediately due to Heb. xi 5.

THE BISHOP'S ORDINATION PRAYER 31

a passage from the liturgical Preface, which has already provided one remarkable literary parallel to the A. C. text of the bishop's prayer. The reference is A. C. viii 12 (Funk I p. 502 l. 16 ff.).

Ordination prayer	Liturgical Preface
"Ἀβελ ἐν πρώτοις,	καὶ τοῦ μὲν "Ἀβελ...προσδεξάμενος τὴν θυσίαν,...
Σὴθ καὶ Ἐνὼς καὶ Ἐνὼχ καὶ Νῶε καὶ Μελχισεδὲκ καὶ Ἰώβ·	τὸν Σὴθ καὶ τὸν Ἐνὼς προσελάβου καὶ τὸν Ἐνὼχ μετατέθεικας......,
ὁ ἀναδείξας Ἀβραάμ...σὺν τοῖς πιστοῖς σου θεράπουσιν Μωϋσεῖ καὶ Ἀαρὼν καὶ Ἐλεαζάρῳ καὶ Φινεές...	ἀλλὰ ἀναδείξας τὸν ἅγιόν σου θεράποντα Μωϋσῆν...τὸν Ἀαρὼν καὶ τοὺς ἐξ αὐτοῦ ἱερατικῇ τιμῇ ἐδόξασας.

Compare also with the prayer passage A. C. vii 39 (Funk I p. 440): τοὺς δὲ ἁγίους ἐδόξασεν...τὸν Σήθ, τὸν Ἐνώς, τὸν Ἐνώχ, τὸν Νῶε, τὸν Ἀβραάμ...τὸν Μελχισεδὲκ καὶ τὸν Ἰὼβ καὶ τὸν Μωϋσέα, Ἰησοῦν τε καὶ Χαλὲβ καὶ Φινεὲς τὸν ἱερέα. A similar list in A. C. ii 55 (Funk I p. 155) mentions in the following order *Abel, Sem, Seth, Enos, Enoch, Noe, Lot, Melchisedek, Job, Moses, Jesus* (son of Nun), *Caleb, Phinees*. We notice in all these passages the constant group Seth, Enos, Enoch, and the association of Job with Melchisedek in the ordination prayer and in the last two passages. The passage ii 55 is interpolated into the *Didascalia*.

4. In no. (34) of the synopsis the words μεσιτείᾳ τοῦ Χριστοῦ σου δι' ἡμῶν are peculiar to A.C. Compare with them:

διὰ τῆς μεσιτείας τοῦ Χριστοῦ αὐτοῦ (viii 13; Funk I p. 514 l. 16).

διὰ τῆς μεσιτείας τοῦ μονογενοῦς σου υἱοῦ (viii 18; Funk I p. 524 l. 8)[1].

διὰ τῆς μεσιτείας τοῦ ἠγαπημένου παιδὸς αὐτοῦ Ἰησοῦ Χριστοῦ (viii 48; Funk I p. 594 ll. 1–2).

5. With no. (60)—ἐπισυναγαγεῖν τὸν ἀριθμὸν τῶν σωζομένων—compare viii 8 (Funk I p. 484 ll. 3–4), ἑνώσῃ καὶ συγκαταλέξῃ αὐτοὺς μετὰ τῶν σωζομένων; and *ib.* l. 14 τῆς μετὰ τῶν σωζομένων ἐπισυναγωγῆς.

6. In no. (76) the adverbs ἀτρέπτως, ἀμέμπτως, ἀνεγκλήτως are found only in the A. C. text. These three adverbs, or the corresponding adjectives, occur together and in the same order

---

[1] This comes in the ordination prayer for a deacon; but there the clause is peculiar to the A. C. and Ep. texts, which are identical.

five times elsewhere in A. C. viii, viz. in c. 11 (Funk p. 492 l. 18); c. 12 (p. 514 l. 6); c. 18 (p. 524 l. 7)¹; c. 41 (p. 552 l. 16); c. 48 (p. 592 l. 16).

7. Just before the doxology, in no. (80), comes a passage, peculiar to A. C., which must be set alongside of two others in A. C. viii:

Ordination prayer

προσφέροντά σοι²   (viii 46; p. 562 l. 7) ἡμεῖς προσε-
                                                           νεγκόντες
καθαρὰν καὶ ἀναίμακτον θυσίαν, ἣν   κατὰ τὴν διάταξιν αὐτοῦ θυσίαν κα-
διὰ Χριστοῦ διετάξω,   θαρὰν καὶ ἀναίμακτον.
τὸ μυστήριον τῆς καινῆς διαθήκης.   (viii 12; p. 508 l. 21) τοῦτο τὸ
                                                         μυστήριον τῆς καινῆς διαθήκης³.

8. Finally, there is the word σέβας in the doxology where the parallel texts, except C. H., have κράτος or its equivalent. The three ascriptions in A. C. are δόξα, τιμὴ καὶ σέβας. The Latin of Eg. C. O. has 'gloria et *potentia* et honor,' the Ethiopic 'glory and *might* and honour'; Ep. has δόξα, κράτος, τιμή. C. H. has only 'gloria.' Now this avoidance of κράτος and use of σέβας is characteristic of the doxologies in A. C.: while σέβας is all but invariable, I find κράτος only in vii 49⁴. Moreover the three ascriptions in the form and order δόξα, τιμὴ καὶ σέβας are found seven times elsewhere in A. C. viii, viz. Funk I pp. 482 l. 27; 484 l. 15; 520 l. 5; 522 l. 24; 524 l. 9; 526 l. 8; 532 l. 13; and in vii 47 (p. 456 l. 8).

As a result of the investigation, just concluded, into the nature of the matter which is peculiar to A. C. in the prayer, I think that no one will demur to this further conclusion, *that the Eg. C. O. text* (identical, it will be remembered, with that of Ep.) *could not conceivably have been derived by epitomization and alteration from*

---

[1] This again is the deacon's ordination prayer, and again the words in question are found there in none of the parallel documents except Ep.

[2] This much is in four of the parallel texts of the prayer.

[3] This refers (as in the ordination prayer) to the Eucharist, being introduced as part of the words of Institution.

[4] The prayer, in the doxology of which κράτος there occurs, is not one of the redactor's own composing; it is found in St Chrysostom *Hom. 55 in Matth.* c. 5 (*P. Gr.* LVIII 545 [561]) and also (as part of a grace before meat) in Ps.-Athanasius *de Virginitate* c. 12 (*P. Gr.* XXVIII 265), and in both places it has κράτος in the doxology. See Funk's note *in loc.*

the A. C. text. The evidence just collected renders it, to my mind, certain that A. C. does not give us an original form of the bishop's prayer, but contains a large number of interpolations, and some alterations, introduced by the A. C. compiler himself into an earlier form of the prayer. The force of this evidence lies, it need hardly be said, not in the mere fact that the A. C. text of the prayer has a number of remarkable literary and other coincidences with the rest of A. C., but in the fact that these coincidences are confined to those parts of the prayer which are peculiar to the A. C. text. Any one who is inclined to question this may confidently be challenged to produce from the very considerable remainder of the A. C. text of the prayer (that which it has in common with Eg. C. O.) a single further parallel with the rest of A. C. which will bear comparison with one of the couple of dozen and more cited above.

Unless, then, both A. C. and Eg. C. O. here rest upon some common lost source, it seems evident that the A. C. text is immediately derived from that found in Eg. C. O. and Ep.[1].

The 'Lost Church Order.'

Let us now take hypothesis *c.* (see p. 28 above)—that of Dr Wordsworth—and let us suppose that the Eg. C. O. and A. C. forms of the prayer both rest on a lost text.

Any one who will look at the synopsis of the prayer already given can verify the following statement: that *the whole of that matter in the A. C. text which is not entirely peculiar to it is to be found also in the Eg. C. O.-Ep. text*[2]. On the other hand it has just been shewn, as regards practically the whole of the peculiar matter in the A. C. text, that this is interpolation due to the

[1] It is further evident that if there is any truth in Achelis's view, that the Ep. (here=Eg. C. O.) text of the prayer was drawn from an earlier form of A. C. viii than the existing one, *it was the original compiler of A. C. himself who made the alterations to the present A. C. form of the prayer*—in other words, the compiler of A. C. made a second edition of his eighth book. This is a point which does not seem to have been noticed by Achelis, and which it will be well to remember when we come to deal with the relation of Ep. to A. C.

[2] This is really contained in the proposition (verifiable by reference to the synopsis) that ' *no two of the other documents anywhere agree together* [so far as this prayer is concerned] *without also agreeing with Eg. C. O.*' (see p. 26 above).

A. C. compiler. Now, as the sole ground for postulating a lost source of these documents is to account for their '*common matter*,'[1] and as we find in Eg. C. O. all the matter which the A. C. text of the bishop's prayer has in common with any of our documents, I can only ask, Where is the necessity for postulating any source for the A. C. text of this prayer other than the Eg. C. O. text?

But it will naturally be asked, What of other parts of A. C. viii in which it has matter in common with one or other of the remaining documents? Can we in *all* such passages assert a similar dependence on Eg. C. O.?

We have already seen (at p. 27 above) that neither C. H. nor Test. could have stood as an intermediate source between A. C. and Eg. C. O. It is therefore antecedently probable that the dependence of A. C. on Eg. C. O. which we have found in the case of the bishop's ordination prayer extends to every part of A. C. viii which contains matter belonging to the cycle of documents we are considering. But we are not left with a mere probability. Achelis, who thoroughly examined the matter, asserts (*op. cit.* p. 27) that 'there is not a word common to C. H. and A. C. viii that is not found in Eg. C. O. as well.' This statement I believe to be essentially true not only of A. C. in relation to C. H., but also of A. C. in relation to Test. Eg. C. O. is, so far as I can discover, *the common measure of all matter shared by any two, or more, of the documents C. H., A. C. and Test.*[2] But if each of our documents were directly based on a lost work, it is morally certain that A. C. would present some clear cases of agreement with C. H. and Test. against Eg. C. O., viz. by adhering to the original text where Eg. C. O. had departed from it.

[1] So Dr Wordsworth (*op. cit.* p. 18): 'Next to the "Didaché" we must place a lost book of which we infer the existence from the common matter contained in a number of others.'

[2] This does not prove outright that Eg. C. O. is the immediate source of *all* these documents; for if we suppose, for example, that C. H., Eg. C. O. and Test. stand in a direct line of derivation, and that Eg. C. O. stands *second* in the line, it is clear that it will still be the measure of the common matter in C. H. and Test., since everything that has passed from one to the other of these two documents must have passed through it. We have still (as in the case of A. C.) to compare C. H. and Test. with Eg. C. O. separately and on their merits.

That Eg. C. O. was the immediate source of all that matter in A. C. viii which belongs to this group of documents, I hold with Achelis to be an unassailable fact.

iii. The relation of Test. to the other documents.

This question is one into which I consider it unnecessary to enter in any detail. Funk and Achelis are agreed that Eg. C. O. is the direct source of Test. for that matter which belongs to this family of documents. It is quite possible, and even probable, that the author of Test. used other sources as well, but not for any of the matter represented in other documents of this group.

Funk's view of the relation of Test. to the rest of our Orders is shewn by the following *stemma*, taken from his book *Das Testament unseres Herrn* p. 293:

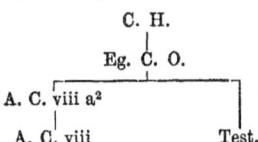

Achelis's view may be represented thus[1]:

```
            C. H.
              |
           Eg. C. O.
              |
       ┌──────┴──────┐
   A. C. viii a[2]
       |
   A. C. viii        Test.
```

An adequate examination of the documents must, in my opinion, result in the conclusion that Funk and Achelis are right in deriving Test. immediately from Eg. C. O.[3]. The proof of this would run on closely parallel lines to that already given for the dependence of A. C. on Eg. C. O. (see p. 26 ff. above).

One instance may suffice to demonstrate the independent use of Eg. C. O. by the compiler of Test. The eucharistic prayer in

---

[1] See Funk *Das Test. unseres Herrn* p. 294.

[2] That is, an earlier form of A. C. viii, which earlier form is now represented only by Ep., which is an excerpt from it (so Achelis).

[3] Schwartz (*Über die pseudoapostolischen Kirchenordnungen* p. 8) takes this to be obvious, describing Test. as 'the compilation of an apocalypse with a redaction of KO' (=Eg. C. O.).

Eg. C. O., which does not appear at all in C. H. or Ep. and is but slightly used in A. C., is embodied nearly in its entirety in Test. i 23.

I do not know of any satisfactory evidence of a literary connexion between Test. and C. H. or A. C. which cannot be traced back to Eg. C. O. If there be any such connexion its effects have been very slight indeed. Moreover, we should be cautious in accepting any particular instance of it that may be alleged. It is to be remembered that the text of Eg. C. O., as it has reached us, has a considerable history behind it and has suffered not a little in the course of its transmission. A comparison of the Ethiopic, Coptic and Latin versions will satisfy anyone who cares to undertake it on this point. Sometimes one version will contain a passage not found in the others, yet shewn, at the least, to have had a place in the Eg. C. O. text at an early date by its appearance, in some form, in one or other of the related Church Orders (C. H., etc.). Thus we have in some cases to control the text of one version by that of another. But further: as in the case of the New Testament we have in the quotations of early Fathers a source of information as to its text additional to that supplied by the MSS and versions; so in the case of Eg. C. O. we have, besides the extant versions of the text, at least two ancient documents (A. C. and Test.) which have made use of it; and we must recognize the possibility that any one or more of the parallel documents may preserve original features which the existing versions have not preserved. If we should find, therefore, that Test. and A. C., or Test. and C. H., or C. H. and A. C. have minor points of coincidence that are not shared by any existing version of Eg. C. O., we must not too hastily conclude that such coincidence is the result of some direct literary connexion between any two or more of those documents. The discovery of the Latin version and the publication of the full text of the Ethiopic have already restored several considerable passages to Eg. C. O. which it was not previously known to contain[1]; and the probabilities are that

---

[1] Namely, (a) the Eg. C. O. preface (Lat. and Eth.)—see p. 4 above; (b) a passage in Eth. (Horner p. 157 ll. 2-11) on the Sabbath and Sunday Eucharist, parallel to C. H. xxx (*fin.*)—xxxi (*init.*), or §§ 214-216 of Achelis's rearrangement; (c) a passage on 'gifts to the sick' (Eth.: Horner p. 159 ll. 19-26 *plus* some words

THE BISHOP'S ORDINATION PRAYER 37

if ever a Greek text of Eg. C. O., or even a new version (say, in Syriac), were discovered, we should find that it presented some points of agreement with one or more of the other Orders which do not appear in any of the known versions of Eg. C. O.

iv. The relation of Ep. to A. C. viii.

In considering the relation of Ep. to A. C. viii we must start from the undisputed fact that Ep., though considerably shorter, is, so far as it goes, usually *in verbal agreement with A. C.* There are, it is true, a few places in which it seems clear that the text has been purposely modified on one side or the other, and there are others that exhibit variants which seem due to the ordinary accidents attending the textual transmission of ancient documents. But these differences are not such as to raise any difficulty in the way of what must be regarded as the simplest and most obvious explanation of the relation of Ep. to A. C., viz. that it is an excerpt from A. C. viii, made by another and later hand than that of the original compiler. The essential difference between the two documents is one of extent; and it was produced by making a number of quite clean-cut omissions or additions, as the case may be[1].

There are, however, two passages in Ep. to which what has just been said does not apply. The first of these is the bishop's ordination prayer. We have seen that the Ep. text of this prayer is identical with that found in Eg. C. O., and so represents the original text worked over by the compiler of A. C. (see pp. 21 ff. and 28 ff. above). Thus the epitomist of A. C. viii did not derive the prayer from A. C. viii. It will be instructive to see how recent scholars who have dealt with these documents have faced this difficulty.

1. Achelis attempts to surmount the difficulty by supposing that Ep. is, indeed, an excerpt from A. C. viii, but from an earlier

---

omitted in Horner's translation, but supplied by him in his Collation p. 384), parallel to C. H. xxxii §§ 160–163 and Test. ii 11 (*init.*); (*d*) a passage on the service of the evening lamp (Eth.: Horner p. 159 l. 27—p. 161 l. 6), parallel to C. H. xxxii §§ 164–168, Test. ii 11, and A. C. viii 35 (*fin.*)–37.

[1] The tables printed in Appendix A, at p. 170 below, will help to a due recognition of this cardinal fact.

form of that book than the one that has come down to us[1]. That earlier form must, he thinks, have contained this prayer in the form in which it now stands in Ep. and Eg. C. O.[2]. Achelis's view of the relation of Ep. to A. C. is now shared by Dr A. J. Maclean, Bishop of Moray[3].

2. Funk boldly overrode the difficulty, maintaining that the Ep. form of the prayer was produced by epitomization of the present A. C. form, in the same way that he held the rest of Ep. to have been derived from A. C. viii[4]. He then made Ep. the step between A. C. viii and Eg. C. O. in the order (1) A. C., (2) Ep., (3) Eg. C. O.[5]. But finding that A. C. viii has some passages in common with Eg. C. O. that do not appear in Ep., he was driven to suppose that Ep., as we have it, is incomplete, and has somehow lost those passages[6].

3. Bishop Wordsworth says (*op. cit.* p. 33): 'This book [sc. Ep.] is usually considered to be the first draft of the central and latter part of the eighth book of the "Apostolic Constitutions."' So formerly Dr Maclean: '*The Constitutions through Hippolytus*

---

[1] Cf. *Die Can. Hip.* pp. 3-4, 27, 242-3, and (most clearly) 271. It is well to remember that Achelis does not assert that the earlier form of A. C. viii differed materially from the present one; in fact he only postulates it to meet the case of the bishop's ordination prayer and that of the Ep. text regarding the appointment of a reader. See above, p. 9 note 1.

[2] *Ibid.* pp. 242-3.

[3] *Ancient Church Orders* (1910), p. 154.

[4] See *Didasc. et Const. Apost.* vol. II pp. xi-xvi.

[5] *Ibid.* pp. xix-xxii.

[6] In *Didasc. et Const. Apost.* II p. xx he speaks of only two (evidently A. C. viii 3 and a liturgy); but in *Das Test. unseres Herrn*, p. 127, he mentions A. C. viii 40 also as certainly represented once in Ep. This contains the prayer over firstfruits, much of which is found also in Eg. C. O. (cf. Hauler p. 115). Funk's view (and his arguments for the same in *Das Test. u. Herrn* p. 128 ff.) that the Eg. C. O. eucharistic prayer is an epitomization of the liturgy in A. C. viii can only excite astonishment. But here too he supposes that the Eg. C. O. prayer came from A. C. through Ep., and consequently that Ep. has lost a passage on the liturgy. Two other points of contact between A. C. and Eg. C. O. not shared by Ep. which Funk-seems not to have noticed are (*a*) the words καὶ νῦν, κύριε, παράσχου, ἀνελλιπὲς τηρῶν ἐν ἡμῖν τὸ πνεῦμα τῆς χάριτός σου in the prayer for ordination of a presbyter (see p. 50 below); and (*b*) the words ὁ διαγαγὼν ἡμᾶς τὸ μῆκος τῆς ἡμέρας καὶ ἀγαγὼν ἐπὶ τὰς ἀρχὰς τῆς νυκτός in the prayer for the evening lamp service (A. C. viii 37): see p. 113 below. Ep. omits the former words from the presbyter's prayer, and the whole service in which the latter words occur in A. C.

[i.e. Ep.]..., so called, are usually thought to be a first draft of part of the eighth book of the Apostolic Constitutions.'[1] Mr Brightman favours this solution, but leaves open the possibility that Ep. may be an excerpt from such an earlier form of A. C. viii[2] (Achelis's view). Mr C. H. Turner, too, speaks of Ep. as 'perhaps a preliminary draft by the compiler of the *Apostolic Constitutions*,' with a reference to Mr Brightman (*L. E. W.* I xx)[3].

The second of these hypotheses (that of Funk) has already been shewn to be impossible (see above p. 26 ff.). The A. C. form of the bishop's prayer is simply a worked-up version of the Ep.-Eg. C. O. text; and the person who made this version was the A. C. compiler himself.

The first and third of the hypotheses have this in common, that they both seek to find a place for the Ep. form of the bishop's ordination prayer *behind* the A. C. form, the one by postulating an earlier text of A. C. viii, in which the prayer stood as it now stands in Ep., the other by viewing Ep. itself as a first edition of A. C. viii.

Before we make any attempt to account for the peculiar phenomenon presented by the Ep. form of the prayer it will be well to arrive, if possible, at a clear understanding of the implications of the first and third of the above hypotheses, considered as answers to the question, In what relation does Ep. *as a whole* stand to A. C. viii? I begin with the hypothesis of Achelis and Dr Maclean.

The hypothesis of Achelis.

When a tiresome literary problem has to be solved, the appeal to a second edition of an ancient work, emanating from the original author, may usually be regarded as a counsel of despair. Now it is true that Achelis does not say in so many words that the postulated earlier text of A. C. viii—from which he takes Ep. to be an excerpt—was altered to its present form by the actual compiler of A. C.; but whatever his view on this point, it is certain that, if his main contention be true, the alteration of the text of the bishop's prayer from the Ep. form to the present A. C. form

---

[1] *The Testament of our Lord* (1902), p. 10.
[2] *Liturgies Eastern and Western*, I p. xx ll. 1-4, 28-29.
[3] *Journal of Theological Studies*, vol. XVI (July, 1915) p. 545 n. 1.

was made by the A. C. compiler himself. This is abundantly proved by the marks of the compiler's hand which we have found in those parts of the prayer (and those only) which are peculiar to the present A. C. text[1].

Another fact that has to be faced if Achelis's view be adopted is this, that while several copies of an excerpt (= Ep.) from the first edition of A. C. viii have come down to us, not a single copy of the complete first edition is preserved among the numerous manuscripts containing the work.

But besides these general considerations there are textual difficulties in the way of Achelis's solution which are not easily to be got over. If the synoptic table of the bishop's prayer (at p. 12 ff.) is consulted at nos. (37)–(40), nos. (47)–(49) and no. (82)—the doxology—it will be seen that Ep. has a certain few modifications of the Eg. C. O. text of a kind that cannot be explained as mere accidental variants, and which yet are not shared by the A. C. text. Hence, if the Ep. and A. C. texts of the prayer are both held to be due to the compiler of A. C., and the Ep. text to be that of his earlier edition of A. C. viii, we shall be obliged to suppose that the compiler first made some slight alterations in the Eg. C. O. text of the prayer (those now found in Ep.), and afterwards, in his second edition, rejected them and went back to the original Eg. C. O. text. For a detailed discussion of the passages in question see the Additional Notes to this volume (pp. 150 ff.).

Achelis's theory further fails to account for the presence of the name of Hippolytus in the second part of Ep. He held that this was one of the features which Ep. derived from the earlier edition of A. C. viii (*op. cit.* p. 243, *fin.*). But he failed to observe that the presence of Hippolytus's name, as that of author, in any edition of A. C. viii is rendered impossible by the Clementine pretence which pervades the whole of A. C., and is actually found in Ep. itself[2].

---

[1] See p. 29 ff. above. That Achelis himself regarded the A. C. compiler as the author of the earlier form of A. C. viii is to be inferred from p. 278 of his book, where he speaks of viii 1–2 (which is also in Ep., and so, *ex hypothesi*, part of the original form of A. C. viii) as the work of the 'pseudo-Clement' (see p. 139 below).

[2] On the connexion of Hippolytus's name with Ep. and C. H. see pp. 135 ff. below; and on the Clementine pretence p. 138 ff.

The hypothesis of a 'first draft.'

I now take the hypothesis mentioned by Dr Wordsworth—that Ep. is itself a first draft of A. C. viii. Here the expedient of postulating a double edition by the same author is openly resorted to. But in this case there are some difficulties that do not attend Achelis's theory. In the first place, the hypothesis does not square with the following facts, which may be stated in the words of Dr Maclean[1]:

'We must first notice that in both documents [Ep. and A. C. viii] the sections are divided among the Apostles, and that both enumerate fourteen as being present, the Twelve, St Paul and St James (A. C. viii 4, Const H[2] 3). But in Const H [= Ep.], of the fourteen only ten[3] have sections assigned to them, while in A. C. all fourteen have sections, and the four omitted in Const H have in A. C. those sections assigned to them which Const H has not got. Moreover in A. C. viii 29 Matthias has assigned to him the section about oil and water (which is not in Const H) as well as viii 30: "I the same...." But Const H 20 (which corresponds to A. C. viii 30) is assigned to Simon the Cananaean (to whom both works assign the sections preceding that about oil and water). It begins "I, the same Simon the Cananaean command...."'

The gist of this is that Ep., like A. C., enumerates (in § 3 = A. C. viii 4) fourteen apostles as present, and aims at dividing the enactments among them. But while A. C. accounts for them all, Ep. accounts for only nine. Of the five missing names three disappear along with the matter ascribed to them in A. C.; Matthew disappears because the enactment assigned to him in A. C. viii 22 (that on the reader) is completely altered in Ep., and reduced from 22 lines (including a prayer) to a line and a half[4]; Matthias goes out with the *first* of the three enactments given to him in A. C. (i.e. the one to which his name is there attached), and his other two enactments go back to Simon the

---
[1] *The Ancient Church Orders*, pp. 150-1. The argument was also used by Funk, *Das Testament unseres Herrn* (1910), p. 190 ff.
[2] That is 'Constitutiones per Hippolytum' (=Ep.).
[3] I count only nine in Funk's edition, exclusive of the section (23) given jointly to Paul and Peter.
[4] On this see further p. 46 below.

Cananaean, the last name previously mentioned. Dr Maclean reasonably concludes: 'Thus it appears that Const H [= Ep.] is an excerpt from a work in which all fourteen Apostles had sections assigned to them.'

This piece of evidence seems sufficiently conclusive; but it does not stand alone. A. C. has a number of passages which are derived from Eg. C. O. but which do not appear in Ep. For instance, in the prayer for the ordination of a presbyter it has the words καὶ νῦν, κύριε, παράσχου, ἀνελλιπὲς τηρῶν ἐν ἡμῖν τὸ πνεῦμα τῆς χάριτός σου, which exactly represent 'et nunc, domine, praesta indeficienter conservari in nobis spiritum gratiae tuae' of Eg. C. O. (Hauler p. 109)[1], but which are absent from Ep. It may, of course, be said that the compiler of A. C. viii, in expanding his first draft, went back upon his original source document (Eg. C. O.) and took a little more from it than he had formerly done. But there is one passage at least which definitely excludes this explanation. This is A. C. viii 3. Ep. has A. C. viii cc. 1–2, and c. 4 seqq., but it has not got c. 3. Chapters 1 and 2 deal with the subject of *charismata*, and in particular with the gift of prophecy and the power of working miracles, and close with the following passage: 'Therefore, if there be any man, or woman, among you who chances to have a grace of this sort, let him be lowly-minded, that God may have pleasure in him; for "To whom," saith he, "will I have regard, but to him that is lowly and quiet and trembleth at my words?"' (Is. lxvi 3). Then Ep. § 3 goes on: Ἅμα τοίνυν ὑπάρχοντες ἡμεῖς οἱ δώδεκα τοῦ κυρίου ἀπόστολοι τάσδε τὰς θείας ὑμῖν ἐντελλόμεθα διατάξεις περὶ παντὸς ἐκκλησιαστικοῦ τύπου....πρῶτος οὖν ἐγώ φημι Πέτρος...(Here follows the prescription as to the ordination of a bishop).

It is obvious that there is a want of connexion between the close of § 2 and the beginning of § 3 in Ep., and that τοίνυν has not a natural *raison d'être* and only aggravates the abruptness of the transition. Put back A. C. viii 3 between §§ 2 and 3 of Ep., and not only is the connecting link supplied, and the grammatical force of the τοίνυν made apparent, but it is seen that the wording of A. C. viii 3 is echoed and presupposed in Ep. § 3 (= A. C. viii 4): Τὰ μὲν οὖν πρῶτα τοῦ λόγου ἐξεθέμεθα περὶ τῶν χαρισμάτων...

[1] On this see p. 52 below.

THE BISHOP'S ORDINATION PRAYER 43

νυνὶ δὲ ἐπὶ τὸ κορυφαιότατον τῆς ἐκκλησιαστικῆς διατυπώσεως ὁ λόγος ἡμᾶς ἐπείγει κτλ. Here the statement that the author is about to pass from one subject to another fully explains the use of τοίνυν at the beginning of § 3; while the expression τῆς ἐκκλησιαστικῆς διατυπώσεως of A. C. viii 3 supplies a point of reference for, and appears to me obviously to be presupposed by, the similar expression παντὸς ἐκκλησιαστικοῦ τύπου in A. C. viii 4 (= Ep. § 3). Thus on internal grounds it seems that A. C. viii 3 must already have been penned when c. 4 (= Ep. § 3) was first written. This conclusion is supported by some external indications. A. C. viii 1–2, on *charismata*, is not found in Eg. C. O., the principal source of bk viii; so that this passage was either composed in its entirety by the A. C. compiler himself, or based by him on some document other than Eg. C. O.[1]. Nor was it known until comparatively recently that viii 3 (the link passage between cc. 1–2 and 4) had any basis in Eg. C. O. It was thought by Achelis, for instance, to be merely an artificial device of the A. C. compiler for connecting cc. 1–2 with c. 4 seqq.[2]. But with the publication, in 1900, of the Verona Latin fragments came the discovery that Eg. C. O. opened with a short preface, not found in the Coptic versions, in which alone the complete document was previously known, and not occurring among the extracts from the Ethiopic version published by Ludolf. But again, with the publication of the full text of the Ethiopic by Mr Horner, in 1904, this prefatory passage appeared in that version also—not, however, at the beginning, but about the middle of the document (Horner p. 162)[3].

[1] The fact that Hippolytus is known to have written a work with the title Περὶ χαρισμάτων combined with the further fact that his name is found connected with two documents of this cycle (C. H. and Ep.) has given rise to the belief that the A. C. compiler, in writing viii 1–2, made use of Hippolytus's lost work. But it is certain, in any case, that much of cc. 1–2 is the compiler's own (see Funk *Die apostolischen Konstitutionen* pp. 139–141; Achelis *Die Can. Hip.* pp. 272–274, 278–280; Brightman *L. E. W.* ɪ p. xix), and the question whether he wrote the whole himself or used some earlier source does not concern us here: it will be dealt with later (see p. 148 f.).   [2] *Op. cit.* pp. 251–252, 270 (*fin.*).

[3] Horner's publication (*The Statutes of the Apostles*), as we have seen, gave also the first edition of the Arabic version; but this, like the Coptic, does not contain the passage at all. That the passage really belongs as a preface to the beginning of Eg. C. O. there can be no reasonable doubt (see p. 4 above, and p. 142 below).

When this preface of Eg. C. O. is compared with A. C. viii c. 3, it is apparent that the latter chapter is based upon it.

Eg. C. O. (*Latin*)	*A. C.* viii 3
Ea quidem, quae verba fuerunt, digne posuimus de donationibus, quanta quidem Deus a principio secundum propriam voluntatem praestitit hominibus.... Nunc autem...producti ad verticem traditionis, quae catecizat, ad ecclesias perreximus[1], ut ii, qui bene ducti sunt, eam, quae permansit usque nunc, traditionem exponentibus nobis custodiant....	Τὰ μὲν οὖν πρῶτα τοῦ λόγου ἐξεθέμεθα περὶ τῶν χαρισμάτων, ὅσαπερ ὁ θεὸς κατ' ἰδίαν βούλησιν πάρεσχεν ἀνθρώποις.... νυνὶ δὲ ἐπὶ τὸ κορυφαιότατον τῆς ἐκκλησιαστικῆς διατυπώσεως ὁ λόγος ἡμᾶς ἐπείγει, ὅπως καὶ ταύτην μαθόντες παρ' ἡμῶν τὴν διάταξιν[2]...πάντα κατὰ τὰς παραδοθείσας ἡμῖν ἐντολὰς ποιῆσθε....

Knowing, as we do, that A. C. viii is directly based on Eg. C. O., it is plain from the above texts that the compiler of A. C. had before him a copy of Eg. C. O. which, like our Latin version, opened with a prefatory passage containing an allusion to a previous treatise 'de donationibus,' περὶ χαρισμάτων. More will have to be said about this preface to Eg. C. O. later[3]. Here the one point to be noted about it is this, that it evidently suggested to the compiler of A. C. viii the idea of inserting at the beginning of this book a passage on *charismata* (viii 1–2 = Ep. §§ 1–2). This being so, it is highly improbable that when cc. 1–2 were first written they were not immediately followed by c. 3— an adaptation of the Eg. C. O. preface which suggested them, and a necessary link between them and c. 4 seqq.[4]

---

[1] I keep Hauler's punctuation of this clause. As the Latin text stands it is perhaps the most natural one; and it is possibly supported by Test. i 14 (see Additional Note vi).

[2] The words here omitted introduce the usual apostolic pretence—οἱ ταχθέντες δι' ἡμῶν γνώμῃ Χριστοῦ ἐπίσκοποι.

[3] See pp. 140 ff.

[4] Achelis (*op. cit.* p. 270) says of cc. 1–2 and 4 that they represent two sources 'of entirely different content, which have been clumsily pieced together by a redactor through the insertion of c. 3, so that even now the joint is distinctly noticeable.' And again (pp. 251–252) he says that in cc. 1, 2 we have 'a treatise on charismatic gifts which is only artificially brought into connexion with the rest of A. C. viii by means of c. 3.' Achelis did not then know that c. 3 was based on Eg. C. O., like A. C. viii 4 ff., but he saw that some link between cc. 1–2 and 4 was indispensable.

In view of these considerations I cannot but think that the hypothesis of 'a first draft,' as an explanation of Ep. in its relation to A. C. viii, is based on insufficient examination of the documents. At least, it cannot be accepted as a solution of the problem presented by the identity of the Ep. text of the bishop's ordination prayer with that of Eg. C. O. and its evident priority to the text of A. C.

There is no escape that I can see from either of two seemingly contradictory propositions: (1) that Ep. contains the Eg. C. O. form of the prayer which lay before the compiler of A. C., and which was interpolated and altered by him; and yet (2) that the body of Ep. was produced (as Funk held the whole to have been) by epitomization of—or better, by excerption from—the existing text of A. C. viii.

It is evident that *no one literary theory as to the genesis of Ep. can be found that will cover the phenomena presented by the bishop's ordination prayer on the one hand and by the body of the document on the other.* The document, as one whole, cannot have stood between Eg. C. O. and our present form of A. C. viii, nor can it (again, as one whole) have been produced by abbreviation of A. C. viii.

The true explanation of the phenomena it presents is, I believe, that the epitomist of A. C. viii knew independently the compiler's source[1] for this part of his work, and preferred to substitute the simple form of prayer in Eg. C. O. for the worked-up form which lay before him in A. C. viii[2].

I think it has been proved in the foregoing pages that Eg. C. O. was used quite independently by the compilers of A. C. viii and Test.; and we have, moreover, a Coptic and a Latin version of it, both almost certainly made from the original Greek, and probably

[1] I.e. Eg. C. O. I do not suggest that he was actually conscious of the fact that this document was originally used in the composition of A. C. viii.

[2] Cf. Schwartz (*op. cit.* p. 31): 'There remains no alternative solution but to suppose that it (the bishop's prayer) was taken from this (Eg. C. O.) and inserted in the Epitome in place of the prayer of the *Constitutions.*' The cardinal fact is that we have here a case of pure *substitution*, and not any kind of *literary derivation.* The person who made the substitution knew Eg. C. O.; and it is as easy to believe that he was the epitomist of A. C. viii as anyone else: though whether he was or not is quite immaterial.

46   THE SO-CALLED EGYPTIAN CHURCH ORDER

at comparatively early dates. Thus the document had a considerable currency in the fourth and succeeding centuries; and so a first-hand knowledge of it on the part of the epitomist of A. C. viii is no extravagant supposition. Is there any other indication that this was actually the case?

The section on the Reader.

It has been mentioned more than once that Achelis considered that there are *two* passages in Ep. which require for their explanation the hypothesis of an earlier text of A. C. viii. One of these, the bishop's ordination prayer, has now been considered. The second passage is that which deals with the appointment of a reader (Ep. § 13; A. C. viii 22). The substantive points of difference here are that A. C. prescribes imposition of hand and provides a prayer, while Ep. forbids the former and omits the latter. Let us have the texts before us. As the passage is wanting in the Latin of Eg. C. O. I represent this document by the Ethiopic and Coptic versions.

Eth.	*Copt.*	*Ep.*	*A. C.*
(Horner p. 147)	(Horner p. 309)	(Funk II p. 82)	(Funk I p. 526)
To the reader who is ordained the bishop shall deliver the scripture, and shall not lay hand upon him.	The reader shall be appointed (καθιστάναι) by the bishop giving to him the book of the apostle, and praying over him, but he shall not lay hand upon him.	Ἀναγνώστης καθίσταται, ἐπιδιδόντος αὐτῷ βιβλίον τοῦ ἐπισκόπου. οὐδὲ γὰρ χειροθετεῖται.	Περὶ δὲ ἀναγνωστῶν ἐγὼ Ματθαῖος ...ἀναγνώστην προχείρισαι ἐπιθεὶς αὐτῷ τὴν χεῖρα, καὶ ἐπευξάμενος πρὸς τὸν θεὸν λέγε· [follows the prayer].

It has been pointed out (at p. 39) that if Achelis's view (that Ep. is excerpted from an *earlier* text of A. C. viii) be accepted, it is necessary to assume that the present text of A. C. viii is the original compiler's own second edition of his work[1]. Hence the alteration in the prescription as to the reader will, on the supposi-

---

[1] The proof of this lies in the present A. C. text of the bishop's prayer: for it is just those passages in which the A. C. text differs from that of Ep. that have been shewn to belong to the compiler, not merely of A. C. viii, but of the whole of the *Apostolic Constitutions*. See p. 29 ff. above.

THE BISHOP'S ORDINATION PRAYER 47

tion that Ep. here reproduces the 'earlier text' of A. C. viii[1], merely mark a change of mind on the part of the original compiler. This being so, we cannot well suppose that any considerable time had elapsed between the writing of the original prescription (as in Ep.) and its altered form (now found in A. C.). And so it can hardly be assumed that the compiler's change of mind was due to some general change in ecclesiastical practice which had taken place meantime. The discrepancy, then, between Ep. and A. C. does not receive a very convincing explanation on the supposition either that Ep. is an excerpt from an earlier form of A. C. viii or that it is a first draft of that book[2].

It appears to me that the true solution is forthcoming only if we follow the indications of the general evidence and regard Ep. as (with the exception of the cases here dealt with) a series of excerpts from the present A. C. viii by a later hand. The laying on of hands in ordaining a reader is, on any view, an innovation in A. C.; and if the practice had not generally established itself when the epitome was made (did it ever do so?), it would be natural for the epitomist to reject the novel prescription in favour of the received usage of his time and locality. But here another question meets us: Did he simply re-write the section on his own account, or did he substitute for it a prescription found in another document?

[1] And, of course, also on the view that Ep. is the compiler's own first draft of A. C.

[2] Dr Maclean (*Ancient Church Orders*, p. 152) thinks that both the Ep. and A. C. texts are due to the compiler of A. C., and that the latter of the two texts shews that 'the A. C. compiler was gradually feeling his way.' He asks: 'Why did he only forbid it [imposition of hands] in the case of readers, and leave it for subdeacons and deaconesses?' Dr Maclean is here arguing against Funk's contention, that the epitomist of A. C. viii, who made the change in question, was a different person from the A. C. compiler, and the pronoun 'he' refers to this epitomist. But might we not ask, Why did the A. C. compiler himself, in his earlier edition (represented, according to Dr Maclean, by Ep.), do the very same thing? for there it stands in Ep. An intelligible reason why the epitomist acted as he did would seem to be that when and where he lived it was the custom to lay hands on a subdeacon but not on a reader. We may notice that both Ep. and A. C. place the reader *after*, and so evidently *below*, the subdeacon, which is not the case in Eg. C. O. I fail to see that the idea of the A. C. compiler being responsible for both the Ep. and A. C. forms of the section, and having changed his mind and altered his original prescription to its precise opposite, has any sort of probability.

That the Ep. passage on the reader is not the composition of
the compiler of A. C. is argued by Funk (in *Das Test. u. Herrn*,
pp. 189–197) in a way that is to my mind convincing. The chief
points of his argument are:

(*a*) In A. C. the section on the reader is ascribed to
St Matthew. Elsewhere when Ep. has a corresponding section to
one in A. C. it attributes it to the same apostle as A. C. does;
where it omits the name of an apostle it also omits the piece to
which in A. C. his name is attached. But here Ep. *has* a section
on the reader, but omits the name of the apostle to whom it is
given in A. C. This is unique.

(*b*) The terminology here in A. C., and the prayer prescribed,
are due to the A. C. compiler himself, being obviously on the same
pattern as the sections on the other orders which precede and
follow. This no one, probably, will be found to question.

When the compiler of A. C. wishes to say that any order of the
ministry shall *not* receive imposition of hands at ordination, he
says οὐ χειροτονεῖται. He so says of a confessor, virgin, widow,
exorcist; and in each of these cases Ep. has the same expression.
But of a reader, who in A. C. *receives* imposition of hands, Ep.
says οὐ χειροθετεῖται. This again is unique.

But further, we know from the A. C. compiler's own definition
that χειροτονεῖν, and not χειροθετεῖν, is (in bk. viii) his word for
that kind of imposition of hand which is given in ordination.
In viii 28, distinguishing between the powers of bishop and
presbyter, he says: ἐπίσκοπος...χειροθετεῖ, χειροτονεῖ, προσφέρει
...πρεσβύτερος...χειροθετεῖ, οὐ χειροτονεῖ. This definition is
repeated in Ep.; and hence if Ep. is here by the same hand as
A. C. there is no obvious reason why (even in his first draft) the
compiler should have said in the single case of a reader οὐ
χειροθετεῖται—thus both abandoning his normal expression and
departing from his own definition. It may be mentioned in
passing that οὐ χειροθετεῖται does not occur in A. C. viii at all.

Dr Maclean (*Ancient Church Orders*, p. 154) does not allow the
validity of this argument. He thinks the reader is 'ordained' in
Ep., but without laying on of hands, while the succeeding orders
are not 'ordained' at all. He points out (p. 155) that in A. C. iii
11 the compiler applies χειροτονεῖν to 'all minor orders, including

singers and doorkeepers.' But it is evident that in bk. viii the compiler has definitely revised his terminology and restricted the sense he gives to this verb; otherwise he could not say (as he does in bk. viii) of the confessor, virgin, widow and exorcist οὐ χειροτονεῖται. There is the outstanding difficulty, that the compiler says in A. C. that the reader *is* to have hand laid on him; and the supposition that this represents a change of mind on his part seems to elude rather than account for the facts.

The weakness of Funk's argument, as stated by him, lies in this, that he does not take it to its logical conclusion. He sees that the Ep. text on the reader marks a complete departure from the A. C. compiler's general use and manner; but he fails to notice that it presents an equally striking departure from the usual methods of the epitomist himself, and that the latter, in dropping here the regular A. C. practice of attributing each section to an apostle, and in altering its stereotyped phraseology, is quite unlike himself. Had he not some definite reason for departing from his customary procedure?

It is my belief that the passage on the reader in Ep. presents exactly the same case as that of the bishop's ordination prayer, and that, like the latter, it was taken straight from Eg. C. O. and substituted for the section in A. C.

Let us look at the Ep. and Eg. C. O. texts printed out on p. 46 above. Following the frequently superior textual witness of the Ethiopic we shall be safe in eliminating the words 'of the apostle' and 'praying over him,' found in the Coptic. But as the Coptic is doubtless a direct translation from the Greek, we may follow its construction in the first clause. We thus arrive, as nearly as may be, at the genuine Eg. C. O. text. When this is placed beside the Ep. text it is seen that the two are, as in the case of the bishop's prayer, really identical[1]:

Eg. C. O.	*Ep.*
The reader (ἀναγνώστης) shall be ordained (καθιστάναι) by the bishop giving him the book; but he shall not lay hand on him.	Ἀναγνώστης καθίσταται, ἐπιδιδόντος αὐτῷ βιβλίον τοῦ ἐπισκόπου· οὐδὲ γὰρ χειροθετεῖται.

[1] Schwartz (*op cit.* p. 32) neglects the evidence of the Ethiopic here, and wrongly, as I think, describes the Ep. clause as 'a bad redaction of canon 35 of KO,' that is, of *Statute* 35 of (the Coptic of) Eg. C. O. (Horner p. 309).

It appears to me that such an agreement in form and matter as these two texts present cannot be due to mere coincidence. On the other hand, the evidence forbids us to explain the complete discrepancy between this Eg. C. O.-Ep. prescription and that of A. C. by treating Ep. either as a first draft of A. C. or as an excerpt from an earlier form of the same document. And here again, as in the case of the bishop's ordination prayer, we are forced to the conclusion that the Ep. text is merely that of Eg. C. O., *substituted* for that of A. C. by an epitomist of A. C. viii who had a first-hand acquaintance with Eg. C. O.[1]. It is certain, in any case, that Ep. has the Eg. C. O. text here, just as it has the Eg. C. O. text of the bishop's prayer; and the Ep. text of the section on the reader could not have been derived—in the way the body of Ep. was derived—from the A. C. text any more than could the Ep. text of the prayer.

That the epitomist drew yet another feature directly from Eg. C. O.—and one which could not possibly have stood in an earlier text of A. C. viii—can, I think, be shewn to be so very probable as to be almost certain[2].

The ordination prayer for a Presbyter.

In order to shew clearly how different are the phenomena presented by the Ep. text of the bishop's ordination prayer and the passage on the reader from those that meet us in the rest of this document, I must say something about yet another passage.

It is a fact that has often been remarked upon, that not only is the bishop's prayer in Ep. shorter than that in A. C. viii, but the prayer for ordination of a presbyter is so too; and it appears sometimes to be supposed that the Ep. forms of these two prayers stand on the same footing and form parts of one and the same literary problem. Thus Mr Brightman says (*L. E. W.* I p. xx): 'On the other hand, the prayers for the consecration of the

---

[1] So Schwartz in effect (p. 32). He concludes (*ib.*); 'Thus the Epitomist in two passages [the bishop's prayer and the passage on the reader] has worked in KO [=Eg. C. O.] into his excerpt from the *Constitutions.*'

[2] The feature in question is the name of Hippolytus placed, as that of author, just after Ep. § 2, and before that part which answers in content to Eg. C. O. This matter is dealt with later on (pp. 135 ff.).

THE BISHOP'S ORDINATION PRAYER 51

bishop,...and for the ordination of the presbyter,...are in a shorter form than in A. C. viii 5, 16, *and the passages they omit are those in which the compiler's hand is most clearly marked; so that the omissions can scarcely be the result of excerption.*'[1] Dr Maclean similarly puts the two prayers on the same footing[2]. But that the case of the presbyter's prayer is wholly different from that of the bishop's will appear from the following comparison of the Eg. C. O., Ep. and A. C. texts.

	Eg. C. O. (Hauler p. 108)	*Ep.* (Funk II p. 79)	*A. C.* (Funk I p. 522)
(1)		Κύριε παντοκράτορ, ὁ βασιλεὺς ἡμῶν, ὁ διὰ Χριστοῦ τὰ πάντα δημιουργήσας καὶ δι' αὐτοῦ τῶν ὅλων προνοῶν·	Κύριε παντοκράτορ, ὁ θεὸς ἡμῶν ὁ διὰ Χριστοῦ τὰ πάντα δημιουργήσας καὶ δι' αὐτοῦ τῶν ὅλων προνοῶν καταλλήλως·
(2)			ᾧ γὰρ δύναμις διάφορα ποιῆσαι, τούτῳ δύναμις καὶ διαφόρως προνοῆσαι· διὰ γὰρ αὐτοῦ, ὁ θεός, προνοεῖς τῶν μὲν ἀθανάτων φυλακῇ μόνῃ, τῶν δὲ θνητῶν διαδοχῇ, τῆς ψυχῆς φροντίδι νόμων, τοῦ σώματος ἀναπληρώσει τῆς ἐνδείας·
(3)		ἐπίβλεψον καὶ νῦν ἐπὶ τὴν ἁγίαν σου ἐκκλησίαν καὶ αὔξησον αὐτὴν καὶ πλήθυνον τοὺς ἐν αὐτῇ προεστῶτας καὶ δὸς δύναμιν πρὸς τὸ κοπιᾶν αὐτοὺς λόγῳ καὶ ἔργῳ πρὸς οἰκοδομὴν τοῦ λαοῦ σου.	αὐτὸς οὖν καὶ νῦν ἐπίβλεψον ἐπὶ τὴν ἁγίαν σου ἐκκλησίαν καὶ αὔξησον αὐτήν, καὶ πλήθυνον τοὺς ἐν αὐτῇ προεστῶτας καὶ δὸς δύναμιν πρὸς τὸ κοπιᾶν αὐτοὺς λόγῳ καὶ ἔργῳ εἰς οἰκοδομὴν τοῦ λαοῦ σου.
(4)	Deus et pater domini nostri Iesu Christi,		
(5)	respice super servum tuum istum	καὶ ἔπιδε ἐπὶ τὸν δοῦλόν σου τοῦτον	αὐτὸς καὶ νῦν ἔπιδε ἐπὶ τὸν δοῦλόν σου τοῦτον
(6)		τὸν ψήφῳ καὶ κρίσει τοῦ κλήρου παντὸς εἰς πρεσβυτέριον ἐπιδοθέντα	τὸν ψήφῳ καὶ κρίσει τοῦ κλήρου παντὸς εἰς πρεσβυτέριον ἐπιδοθέντα,
(7)	et inpartire spiritum gratiae et consilii	καὶ ἔμπλησον αὐτὸν πνεῦμα χάριτος καὶ συμβουλίας	καὶ ἔμπλησον αὐτὸν πνεῦμα χάριτος καὶ συμβουλίας
(8)	presbyteris[3] ut adiuvet	τοῦ ἀντιλαμβάνεσθαι	τοῦ ἀντιλαμβάνεσθαι
(9)	et gubernet plebem tuam in corde mundo, sicuti respexisti super populum electionis tuae et praecepisti Moysi, ut elegeret presbyteros, quos replesti de spiritu tuo,	καὶ κυβερνᾶν τὸν λαόν σου ἐν καθαρᾷ καρδίᾳ, ὃν τρόπον ἐπεῖδες ἐπὶ λαὸν ἐκλογῆς σου καὶ προσέταξας Μωϋσεῖ αἱρετίσασθαι πρεσβυτέρους, οὓς ἔπλησας πνεύματος,	καὶ κυβερνᾶν τὸν λαόν σου ἐν καθαρᾷ καρδίᾳ, ὃν τρόπον ἐπεῖδες ἐπὶ λαὸν ἐκλογῆς σου καὶ προσέταξας Μωϋσεῖ αἱρήσασθαι πρεσβυτέρους, οὓς ἐνέπλησας πνεύματος.

[1] The italics are mine.
[2] *The Ancient Church Orders*, p. 77, note.
[3] Read (?) 'presbyterii,' with Eth. (MSS b, e) and Test.

4—2

52   THE SO-CALLED EGYPTIAN CHURCH ORDER

Eg. C. O.	Ep.	A. C.
(10) quod tu donasti famulo tuo[1];		καὶ νῦν, κύριε, παράσχου,
(11) et nunc, domine, praesta[2] indeficienter conservari in nobis spiritum gratiae tuae		ἀνελλιπὲς τηρῶν ἐν ἡμῖν τὸ πνεῦμα τῆς χάριτός σου,
(12)	ὅπως ἐμπλησθεὶς ἐνεργημάτων ἰαματικῶν καὶ λόγων διδακτικῶν ἐν πραότητι παιδεύῃ ⟨τὸν λαόν⟩ σου τοῦτον	ὅπως, πλησθεὶς ἐνεργημάτων ἰατικῶν καὶ λόγου διδακτικοῦ, ἐν πραότητι παιδεύῃ σου τὸν λαὸν
(13) et dignos effice,		
(14) ut credentes tibi ministremus		καὶ δουλεύῃ σοι
(15) in simplicitate cordis	εἰλικρινῶς ἐν καθαρᾷ διανοίᾳ καὶ ψυχῇ θελούσῃ,	εἰλικρινῶς ἐν καθαρᾷ διανοίᾳ καὶ ψυχῇ θελούσῃ,
(16) laudantes te,		
(17)	καὶ τὰς ὑπὲρ τοῦ λαοῦ σου ἱερουργίας ἀμώμως ἐκτελῇ διὰ κτλ.	καὶ τὰς ὑπὲρ τοῦ λαοῦ σου ἱερουργίας ἀμώμους ἐκτελῇ διὰ κτλ.
(18) per (etc.)		

A glance at the first and third columns will shew what the compiler of A. C. has added to or omitted from the Eg. C. O. text[3], which clearly lay before him. Nos. (1), (2), (3), (6), (12), (17) shew interpolations. At nos. (4), (10), (13), (16) there are omissions.

If we next look at the second column, we see that, (*a*) Ep. omits all the pieces of Eg. C. O. text *that A. C. omits*; but (*b*) it also omits the *pieces of Eg. C. O. text which A. C. has kept* at nos. (11) and (14); and (*c*) it *omits a piece of the A. C. interpolations* as well, viz. that at no. (2).

Ep. therefore, while it has no part of the original Eg. C. O. text which is not also found in A. C., omits indifferently matter that is peculiar to A. C. and matter that A. C. has derived from Eg. C. O. But this is merely the normal result of a simple process of abbreviation. It is true, certainly, that in slightly shortening the presbyter's prayer the 'Epitomist' of A. C. viii has departed from his general practice of merely excerpting without otherwise modifying the passages extracted; but it is not the case that this prayer in Ep. presents any parallel to that for the bishop. It is simply the A. C. prayer with a couple of pieces

---

[1] Similarly Test.; Eth. adds 'and minister Moses.'

[2] Eth. adds 'to this thy servant,' and continues: 'the grace which fails not, preserving to us the spirit,' etc.; though most MSS omit 'the grace.'

[3] Mere modifications of the Eg. C. O. text may here be disregarded.

omitted; the bishop's prayer is *not* the A. C. prayer, and could not have been derived from it.

I cannot help thinking that the *fons et origo* of much of the confusion that has prevailed in regard to the relation of Ep. to A. C. viii is the failure to recognize that the bishop's ordination prayer and the passage on the appointment of a reader[1] stand on an entirely different footing from the rest of Ep.—that *they could not have come into this document by the same literary process as produced the rest of Ep.* Most of the arguments usually adduced for the priority of Ep. (as one whole) over A. C. are based on these two passages. On the other hand, Funk's otherwise correct judgment, that Ep. is a series of excerpts from A. C. viii, has been undeservedly discredited by reason of his failure to observe that these two passages stand quite apart from the main content of Ep., and his manifestly wrong contention that the bishop's ordination prayer is an 'epitome' of that in A. C. This last error led him to a further one, viz. to the idea that Eg. C. O., which has the same text of the prayer as Ep., must have been based on Ep., and so must be later than A. C.[2]

But others besides Funk have been led to untenable conclusions by regarding the bishop's prayer and the passage on the reader as normal parts of the text of Ep. Achelis and others started from the fact that the Ep. form of the bishop's prayer (at all events) *could not* have been produced by epitomization of the A. C. form; and they were led to adopt other expedients which will not stand the test of examination: either that of postulating an earlier form of A. C. viii from which Ep. might be regarded as an excerpt, or that of treating Ep. as a first draft of A. C. viii.

Summary of conclusions hitherto drawn.

Before we approach the next question to be considered—the relation subsisting between Eg. C. O. and C. H.—it will be well to tabulate the conclusions hitherto arrived at. They are:

[1] I would add also the presence of Hippolytus's name in Ep. (see p. 50 note 2 above, and pp. 137-8, 144 below).

[2] As to this Mr Brightman says truly (*L. E. W.* I p. xxi ll. 36 ff.): 'it is impossible to put it [Eg. C. O.] later than the latter [A. C. viii] or to regard it as derived from it, unless it is to be regarded as an elaborate and successful piece of antiquarianism.'

54 THE SO-CALLED EGYPTIAN CHURCH ORDER

1. That the Ep. text of the bishop's ordination prayer is in reality nothing but a Greek text of the prayer found in Eg. C. O.: and the same is to be said of the passage in Ep. on the appointment of a reader—it gives us, without doubt, the original Greek of the same prescription in Eg. C. O.

2. That A. C. viii and Test. are both directly based on Eg. C. O., not on C. H. or any lost document.

3. That Ep. is—apart from the bishop's prayer and the passage on the reader—an excerpt from A. C. viii as we now have it, not an excerpt from an earlier form of A. C. viii, nor yet a first draft of the present form; that the bishop's ordination prayer in Ep. is not an epitome of the prayer in A. C., but was taken over by the epitomist of A. C. viii from Eg. C. O. (with which document he had an independent first-hand acquaintance) and substituted for the A. C. text. The same explanation is to be given of the Ep. section on the appointment of a reader.

These results may be summarized in tabular form thus[1]:

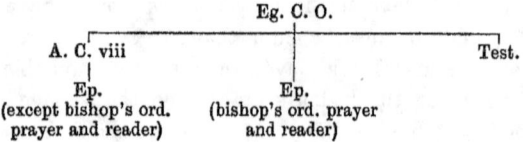

[1] I am not here concerned with the relative antiquity of A. C. and Test., or of Ep. and Test., and the table given is not intended to indicate any view on this matter.

CHAPTER II

EG. C. O. IN RELATION TO C. H.[1]

WE now come to the question of the relations subsisting between the 'Egyptian Church Order' and the 'Canons of Hippolytus.' I have already drawn the conclusions that A. C. viii and Test. are both based immediately on Eg. C. O. That neither A. C. nor Test. stands between Eg. C. O. and C. H., as the immediate source of the latter, follows at once when we observe that C. H. has a great deal in common with Eg. C. O. that is not found in either A. C. or Test. It remains, therefore, to determine, if possible, whether

(a) C. H. is immediately derived from Eg. C. O.; or

(b) Eg. C. O. is immediately derived from C. H.; or

(c) both are based on some lost document.

The first point to which I direct attention is no. (56) in the synopsis of texts of the bishop's ordination prayer (see p. 18 above). That item is peculiar to C. H. Now, if we examine the various texts of the ordination prayer for a deacon, we find that there also C. H. has a passage to which there is nothing even remotely corresponding in any of the other Orders. Let us compare this with no. (56) of the bishop's prayer.

---

[1] I devote a special chapter to this question because it takes us beyond the bishop's ordination prayer, which formed the basis of the preceding investigations.

56   THE SO-CALLED EGYPTIAN CHURCH ORDER

Bishop's prayer	*Deacon's prayer*
Effice etiam, *ut mores eius sint superiores omni populo* sine ulla declinatione. Effice etiam, *ut propter praestantiam illi ab omnibus invideatur*, et accipe orationes eius...	...utque illi concedas vim vincendi omnem potestatem dolosi signo crucis tuae, quo ipse signatur; utque concedas ipsi *mores sine peccato coram omnibus hominibus, doctrinamque*[1] pro multis, qua gentem copiosam in ecclesia sacra ad salutem perducat *sine ullo scandalo*. Accipe omne servitium eius...

I think it will be recognized that these two passages have in common a fairly distinctive idea. This I should express as follows: that the ordinand's way of life should be such as to be *a source of edification to all*.

With these two passages from the ordination prayers for bishop and deacon we must now compare two more, occurring in other parts of C. H., and there also peculiar to this document.

(*a*) After the account of baptism C. H. (can. xix, § 149 of Achelis's arrangement of the text) says of the newly baptized:

Iam vero facti sunt Christiani perfecti, qui fruuntur corpore Christi et progrediuntur in sapientia, *ut illustrentur mores corum virtutibus, non tantummodo coram se ipsis sed etiam coram omnibus gentibus*[2], *quae non sine invidia*[3] *admirabuntur profectum eorum qui gloriantur ipsorum mores superiores et praestantiores esse moribus ceterorum hominum*[4].

This passage links up in a remarkable way the language of the two pieces (cited above) in the C. H. texts of the ordination prayers for bishop and deacon; it reiterates with emphasis their common idea, and at the same time reproduces forms of expression peculiar to each.

(β) Speaking of behaviour at memorial suppers for the departed, the author of C. H. deprecates much talking and clamour, lest 'in contumeliam vertatur qui vos invitavit.' Then he adds (can. xxxiv, § 175):

---

[1] Professor Burkitt translates this word 'and an example.' See *Journal of Theological Studies* vol. xvi p. 353 (*fin.*), in an article by Dr W. H. Frere, for whom Prof. Burkitt made an English translation from the Arabic of parts of C. H. Riedel renders ' and for a lesson ' (' Lehre ') (p. 203).

[2] Compare with the italicized words thus far: ' concedas ipsi *mores sine peccato coram omnibus hominibus*,' in the deacon's prayer.

[3] Compare in the bishop's prayer: ' *ut...illi ab omnibus invideatur.*'

[4] Compare in the bishop's prayer: ' *ut mores eius sint superiores omni populo.*'

sed potius invitent eum constanter et totam familiam eius *et videat(ur) modestia uniuscuiusque nostrum et obtineatur magna dignitas exemplis*[1] *illis, quae in nobis conspiciuntur.*

Here again, though the expression differs somewhat, we have the same idea as in the three foregoing passages—edification to others by exceptionally good behaviour. This passage again is peculiar to C. H., though Eg. C. O. runs closely parallel just before and just after it (see Achelis's synopsis, *Die Can. Hip.* p. 108). These four passages must give any one pause who is inclined to accept Achelis's judgment, that Eg. C. O. is derived from C. H. The point to be noted is not so much that these passages occur in none of the other documents[2], as that none of them occurs in Eg. C. O. Is there any antecedent probability that the author of Eg. C. O.—supposing that he is working on the basis of C. H.— would omit all these passages? I can see none: the idea expressed in them is surely a perfectly harmless and quite edifying one. Were it the case that Eg. C. O. lacked only one, or even two, of the passages, little significance might be attached to this fact; the chances would be that out of four a redactor might pass over one or two. But that without any assignable motive he should omit all four is not antecedently probable. In the case of the passage in the bishop's prayer and of (β) the theory of omission offers particular difficulties; for in the prayer practically every other item of the C. H. text is represented in Eg. C. O., while in the case of passage (β) Eg. C. O. and C. H. are in close agreement just before and again just after the 'edification' piece in the latter document. The two contexts of this passage are worth comparing.

Eg. C. O. (Lat.)	*C. H.* c. xxxiii–xxxiv
(Hauler p. 113) Edentes vero et bibentes cum honestate id agite et non ad ebrietatem	(§ 173) Edant bibantque ad satietatem, neque vero ad ebrietatem, sed in divina praesentia cum laude Dei. (xxxiv § 174) Ne quis multum loquatur neve clamet,

[1] Cf. the deacon's prayer, and the note there on 'doctrinamque.'
[2] Because we have seen that A. C. and Test. are directly based on Eg. C. O.; and if we suppose that Eg. C. O. is based on C. H., then as Eg. C. O. omits the passages, they will necessarily be absent from A. C. and Test. as well.

58   THE SO-CALLED EGYPTIAN CHURCH ORDER

Eg. C. O. (Lat.)
et non ut aliquis inrideat,

aut tristetur qui vocat vos in vestra inquietudine,

sed ut oret, ut dignus efficiatur ut ingrediantur sancti ad eum. 'Vos enim,' inquit, 'estis sal terrae.'

C. H. c. xxxiii–xxxiv

neve sint scandalo hominibus[1], ita ut in contumeliam vertatur qui vos invitavit, cum appareat vos a bono ordine aberrare.

(§ 175) Sed potius...*etc.* [as at (β) above]

(§ 176) Oret autem quisque ut sancti introeant sub tectum eius. Dicit enim Salvator noster: 'Vos estis sal terrae[2].'

Now there is one passage in Eg. C. O. in which the idea of 'edification' may just be articulated; and there for the fifth time it appears prominently in C. H. Let us compare the two texts.

Eg. C. O. (Lat.)
(Hauler p. 114) Si laici fuerint in unum, cum moderatione agant. Laicus enim benedictionem facere non potes.

Unusquisque in nomine domini edat. Hoc enim deo placet, *ut aemulatores etiam aput gentes simus*, omnes similes et sobrii.

C. H. c. xxxv
(§ 181) Laico autem non convenit ut signet panem, sed tantummodo frangat, nihil praeterea faciat.

(§ 182) Si clericus omnino non adest, quilibet suam partem comedat cum gratiarum actione, *ut videant gentes mores vestros cum invidia*.

For the last clause in Eg. C. O. the Ethiopic has: 'Because this is due to God, that we should be zealots among the peoples, all of us equal and quiet and pure and without fault' (Horner p. 159). The Coptic (Sahidic) has: 'for this is proper for godliness, that we should be sober ($\nu\acute{\eta}\phi\epsilon\iota\nu$) and that the heathen ($\ddot{\epsilon}\theta\nu o\varsigma$) may envy us' (Horner p. 322).

It would seem to be suggested by the Coptic that 'aemulatores' in the Latin should have a passive rather than an active sense, standing for $\zeta\eta\lambda\omega\tau o\acute{\iota}$ rather than $\zeta\eta\lambda\omega\tau a\acute{\iota}$. If this be so, then the Ethiopic, like the Latin, has attempted to translate literally, and so has obscured the sense; while the Coptic has preserved the sense by having recourse to a circumlocution. But C. H. can hardly represent a similar periphrastic *translation* of $\zeta\eta\lambda\omega\tau o\acute{\iota}$: '*ut videant gentes mores vestros* cum invidia[3]' goes

---

[1] Note that this also (again absent in Eg. C. O.) is part of the 'edification' thought of C. H. Cp. 'sine ullo scandalo,' in the deacon's prayer.

[2] Riedel has this last clause in a form nearer to Eg. C. O.; viz. by omitting 'quisque,' he makes *the host* the subject of 'oret,' not 'each one' of the guests—who of course are themselves the 'sancti.'

[3] Riedel has 'and envy you' for 'cum invidia.'

beyond a translation of any Greek text underlying Eg. C. O., and must represent a different set of Greek words. The difference, then, between C. H. and Eg. C. O. cannot be explained as due merely to translation. A comparison with the phraseology of the 'edification' passages already quoted will confirm this judgment. In the deacon's prayer we read: 'concedas ipsi *mores* sine peccato coram omnibus hominibus.' In passage (*a*) we have: 'sed etiam coram omnibus gentibus, quae *non sine invidia* admirabuntur profectum eorum qui gloriantur ipsorum *mores* superiores...esse *moribus* ceterorum hominum.' And in passage (β) the idea that others may *see* us is found: 'exemplis illis, quae in nobis *conspiciuntur.*' Thus in our present passage it is just where the C. H. form of expression differs from that of Eg. C. O. that it shews its affinity with the other 'edification' passages, which are peculiar to C. H.; so that while Eg. C. O. barely, if at all, expresses the idea of good example, C. H. enunciates it in terms that are quite unequivocal. There is then a good presumption that it is Eg. C. O. that is here original, and that C. H. has a text that is modified into accord with a favourite idea of the compiler and his characteristic mode of expressing that idea.

Before going further with the present inquiry, it may be well that I should state the conclusion to which I have been led by an exhaustive comparison of C. H. with Eg. C. O. My conclusion is that it is C. H. that is directly based on Eg. C. O., and not *vice versa*; and that C. H. is an appreciably later and very unskilful redaction of Eg. C. O.

In order to come to a judgment on this question I wrote out for myself in parallel columns the whole of C. H. and Eg. C. O. This was done without any direct reference to the similar scheme of Achelis; though I used, and was much helped by, his rearrangement of the order of C. H. Moreover, instead of the Coptic (Sahidic) of Eg. C. O., used by Achelis, I employed for this document the Latin and Ethiopic versions—the one entirely and the other for the most part unknown to him when he wrote *Die Canones Hippolyti*—filling the gaps of the Latin from the Coptic. My method was to break the text up into small pieces (as in the table already given of the bishop's prayer), so as to be able to see at a glance every item represented in both documents and everything peculiar to one or the other. A system of cross references drew attention to any discrepancies of order between the documents (other than those already rectified by Achelis), and also indicated repetitions of the same passages, ideas, phraseology, in either work[1]. By this means I was afterwards enabled to make not a few corrections in the synopsis given by Achelis.

The general result is that, whereas I have nowhere found evidence of a dependence of Eg. C. O. on C. H., the reverse conclusion has been forced upon me by passage after passage. The author of C. H., while he seems to have had mainly an academic interest in the subject-matter, and did not trouble to alter his source in such a way as to produce a more or less practical manual for his own times—as the compiler of A. C. did to a considerable extent—yet appears to me to betray, time after time, a later ecclesiastical standpoint than is found in Eg. C. O. He shows a knowledge of later institutions and an ignorance of early ones, and more than once fails altogether to grasp the meaning or appreciate the ideas of the document he is using, either substituting commonplace and conventional conceptions for those that in Eg. C. O. are distinctive—and to us unfamiliar or even startling—or else omitting these latter altogether.

I know that it is commonly said that C. H., as we have it, is 'interpolated'—in the sense, I must suppose, that while the general content (though, in this case, not the order) of the original document has been more or less faithfully preserved, it has suffered from additions and glosses, due to translation, copying, or what not, that can without much difficulty be detached from the original matter. Interpolation of this sort might, obviously, have taken place at almost any date down to that of the earliest existing manuscript of the work; and doubtless C. H., like many a work with a long textual history, has suffered somewhat from this kind of corruption. But no one who carefully and without prepossession

[1] Such repetitions (e.g. the 'edification' passages, treated of above), except in cases which might easily be explained as 'transmissional'—due to the carelessness of scribes, and the like—I found to be confined almost entirely to C. H., but to be very frequent in this document, which deals largely in 'doublets' and even 'triplets.'

studies the text of C. H. in comparison with that of Eg. C. O. can rest satisfied with an 'interpolation' theory of this kind, or fail to see that C. H., as it has come to us, is the outcome not of a certain amount of fortuitous textual accretion or corruption, but of a deliberate process of redaction perpetrated on some really early document.

Take the matter of order. Achelis holds that the order of contents in C. H. is, after canon xix, an almost complete disorder, and is to be rectified by conforming it to the arrangement of the corresponding matter in Eg. C. O. This judgment of Achelis seems now to be universally accepted; and it is doubtless correct in this sense, that the order of Eg. C. O. is manifestly superior and almost certainly original. But whether the document known to us as the 'Canons of Hippolytus' ever had its contents disposed in this order, is quite another question. When we add to this defect of order in C. H. the large amount of 'interpolated' matter that has to be eliminated in order to assign the rest to an early date, I think it will appear that the original C. H., postulated by Achelis, must have suffered in quite an exceptional way in the course of its textual transmission.

Achelis essayed, by the use of brackets, to get rid of all passages which he thought could not have formed part of C. H. in its original form[1]. But then he was guided by the supposition

[1] He thought (*op. cit.* p. 147) that, apart from a couple of doubtful cases, the interpolators of C. H. did not alter the text before them, for which, he says, they evidently had a great respect. If they disagreed with what they found, they merely *added* their own view—as though some one interested in comparing present practice should make some marginal entries in an old book. Hence 'their work is scarcely to be called a *redaction*: it is an *interpolation*.' To prove that there actually are interpolations in C. H. he adduces as 'the most striking example' the double prescription in can. xvii § 93–6 and can. xviii § 100 as to 'mulieres puerperae.' In can. xvii they are (according to his text) ordered to abstain from Communion for 20 days if the child is a boy, for 40 days if it is a girl; while in can. xviii the periods are 40 and 80 days respectively. But from Riedel we learn that the women in question in can. xvii are not 'puerperae' but midwives: so that the two prescriptions contemplate two different cases; and the fact that the periods specified for a midwife are exactly half those for a 'puerpera' points to both prescriptions being by the same hand rather than by two different hands. See Riedel p. 198, and his third note on p. 209. Achelis elects to bracket out the passage in can. xviii (that which really deals with 'puerperae') as an interpolation, and keeps that in can. xvii (on midwives, as we now know) as original. Neither is found in Eg. C. O.

that C. H. was really the work of Hippolytus; and if this attribution be disallowed and it be suggested that C. H. had no existence until the latter part of the fourth century (or perhaps even till the fifth or sixth), the supposition that it has suffered interpolation or derangement of its parts will be unnecessary. For my part I do not believe it is possible, by any system of brackets or readjustment of its order, to restore the present C. H. to the form of an original document of the third century. If as originally compiled it was not a mere redaction of an earlier work, then it has itself been subjected to a process of redaction that goes far beyond anything that can be covered by the term 'interpolation.' This it will be my main endeavour to shew in the following pages.

It is curious that while Achelis employs Eg. C. O. for the restoration of the order of C. H., and often appeals to it as a positive authority for treating passages in the latter document as interpolations, and sometimes also for correcting the text in other ways; and while he actually holds that the title of Eg. C. O., when it existed, must have borne the name of Hippolytus as that of the author; yet he seems never fairly to have faced the possibility that Eg. C. O. was itself the original form of C. H. which he was trying to restore. He assumes from the outset that C. H. was the source of Eg. C. O. without anywhere undertaking to prove this[1].

I now proceed to adduce a selection of passages which appear to me to bear out what has been said above as to C. H. being the result of a deliberate process of redaction. Achelis's expurgation of the text will not seriously hamper the enquiry, even though it should be admitted that here and there he was right in regarding

[1] In making these criticisms on Achelis I must in justice remind the reader that when his judgment on the interrelation of these documents was formed he lay under a great disadvantage, as compared with more recent writers, in not having before him Hauler's Latin fragments or the full text of the Ethiopic version of Eg. C. O. As Schwartz says (*op. cit.* p. 11): 'That Achelis in his investigation (*T U* 6, 4) started from this unsupported ("isolierten") and late redaction of KO [=Eg. C. O.] was a serious mistake, one, however, which is excused by the fact that the old Latin collection was not then discovered.' In a review of Th. Schermann's *Ein Weiherituale der römischen Kirche, am Schlusse des ersten Jahrhunderts*, in *Oriens Christianus* (neue Serie 4 Band II Heft, 1915, p. 350) Schwartz pronounces C. H. to be 'an inferior, degenerate redaction of KO.' That is an estimate of C. H. to which I have been led quite independently, and which I hope to justify in the following pages.

a piece of text as a later addition to the original form of C. H.; for some of the most convincing evidence, as it appears to me, for the priority of Eg. C. O. over C. H. is to be found in passages to which Achelis takes no exception[1].

For Eg. C. O. I rely mainly on the Latin version, where extant, since in many places it clearly represents a better Greek text than does the Coptic, while as being a direct translation from the Greek it has suffered far less than the Ethiopic from corruptions and obscurities arising out of misunderstandings of the sense; it has, moreover, escaped a number of 'corrections' which in the course of centuries have befallen the last-named version. I think it well, however, to cite also the Ethiopic or the Coptic text, where one or other of these serves to illustrate the sense or control the reading of the Latin. Where the Latin is wanting, I usually cite both the Ethiopic and the Coptic.

A. *Schoolmasters.*

The first passage I adduce is one from a context which deals with various forms of occupation deemed inconsistent with the profession of Christianity and required to be abandoned by one who wishes to become a catechumen. The Latin is here wanting, and so I give the Ethiopic and Coptic texts of Eg. C. O.

Ethiopic	*Coptic*	*C. H.* xii
(Horner p. 148 l. 25 ff.)	(Horner p. 312 l. 10 ff.)	(Achelis §§ 69-70)
And if it was one who teaches children the work of this world, then it is good if he leave off; yet if there is no other occupation by which he may live, he shall be excused.	If he teaches little ones, it is good indeed for him to leave off: if he has no trade (τέχνη), then let him be forgiven.	Γραμματικός, qui parvos pueros instruit, si aliam artem non novit, qua victum quaerat, vituperet quandocunque in iis, quos instruit, aliquid apparet, et sincere confiteatur eos, qui a gentibus dii vocantur, daemones esse dicatque coram illis quotidie: Non est Deus nisi pater et filius et spiritus sanctus. Si autem discipulos omnes docere potest magnam partem (?...), vel si potest ulterius progressus docere eos fidem veram, hoc illi erit merito[2].

[1] For example, the four 'edification' passages, already dealt with, are not suspected by Achelis.

[2] Riedel translates this last sentence: 'If he is capable of teaching all his pupils many of the poets, good; but if he is furthermore capable of teaching them the true faith, he will thereby earn reward.'

64   THE SO-CALLED EGYPTIAN CHURCH ORDER

This passage offers a fair example of the sort of differences which often appear between C. H. and Eg. C. O. It will probably strike most readers as odd that Achelis has not bracketed out as interpolation the whole of the C. H. text after 'victum quaerat.' In Eg. C. O. the question for decision is a very simple one: whether a heathen schoolmaster, after he has become a catechumen, may go on as before. The question was a practical one in Tertullian's day, and he answered it in the negative (*de Idol* c. 10). But C. H. has a later standpoint, and takes us beyond that simple issue. According to this document a heathen γραμματικός, accustomed to teach letters to heathen children, is, on becoming a catechumen, to share the functions of a Christian catechist, and teach those same children the doctrine of the Trinity[1].

B. *Extempore prayer by the Bishop.*

Immediately after the prescriptions as to confessors there is in Eg. C. O. a passage which evidently relates to the eucharistic prayer, ordered in an earlier part of these documents to be said by the bishop after his ordination. C. H. has a piece which evidently stands in an immediate literary relation to the Eg. C. O. text, but has an entirely different application and sense. Let us compare the texts. The Latin of Eg. C. O. is wanting, and we must be content with the Ethiopic and Coptic.

Ethiopic	*Coptic*	*C. H.* vi
(Horner p. 146 l. 14 ff.)	(Horner p. 309 l. 5 ff.)	(Achelis § 47)
And the bishop shall give thanks as we have already said. And it is [*sic*][2] necessary that he should mention the things which we have already said, that he should recite	Now the bishop shall give thanks (εὐχαριστεῖν) according to the things which we said before. It is not altogether (οὐ πάντως) necessary for him to recite the same words	episcopus igitur omittat orationis partem, quae ad spiritum sanctum pertinet.

---

[1] Lay 'teachers' are found in Eg. C. O.; but the mention of them comes later, and the context shews that they are Christian catechists: 'And after the prayer, when the teacher has laid his hand upon the catechumen he shall pray and dismiss them. And if it was one belonging to the church who teaches, or a layman, he shall do likewise' (Horner p. 150). Cf. A. C. viii 32: ὁ διδάσκων εἰ καὶ λαϊκὸς ᾖ, ἔμπειρος δὲ τοῦ λόγου καὶ τὸν τρόπον σεμνός, διδασκέτω· "ἔσονται γὰρ πάντες διδακτοὶ θεοῦ." A special order of 'teachers' is mentioned by Hermas (*Vis.* iii 5), and by Hippolytus (*in Dan.* lib. I, c. 17).

[2] Arabic also (Horner p. 247 l. 9), 'and it is obligatory.'

clearly and carefully, and give thanks to God according as it is proper for each to pray. And if there was one who could pray with devotion or use (make) a grand and elevated prayer, and he himself being good; and if he prayed and speaks praise with moderation, no one shall be prevented from praying, who is truly right (in his faith).

which we said before, as if learning to say them by heart in his thanksgiving (εὐχ.)[1] to God; but according to the ability of each one he is to pray. If indeed he is able to pray sufficiently well with a grand prayer, then it is good; but if also he should pray and recite a prayer in (due) measure, no one may forbid him, only let him pray being sound in orthodoxy.

The first point to be observed is that the omission by the Ethiopic (as also by the Arabic) of the negative—'and it is *not* necessary'—is contrary to the whole tenor of the passage, and that the Coptic preserves the correct reading. The negative is also implied in the 'omittat' of C. H.; and Test. too has (i 39): 'But let him *not* pray over him (sc. the confessor) repeating all these words.' The reason for the omission is easy to see: it appeared strange to some later editor or copyist that a prayer prescribed to be said should immediately be allowed not to be said.

What is the prayer directly in question in Eg. C. O.? From the wording of the text it seems evident that it is not one for the ordination of a confessor, as the position of the passage might suggest, but the eucharistic prayer. This is in reality not a much less natural place in which to speak of the eucharistic prayer than it is to speak of any of the ordination prayers. In either case we have to suppose that the author turns back for a moment to mention a point which would have been more appropriately dealt with just after the prayer alluded to, whichever it be. The immediately preceding context does not actually mention that the bishop is to *pray* in ordaining a confessor; and so the last prayer mentioned is that for the ordination of a deacon. The indications of the passage itself certainly do not suggest an ordination prayer; it speaks twice of the bishop's 'giving thanks' (εὐχαριστεῖν), a word not previously used of any of the ordination prayers, but employed in all texts of Eg. C. O. to introduce the liturgical prayer. The phrase, too, 'but according to the ability of each one he is to pray,' reminds us of Justin's ὅση δύναμις

[1] Achelis (*op. cit.* p. 69) 'wenn er Gott dankt (εὐχαριστεῖν).'

αὐτῷ (1 *Apol.* c. 67). The whole passage is of too general and comprehensive a character to be taken (as C. H. and Test. take it) in reference to the ordination of a specific class of confessors, and it must be understood as constituting an independent paragraph with a retrospective purpose. I am convinced that it is the eucharistic prayer that is in question in Eg. C. O., and that the compilers of C. H. and Test., misled by the position of the passage, have tried to apply it to the ordination of a confessor to the presbyterate[1].

C. *A warning against instability.*

In canon xv (§§ 77, 78) C. H., speaking of the conditions for admitting heathens to Christian instruction, says:

> Trium testium asseveratione opus est, qui testentur illos ab omnibus talibus nefandis operibus iam resiluisse. *Non raro enim fit, ut homines usque ad senectutem propositis suis inhaereant,* nisi summa vi contendant.

To this there is nothing parallel in Eg. C. O. in the same context; but what answers to the italicized words is found in this document in an earlier passage on the appointment of widows, thus:

Ethiopic	Coptic
(Horner p. 146–7)	(Horner p. 310)
And if it was one whose husband had lately died, she shall not be trusted. But even if she is aged, she shall be tried many days, because lust will contend with those who are ordained to a place[2].	But if she has not tarried long since her husband died, trust her not. But (even) if she has become old let them prove (δοκιμάζειν) her by time (χρόνος). *For often the passions even grow old with him who gives place for them in himself.*

[1] Schwartz (*op. cit.* p. 35) takes this view without contemplating the possibility of any other. After giving a Greek translation of the Coptic he says: 'The bishop, then, is at liberty to hold himself independent of the verbal text of the prescribed *eucharistic* prayers, and thus possesses the prerogative which the *Didache* (xi 7) accords only to prophets....That these directions stand at the end of the section on ordinations is explained by the fact that the office conferred by ordination and the ministry of the Eucharist are correlated ideas.' Dr Frere too (*J. T. S.* xvi p. 359) holds the Eg. C. O. text to be original and that of C. H. to be secondary, though he appears to understand that an ordination prayer is in question.

[2] Horner notes on the last clause of the Ethiopic: 'This seems a misunderstanding of the Arabic version.' The Arabic has: 'for solicitations grow old in him who makes place for them in him' (p. 247). The corresponding passage on widows in C. H. (can. ix) is to be sought in Riedel; Haneberg's text has only a fragment of it. It has nothing answering to the italicized clauses above.

It seems fairly evident that, as Mr Horner observes, the Ethiopic has misunderstood the last clause, and that the Coptic (supported by the Arabic) gives the original sense. That this clause is in Eg. C. O. thoroughly appropriate to its context hardly needs to be pointed out: the italicized words naturally presuppose some trial of the fitness of *aged* persons; and this is prescribed in the previous sentence[1]. The clause in C. H. (can. xv §§ 77–8), on converts from heathenism, has no such appropriateness. It does not appear to me credible that the clause, in the position it occupies in Eg. C. O., was borrowed from the context in which it appears in C. H.

D. *Fasting Communion, and the Easter Fast.*

The passages in C. H. and Eg. C. O. in which fasting is spoken of deserve careful attention. In quoting the several texts I italicize certain words and clauses on which I wish especially to comment.

(i)

Eg. C. O.
(Hauler p. 116)

Nemo in pascha, antequam oblatio fiat [Copt.—and Eth. similarly—'before the hour in which it is right to eat'], *percipiat.* Nam qui ita agit, *non illi imputatur ieiunium.*

C. H.
(can. xxii §§ 195-198)

Hebdomas qua Iudaei Pascha agunt ab omni populo summo cum studio observetur, caveantque imprimis ut illis diebus ieiuni maneant ab omni cupiditate, ita ut in omni sermone non loquantur cum hilaritate, sed cum tristitia, [quia norunt dominum universi impassibilem pro nobis passum esse eo tempore, ut nos patientes toleremus dolores, quibus liberari possimus illis tormentis, quae propter peccata nostra meruimus; utque etiam participes facti dolorum, quos pro nobis suscepit, participes simus regni eius.][2]
Cibus autem, qui tempore πάσχα convenit, est panis cum solo sale et aqua.

[1] It may be remarked that this prescription is quite in the spirit of 1 Tim. v: young widows are to be avoided, and even those who are of the requisite age are to have special qualifications.

[2] The words in square brackets here and in the passages that follow are regarded by Achelis as interpolations.

68 THE SO-CALLED EGYPTIAN CHURCH ORDER

Eg. C. O.

Si quis autem in utero habet et *aegrotat* et non potest *duas dies* ieiunari, in sabbato ieiunet propter necessitatem, contenens panem et aquam.

Si quis vero in navigio vel in aliqua *necessitate* constitutus ignoravit diem... post quinquagesimam reddat ieiunium.

C. H.

Si quis *morbo* affectus

vel ruri vitam agit, ubi Christianos non novit, ita ut tempore πάσχα laetitiae se permittat ignorans terminum eius...hi omnes ieiunent post pentecosten.

(ii)

C. H. (can. xix § 150—xx § 156). [Ii vero, qui baptizantur, cum ceteris qui illorum ieiunio sunt adstricti, *nihil gustabunt antequam sumserint de corpore Christi; illud enim non aestimaretur ieiunium*, sed peccatum. Si *huic contrarians* ante communionem corporis aliquid sumserit, *contrariatur Deo* eumque contemnit. Finita autem missa conceditur illi, ut edat quod vult. Omnes autem catechumeni congregentur, ut illis sufficiat doctor unus, qui illos sufficienter instruat orando et flectendo genua, *neque gustent quidquam antequam* ii, qui baptizati sunt, *communionem corporis et sanguinis finierint.*]

(can. xx) Diebus ieiunii, qui constituti sunt *in canonibus*, feria quarta et sexta [et quadraginta] (?ieiunent¹). Qui autem alia ieiunia superaddit ad haec, mercedem acquiret. *Qui autem huic adversatur* neque *morbo* neque infortunio vel *necessitate* excusatus, *extra canonem* versatur *Deoque adversatur*, [qui pro nobis ieiunavit].

(iii)

Eg. C. O.
(Hauler p. 117)

Omnis autem fidelis festinet, *antequam aliquid aliut gustet, eucharistiam percipere.* Si enim ex fide percipit, etiamsi mortale quodcumque datum illi fuerit, post hoc non potest eum nocere.

C. H.
(can. xxviii § 205)

Ne gustet aliquis fidelium quicquam, nisi antea de mysteriis sumserit, praesertim diebus ieiunii sacri.

In these passages there are two special points for consideration: (*a*) 'fasting communion'; (*b*) the Easter fast.

(*a*) In no. (i) it might seem at first sight that C. H. is not the true parallel to Eg. C. O.; it begins differently, and it does not mention the matter of taking no food before the Eucharist. It might therefore be thought that what C. H. has in passage (ii) is the real parallel to the passage in Eg. C. O. (i). But the contexts make it clear that this is not the case: in (i) C. H., like Eg. C. O., is dealing with the paschal fast, and both documents go on to specify certain cases in which the fast is to be kept after Pentecost.

¹ So Achelis conjectures.

In passage (ii), on the other hand, although C. H. has certain remarkable points of literary contact with Eg. C. O. (i), yet what is there said refers to a different matter, viz. the fast of those who are being baptized, and comes immediately after the directions as to the first communion of the newly baptized. C. H. (ii) has really no parallel passage in Eg. C. O., and hence Achelis felt himself at liberty to bracket out most of it as forming no part of the original C. H.—with what justice must now be considered.

In the bracketed portion of C. H. (ii) we find the words 'illud enim non aestimaretur ieiunium.' This phrase occurs nowhere else in C. H., and consequently cannot be a repetition by a later interpolator of something he had read elsewhere in this document; but it does occur, in reference to the same thing—the taking of food before communion, or 'the Oblation'—and in nearly the same words, in Eg. C. O. (i): 'non illi imputatur ieiunium.' Thus the 'interpolator' of the bracketed portion of C. H. (ii) had Eg. C. O. before him.

But again, the 'interpolated' part of C. H. (ii) has also a literary connexion with the non-'interpolated' part; for in the former we read: 'si huic contrarians...sumserit, contrariatur Deo,' and in the latter: 'Qui autem huic adversatur...Deoque adversatur.'

And finally the non-'interpolated' part of C. H. (ii)—equally with the 'interpolated' part—reproduces some of the language of Eg. C. O. (i), viz. in the clause 'neque *morbo* neque infortunio vel *necessitate* excusatus' (cf. Eg. C. O. 'Si quis...*aegrotat*,' and 'vel in aliqua *necessitate* constitutus').

We must then, in the present case, reject Achelis's interpolation theory as inadmissible, and treat the whole of passage (ii) as an integral part of C. H. And the ground being thus cleared, we may proceed to ask, What is the exact meaning of the prescription in the first part of C. H. (ii) as to taking nothing before communion?

The first sentence of this passage, in which its literary relation to Eg. C. O. (i) is manifest, might, taken by itself, legitimately be interpreted as meaning no more than that the reception of communion marks the term of the fast imposed on those who are being baptized. But the clauses that follow appear to go beyond this, and definitely to contemplate fasting communion as the general rule. That this is actually the case will probably appear from C. H. (iii), where the words 'praesertim diebus ieiunii sacri,' following the prohibition 'Ne gustet aliquis...nisi antea de mysteriis sumserit,' shew that the prohibition is a general one.

Let us now turn to Eg. C. O. at (i). That the Latin 'antequam *oblatio fiat*' is, if not the original, at least an early reading, is indicated by the related passage in C. H. at no. (ii), and also by Test. (ii 20), which says that the bishop must give command 'that no one taste anything until *the Offering* is completed.'[1] What then is the meaning of the Eg. C. O. direction? I think that if we look at it fairly, and in conjunction with the reason that is added ('Nam qui ita agit, *non illi imputatur ieiunium*'), it will appear that the writer's intention was merely to fix the term of the Easter fast, and that no ideas connected with 'fasting communion' were present in his mind at all. He is professedly speaking of the fast: it is of two days, and ends after the Easter Mass; if any food be taken before that point the Easter fast is broken.

But what of the Eg. C. O. passage in no. (iii)? We have seen just above that the parallel passage to this in C. H. evidently lays down fasting communion as the rule; this appears from the added words 'praesertim diebus ieiunii sacri.' Now instead of these words of C. H., Eg. C. O. adds the following remarkable reason why the Eucharist should be received before any other food is tasted: that even if one should afterwards be given some deadly poison, this will not hurt him. We find this reproduced in Test. in a form which suggests that the compiler understood the original prescription to mean that the Eucharist was to be received before all meals: 'But *alway* let the faithful take care that *before he eat* he partake of the Eucharist, that he may be incapable of receiving injury' (ii 25). I shall presently have to deal again with the Eg. C. O. passage no. (iii) with reference to the context in which it occurs[2], and I shall then give what appear to me to be good reasons for believing that it refers not to communion in church

---

[1] It is questionable, however, whether the original reading was not προσφέρεσθαι, 'to eat' (so Eth. and Copt.: 'before the hour in which it is right to eat'), which has been corrupted into (or treated as) προσφέρειν, 'to offer.' If so Eg. C. O. at (i) has no allusion to Communion at all.

[2] See p. 77 ff. below.

but to the private reception of the Eucharist at home. Here it is enough to remark that the reason alleged for receiving the Eucharist before other food is tasted (which reason disappears in C. H.) appears to point to ideas very far removed from any thought of a ceremonial fast *in preparation for* communion. The prescription, then, of 'fasting communion,' which we find in C. H., is absent from (or, at least, cannot legitimately be found in) Eg. C. O.

(b) The second point for consideration in the passages we are dealing with is the Easter fast. What are the ideas connected with this in the minds of the respective authors of C. H. and Eg. C. O.?

Here it will be well to have before us the only other passages in these two documents which treat of fasting. Besides passages (i) (ii) and (iii) above, each has two other allusions to this subject. The first refers especially to the fast of those about to be baptized.

Eg. C. O. (Copt.)
(Horner p. 315)
Then let those who are set apart to be baptized be instructed to bathe and make themselves free (from the alien), and wash themselves on the fifth day of the week....Let them who will be baptized fast on the preparation of the sabbath.

C. H.
(can. xix § 106)
Qui autem baptizandi sunt, feria quinta hebdomadis laventur aqua et edant. Feria autem sexta ieiunent.

The next passage concerns fasting in general. Here the Greek text of Eg. C. O. is extant, having been found by Funk in the Vienna MS. hist. gr. 7 fol. 12[1]. I cite also the Coptic text.

Eg. C. O. (Greek)
(Funk II p. 112)
Χῆραι καὶ παρθένοι πολλάκις νηστευέτωσαν καὶ εὐχέσθωσαν ὑπὲρ τῆς ἐκκλησίας.
πρεσβύτεροι, ἐπὰν βούλοιντο, καὶ λαϊκοὶ ὁμοίως νηστευέτωσαν.

Eg. C. O. (Copt.)
(Horner p. 320)
Let the widows and virgins fast often, and let them pray in the church.
Likewise the presbyters and the laymen, let them fast at the time when they wish[2].

C. H.
(can. xxxii §§ 157-9)
Virginum et viduarum est ut saepe ieiunent et orent in ecclesia.
Clericis libera sit facultas voluntarie ieiunandi.

[1] See *Didasc. et Const. Apost.* II p. 112, and Schwartz *op. cit.* pp. 3-4.

[2] The Ethiopic has this clause thus (Horner p. 157): 'And the presbyters and the deacons shall fast at any time they will. And likewise shall the people fast.' Here 'and the deacons' is evidently a later interpolation; otherwise the Ethiopic keeps nearer to the form of the Greek than does the Coptic.

Eg. C. O. (Greek)	*Eg. C. O. (Copt.)*	*C. H.*
ἐπίσκοπος οὐ δύναται νηστεύειν, ἐὰν μὴ ὅτε καὶ πᾶς ὁ λαός.	But it is impossible for the bishop to fast except on the day when *all the people* will fast.	Episcopus autem ieiunio non se obstringat nisi *clerus* cum ipso ieiunet.
ἔσθ' ὅτε γὰρ θέλει τις προσενεγκεῖν, καὶ ἀρνήσασθαι οὐ δύναται· κλάσας δὲ πάντως γεύεται.	For it will happen that some one wishes to take some (food) to the church, and it is impossible for him to be denied; and having broken the bread he shall certainly taste the bread (etc.).	Si quis autem oblationem facere intendit, [quo tempore presbyter in ecclesia non adest, diaconus loco eius fungatur in omnibus rebus, cum exceptione solius portandi sacrificii magni et orationis].

The first of these two passages is, as already observed, connected with the immediate preparation for baptism, and refers solely to the fast of those about to be baptized. The second deals with fasting in general, and so does not enter into the question of the Easter fast; but it is instructive in itself for the purpose of the present enquiry, and will justify a short digression.

In the first couple of clauses of this second passage C. H. does not differ very widely from Eg. C. O.; but in the third there is a significant variation. Eg. C. O. says that the bishop is to fast only when the *people* fast, and adds a practical reason for this, viz. that it may happen that someone will make an offering, of which it is the bishop's duty to partake. Here we seem to be in touch with realities. But C. H. substitutes 'clergy' for 'people,' and alleges no reason why the bishop should fast only when the clergy do so. This alteration—for so it must be regarded—is obviously due to conventional ideas by which the bishop is naturally associated with the clergy. Achelis, no doubt recognizing this, says that we should correct 'clergy' in C. H. to 'people.' He also notices (but fails to account for) a further difficulty connected with the C. H. text, namely this: that what immediately follows in this document clearly has a literary relation to the reason given in Eg. C. O. why the bishop should only fast with the people—the words 'Si quis autem oblationem facere intendit' of C. H. evidently answer to ἔσθ' ὅτε γὰρ θέλει τις προσενεγκεῖν of Eg. C. O. What does this mean? It means that the compiler of C. H., thinking it more proper that the bishop should fast with the clergy than with the people, has turned off the reason alleged in Eg. C. O. for the latter practice and attached it, most abruptly, to a separate formal enactment about the distribution of the 'offering' in question to the people—an enactment which comes some way further on in Eg. C. O. (but in the Ethiopic only[1]). Achelis sees the superiority of Eg. C. O. here, but says that the C. H. text may well be due to a 'misunderstanding on the part of a translator.' He accordingly brackets out as an interpolation the words 'quo tempore presbyter in ecclesia non adest, diaconus loco eius fungatur...orationis,' which follow. This however will not do; for these words are a genuine portion of C. H., and their parallel in Eg. C. O. is preserved in the Ethiopic text (Horner p. 159), thus:

Eg. C. O. (Eth.)	C. H.
If there is no presbyter to give that which was distributed, as much as ought to be received, he (the deacon) shall give thanks and shall take count there of them who take (it) away, that they minister with care and give the eulogia.	quo tempore presbyter in ecclesia non adest, diaconus loco eius fungatur in omnibus rebus, cum exceptione solius portandi sacrificii magni et orationis.

Here the ensuing context in both documents will shew that we have a true literary dependence and not a mere coincidence.

After this digression let us return to the subject of the Easter fast. The two passages last adduced do not directly touch this matter; so that the only texts to be considered are our original passages (i) (ii) and (iii) at pp. 67–68 above.

Of these no. (i) deals specifically with the Easter fast in both Eg. C. O. and C. H. In the second part of no. (ii) C. H. tells us that the regular, or 'canonical,' fasting days are Wednesday and Friday and the 'quadraginta.' In (iii) C. H. prescribes fasting communion, and 'especially *in the days of the holy fast.*'

The point to be particularly noted about no. (i) is that while Eg. C. O. speaks of a paschal fast of only *two days,* C. H. says that the *week* in which the Jews keep the πάσχα is to be carefully noted. It is somewhat striking that in the C. H. passage this week is not described at the outset as a 'fast,' nor is the observance which is specified that of fasting. What is particularly insisted on is mourning, and the avoiding of all 'hilaritas' and 'laetitia.' That the week is really one of fasting as well we learn quite

[1] Horner p. 159 ll. 19–26, *plus* some words accidentally omitted but supplied in the Collation p. 384.

incidentally, when at the end of the passage it is said that anyone who, through ignorance of the time of the πάσχα, 'laetitiae se permittat' is to *fast* after Pentecost. So strong is this emphasis on the sorrowful aspect of πάσχα week that it suggests the question: Is not the compiler of C. H. here possibly concerned with the differentiation of the Holy Week fast from other fasts? When we look at passage (ii) we find it stated that the regular fasts are Wednesday, Friday 'and the *quadraginta*.' Achelis rejects this inclusion of Lent because, he says, it is contradicted by passage (i), which speaks of a paschal fast of only one week. But if C. H. is not earlier than the middle of the fourth century no contradiction is involved. In A. C. v 13 we find the following direction as to Lent and Holy Week:

'After these (festivals) you are to keep the fast of Lent (τῆς τεσσαρακοστῆς), which includes a memory of the Lord's life (πολιτείας) and teaching (νομοθεσίας). But let this fast be concluded before the fast of the πάσχα, beginning on the second day of the week and being completed on the preparation (Friday[1]). After which breaking your fast, begin the holy week of the πάσχα, fasting during it, all of you, with fear and trembling, praying in these (days) for those who are perishing.'

On this Funk remarks: 'Haec disciplina [sc. the keeping of Lent up to the Saturday before Palm Sunday], quam Constitutor quoque sequitur quadragesimam a ieiunio hebdomadis sanctae discernens, paulatim Oriente toto in usum venit.' Thus in the fourth century a Lent of forty days, in addition to an older Holy Week fast of six, was well understood; and on the view here taken of C. H. its prescription of both these fasts is quite consistent. The inclusion of Lent also accords, as we have seen, with the compiler's apparent anxiety to attach a peculiar and distinctive character to the Holy Week fast.

It appears then to be the case that, while the only paschal fast known to the author of Eg. C. O. was one of two days (Friday and Saturday of Holy Week), the compiler of C. H., like the

---

[1] I.e. the Friday before Palm Sunday. Funk notes: 'Sabbato enim praeter sabbatum hebdomadis sanctae Graeci non ieiunabant.' Thus the quadragesima ends on Friday; then there is a break of two days, and the Holy Week fast begins on the Monday following.

author of A. C., contemplates both a full 'quadraginta' and a Holy Week fast of six days.

Of the forty days fast Funk says (I p. 269 note 3): 'Quadragesima primum a synodo Nicaena c. 5 commemoratur et haud dubie non multo ante exorta est. Testimonia, quae praebent Canones qui sub nomine Hippolyti Romani arabice circumferuntur c. 20 et Origenis In Lev. hom. 10, fide non sunt digna.'

On the other hand, the observance of a paschal fast only, of one, two or more days in Holy Week, was a very ancient practice, as St Irenaeus testifies in his letter to Pope Victor (Euseb. *Hist. Eccl.* v 24). For a paschal fast of six days we have the testimony of Dionysius of Alexandria[1]. He blames those who break the Easter fast before midnight and commends those who carry it on to the fourth watch of the night, but does not censure those who leave off for some special cause, adding: ἐπεὶ μηδὲ τὰς ἐξ τῶν νηστειῶν ἡμέρας ἴσως μηδὲ ὁμοίως πάντες διαμένουσιν—some remain without food (ἄσιτοι) for the whole six days, others for two, others for three, others for four, others for none at all. Then he adds, that if any should spend the first four days not merely without abstaining from all food, but not even fasting, and rather in luxuries and banqueting, and then imagine that by abstaining from all food on the last two days (Friday and Saturday) they do something great and fine (μέγα τι καὶ λαμπρόν), he for his part would not make these equal to those who have already exercised themselves (προησκηκόσι) for several days.

This throws some light on the Eg. C. O. text in no. (i) of the passages we are considering. There the strict prohibition against taking any food before a certain fixed point (the Easter Mass), and the clear intimation that the fast lasts two days only, render it practically certain that during these two days no food at all is permitted. It appears to be only in the case of pregnancy or sickness—in which case the Friday's fast is remitted—that bread and water are allowed. C. H. on the other hand, which contemplates a paschal fast of a week, permits bread, water and salt throughout the fast.

There is one striking feature in the C. H. prescription—in passage (i)—as to the paschal fast which I have not hitherto

---

[1] *Epist. Canonica* (Routh, *Reliq. Sacr.* III p. 229). Dionysius was bishop from 248 to 264-5; the date of the letter cannot be fixed more precisely.

adverted to, but which must now be considered, since at first sight it may not unnaturally be regarded as a mark of early date. This is the direction that Holy Week is to be fixed by noting the week in which the Jews keep the Passover. This is not, of course, what is known as the *quartodeciman* method of reckoning Easter, for C. H. makes Easter day Sunday, and not the fourteenth of Nisan. Were it strict quartodecimanism that was ordered, we should know at once that the prescription containing it could not possibly have emanated from Hippolytus, who wrote against the Quartodecimans as heretics. Whether, even as it stands, the prescription could have come from Hippolytus is a point which may well be considered doubtful[1], but which I shall not discuss here. It will be more to the purpose to indicate the possible source of this early-looking feature in a document which contains several marks of post-Nicene influence. There is, I think, a fair probability that the direction as to the Holy Week fast was drawn from the *Didascalia* bk v cc. 18 and 20 (according to Funk).

Didasc. v

c. 20 (Funk I p. 298). Vos ergo, cum populus ille [the Jews] pascham facit, ieiunate et vigilias vestras studete perficere mediis in azymis eorum[2].

(p. 296) Propterea et vos lugeatis pro eis (sc. Iudaeis) die sabbati paschae usque ad tertiam horam noctis sequentis; ac deinde in resurrectione Christi laetamini ac delectamini coram eis et solvite ieiunium vestrum, et reliquias ieiunii vestri sex dierum offerte Domino Deo.

c. 18 (p. 288). Propterea a decima, quae est secunda sabbati, diebus paschae

C. H. xxii

(§§ 195-7) *Hebdomas qua Iudaei pascha agunt* ab omni populo summo cum studio observetur,

caveantque ut illis diebus ieiuni maneant ab omni cupiditate, ita ut in omni sermone non loquantur cum hilaritate, sed cum tristitia, quia norunt Dominum universi impassibilem pro nobis passum esse eo tempore....

Cibus autem, qui tempore πάσχα

---

[1] Dr Wordsworth says of C. H. (*op. cit.* p. 22): 'It cannot, however, I think, be the work of Hippolytus himself, chiefly for two reasons: (1) because the date of the Easter fast is, in it, ordered to be found by observing when the Jews keep the Passover....' And *ibid.*: 'We must therefore probably assign it to a period before A.D. 216-224, when Hippolytus was making his researches into the Kalendar.' And p. 359: 'About the year A.D. 216 he [Hippolytus] determined to try and deliver the Christian world from the necessity of following the Jewish calculation as to the Paschal full-moon, which was not only a humiliating dependence but was found sometimes to lead to wrong results.'

[2] Cf. also *Didasc.* c. xvii *init.* (Funk I p. 286): 'Oportet igitur, fratres, *dies paschae vos accurate inquirere* et ieiunium vestrum facere *cum omni diligentia*. Incipite vero, *cum fratres vestri, qui e populo sunt, pascham faciunt*.'

ieiunabitis atque *pane et sale et aqua solum* utemini hora nona usque ad quintam sabbati: parasceven tamen et sabbatum integrum ieiunate, nihil gustantes.

convenit, est *panis cum solo sale et aqua*[1].

Though these parallels do not amount to evidence that the C. H. compiler has here borrowed from the *Didascalia*, yet on the face of the case it appears to me that there is a strong probability that this is so, and that herein lies the explanation of this divergence of C. H. from Eg. C. O. in the matter of the Holy Week fast[2].

E. *Care of the Holy Eucharist in communicating.*

The passage in Eg. C. O. on the subject of receiving the Eucharist before tasting other food[3] (Hauler p. 117), which has already been considered in connexion with the idea of fasting communion, must now be looked at again in its context and together with the parallel context of C. H. Square brackets in the C. H. text mark pieces which Achelis treats as interpolations.

Eg. C. O.
(Hauler p. 117)

C. H.
(Cann. xxviii, xxix, §§ 205-213)

(1) Fideles vero mox, cum expergefacti fuerint et surrexerint, antequam operae suae contingant, orent Deum et sic iam ad opus suum properent. Si qua autem per verbum catecizatio fit, praeponat hoc, ut pergat et audiat verbum Dei ad confortationem animae suae; festinent autem et ad ecclesiam, ubi floret spiritus.

(2) Omnis autem fidelis festinet, antequam aliquid aliut gustet, eucharistiam percipere.

Ne gustet aliquis fidelium quicquam, nisi antea de mysteriis sumserit, praesertim diebus ieiunii sacri.

---

[1] Riedel: 'ist allein Brot und Salz sowie Wasser.'

[2] The passages cited from the *Didascalia*, in addition to directing a careful observation of the time when the Jews keep the Passover, and extending the fast over a week (six days), coincide with C. H. in permitting 'only bread and salt and water' during the fast. The passage in Eg. C. O. corresponding to the C. H. text speaks only of 'bread and water,' and this in a different connexion—it is allowed, apparently, on the Saturday only, and then only to those who cannot observe the fast in the regular way, that is, by abstaining from all food on the Friday and Saturday.

[3] I.e. passage (iii) at p. 68 above.

Eg. C. O.

(3) Si enim ex fide percipit, etiamsi mortale quodcumque datum illi fuerit, post hoc non potest eum nocere.

(4) Omnis autem festinet, ut non infidelis gustet de eucharistia,

(5)

(6) aut ne sorix aut animal aliud[1],
(7) aut ne quid cadeat et pereat de eo.
(8) Corpus enim est Christi edendum credentibus et non contemnendum.

(9) ⟨Calicem⟩[2] in nomine enim Dei benedicens accepisti quasi antitypum[3] sanguinis Christi.

(10) Quapropter nolito effundere, ut non spiritus alienus velut te contemnente illut delingat:

(11) reus eris sanguinis, tamquam qui spernit prae[pu]tium, quo[d] conparatus est.

(12)
(13) See (10) above

(14)

C. H.

Ceterum *clerici* caveant cum sollicitudine ne quemquam *ad sumenda sacra mysteria invitent*, nisi solos fideles.

[Stet clerus vacans altari (non occupatus prope altare); quando paratum est, stet] ad custodiendum
ne *supervolitet musca*
neve cadat quicquam *in calicem*, [*see also* (13) *below.*]

See (13) *below*

[unde oriatur crimen mortis *pro presbyteris*].

[Ideo unus custodiat locum sacrum.]
Qui autem *distribuit mysterium* quique accipiunt, magna diligentia caveant ne quicquam in terram decidat, ne potiatur eo spiritus malignus.

[Nemo intra velum aliquid loquatur, nisi orationem vel quae pro cultu necessaria sunt, praeterea omnino nihil; ne fiat aliquod opus in loco illo. Ubi autem absolverunt communionem populi, intrent ut recitent. Omni hora intrent propter potestates loci sacri et sint illis psalmi pro tintinnabulis quae erant in tunica Aaronis, neve sedeat quis illo tempore, sed orent, neve aliud quicquam agant, inclinentque genua et prosternentur ante altare. Pulverem autem qui scopis converritur de loco sacro proiciant in aquam maris undosi, neve remaneat(?) conculcandus(?) ab hominibus, sed omni tempore purus sit.]

---

[1] So in the Coptic and Arabic: 'nor a mouse, nor any other creature.'
[2] This word is wanting. Hauler thinks that before this clause a heading has fallen out; he says: '*Suppl. vid.* ⟨Nihil effundendum de calice⟩.'
[3] On this idea of the Eucharist as an 'antitype' of the body and blood of Christ see p. 86 below.

As regards this passage, it is to be remarked that section (1), though occurring in all the versions of Eg. C. O.[1], does not seem to be in its proper place here. The reasons for thinking this are, (a) that the passage is repeated (though in a longer form) a little further on in the Ethiopic (Horner p. 182), Arabic (p. 262) and Coptic (p. 327)[2]—just before a number of directions as to daily prayer; and (b) that it is obviously, from the nature of its contents, in place in the latter context.

The differences which appear between Eg. C. O. and C. H. in the directions which follow—in nos. (2), etc.—are of the utmost significance and importance for determining the relation in which the two documents stand to each other, and they must be considered in some detail.

As regards no. (2), it has already been pointed out that there is nothing in Eg. C. O. to suggest that the author of this document had any idea in his mind of a ceremonial fast in preparation for communion, whereas this idea was clearly in the mind of the compiler of C. H.[3].

Here it is to be noticed in addition that Eg. C. O. gives no indication whatever that the reception of the Eucharist spoken of is that which takes place at a celebration in church. The indications point rather to a private reception at home, in the lay Christian's own house. For in nos. (4)–(11) the cautions as to the safeguarding of the Eucharist are all addressed to the lay communicant himself: the believer ('fidelis') is to see (a) that no unbeliever taste of it, nor (b) a 'mouse or any other creature' eat it, and (c) that it do not fall to the ground and be lost. As regards (a), it seems hardly conceivable that a writer who was thinking of communion in church should warn lay communicants to keep unbelievers—who would not be admitted at all—from 'tasting' the eucharist. As to (b), again, the possibility of mice eating the eucharistic Bread seems a contingency that would hardly occur to a writer who had in mind the public reception of the Holy Communion in church. And observe that it is not said, Beware of letting the Eucharist drop, lest a mouse should

---

[1] Eth., Horner, p. 180; Arab., p. 260; Copt., p. 325.
[2] The Latin is wanting here.
[3] See pp. 68-71 above.

find and eat it; but, Beware 'lest an unbeliever taste of the Eucharist, or a mouse or other animal'; and then is added separately, as meeting a different contingency, the caution against letting it fall; and for this a special reason is assigned, viz. 'ne pereat de eo.'[1]

It may be objected that the direction about the chalice in nos. (9)-(11) is inconsistent with the view that the writer of Eg. C. O., in speaking of the consecrated Bread, is thinking of communion at home, since there seems to be no evidence that part of the contents of the chalice was taken away for private reception, and from the nature of things this would be unlikely. But it appears to me not unnatural that a writer familiar with the practice of taking Holy Communion both in church and at home should speak quite generally of the precautions necessary, whether on the one occasion or the other. As regards the Bread, the chief danger would lie in its reservation in the layman's house and its private reception there; and consequently the precautions recommended would naturally be such as applied especially to that case—as in nos. (4), etc. But having spoken of the Bread,

---

[1] In view of the known custom in early times of reserving at home and privately receiving the Holy Communion, it appears to me that language such as this is most obviously understood to mean that the Eucharistic Bread is to be kept in some safe place, which will not be known to unbelievers or accessible to mice or other creatures.

On such private reservation and communion see Tertullian *ad Uxorem* ii c. 5, who asks the Christian wife of a heathen husband: 'Non sciet maritus quid secreto ante omnem cibum gustes?'; and *de Oratione* c. 19: 'Nonne sollemnior erit statio tua si et ad aram Dei steteris? Accepto corpore Domini et reservato utrumque salvum est, et participatio sacrificii et executio officii' (sc. the observance of the station). St Cyprian (*de Lapsis* c. 26) tells a story of a woman who attempted to receive the Eucharist after partaking of an idol sacrifice: 'Et cum quaedam arcam suam, in qua sanctum Domini fuit, manibus immundis temptasset aperire, igne inde surgente deterrita est ne auderet attingere.' The practice was still kept up in Egypt in St Basil's day. Mr Brightman says (*L. E. W.* i p. 509, n. 27): ' In the fourth century it was usual for the faithful to carry away particles in which to communicate themselves: S. Bas. *ep.* xciii (iii 187 A) ἐν Ἀλεξανδρείᾳ δὲ καὶ ἐν Αἰγύπτῳ ἕκαστος καὶ τῶν ἐν λαῷ τελούντων ὡς ἐπὶ τὸ πλεῖστον ἔχει κοινωνίαν ἐν τῷ οἴκῳ αὐτοῦ καὶ ὅτε βούλεται μεταλαμβάνει δι' ἑαυτοῦ.' From St Jerome *Ep.* xlviii 15 (ad Pammachium) it seems evident that private reservation was still in use in Rome at the end of the fourth century. On the avoiding of irreverence in receiving cf. Tertullian *de Corona* c. 3: 'Calicis aut panis etiam nostri aliquid decuti in terram anxie patimur'; also Origen *hom. in Exod.* xiii 3.

it would be natural that he should also speak of the chalice, even though in this case the danger lay only in its reception in church[1].

I now turn to C. H. Whatever doubt there might be as to whether Eg. C. O. is speaking of public or private communion, there is no room for hesitation in the case of C. H.

At no. (4) it is no longer the lay communicant who is to see that no unbeliever 'taste' of the Eucharist; but the *clergy* are forbidden to 'invite' any 'to receive the holy Mysteries, except only the faithful.'

Then in nos. (5)–(7) we are transported into the church and see the service being ritually carried on. A clerk ['clerus': but no. (12) says 'unus'] is to stand by the altar to see that no insects fly over the chalice and fall into it.

Here, I think, the significance of some of those details noticed above will at once be recognized. In the first place, the mouse spoken of in Eg. C. O. disappears. His place is taken by a fly; and the precaution in Eg. C. O. against *the eucharistic Bread falling on the ground* becomes one against *the fly falling into the chalice*. These variations in detail, trifling as they may appear to the superficial glance, indicate in reality two widely different points of view; they shift the whole scene, and may mark a difference in date of centuries for the two documents concerned. The prescriptions in C. H. conjure up a vision of

[1] I am here supposing that the form of Wine was not reserved for private communion. But we do not really *know* that it was not; and in fact there are some grounds for thinking that it may have been. St Cyprian not only speaks of a daily reception of 'the Eucharist' (*de dom. Orat.* 18), but also of a daily reception of the chalice (*Ep.* 58, Hartel II 657): 'Gravior nunc et ferocior pugna imminet, ad quam fide incorrupta et virtute robusta parare se debeant milites Christi, considerantes idcirco se *cotidie calicem sanguinis Christi bibere* ut possint et propter Christum sanguinem fundere.' Yet Cyprian also alludes to private reservation as a matter of course and something well understood (*de Lapsis* 26; see preceding note): a fact which seems to indicate that in his time there was not, in Africa at least, a daily celebration of the Eucharist at which all might receive the chalice daily. But, if not, then they must have received it at home. If it be suggested that private reservation was allowed only to those who were prevented, by distance or by sickness, from coming daily to church, I would point out that Tertullian *de Orat.* 19 shews that it was allowed even to those who could and did come on the station days, and so presumably to all Christians (see preceding note); and there is no obvious reason for thinking that St Cyprian implies any other usage.

ritual observance, which is first presented to us in A. C. viii 12, and which meets us constantly in eastern descriptions of the liturgy from thence onward down to almost any date. From the indications given it is hardly possible to resist the conclusion that the compiler of C. H. had in his mind's eye a picture of the altar surrounded by ministers, one (or more) of whom, at the beginning of the more solemn part of the liturgy, is deputed to stand by the chalice, doubtless fan in hand, and ward off flies and other insects[1]. Let us see what is said as to this in A. C.:

Ὦν γενομένων οἱ διάκονοι προσαγέτωσαν τὰ δῶρα τῷ ἐπισκόπῳ πρὸς τὸ θυσιαστήριον, καὶ οἱ πρεσβύτεροι ἐκ δεξιῶν αὐτοῦ καὶ ἐξ εὐωνύμων στηκέτωσαν, ὡς ἂν μαθηταὶ παρεστῶτες διδασκάλῳ· δύο δὲ διάκονοι ἐξ ἑκατέρων τῶν μερῶν τοῦ θυσιαστηρίου κατεχέτωσαν ἐξ ὑμένων λεπτῶν ῥιπίδιον ἢ πτερὸν ταῶνος ἢ ὀθόνης, καὶ ἠρέμα ἀποσοβείτωσαν τὰ μικρὰ τῶν ἱπταμένων ζώων, ὅπως ἂν μὴ ἐγχρίμπτωνται εἰς τὰ κύπελλα (viii 12; Funk I pp. 494–6). Then the Preface, or Thanksgiving, immediately follows. Here it may be noted that the point of the service at which in C. H. the 'clerus' is ordered to stand by the altar to keep away insects is, apparently, the same as that in A. C., for at no. (5) it is said: 'Stet clerus vacans altari; *quando paratum est*, stet'; which naturally means, when the gifts have been set in order upon the altar. The fan, though not mentioned in C. H., may perhaps be taken for granted[2].

[1] We can fill in the picture from another passage peculiar to C. H. (can. xxxvii §§ 201-4): 'Quotiescumque episcopus mysteriis frui vult, congregentur diaconi et presbyteri apud eum, induti vestimentis albis pulchrioribus toto populo, potissimum autem splendidis. Bona autem opera omnibus vestimentis praestant. Etiam ἀναγνῶσται habeant festiva indumenta et stent in loco lectionis et alter alterum excipiat, donec totus populus congregetur. Postea episcopus oret et perficiat missam.' Of this passage only the words 'congregentur...apud eum' and 'donec totus populus congregetur' have any parallel in Eg. C. O. (cf. Horner p. 327 l. 4); but the whole of it is, very strangely, accepted by Achelis as part of the original work of Hippolytus. Cf. A. C. viii 12 (Funk I p. 496 l. 6) εὐξάμενος οὖν καθ' ἑαυτὸν ὁ ἀρχιερεὺς ἅμα τοῖς ἱερεῦσιν καὶ λαμπρὰν ἐσθῆτα μετενδύς, κτλ.

[2] We have the fans mentioned in the so-called 'Canons of St Basil,' translated by Riedel from Arabic (but containing a number of Greek words, and probably, as Riedel thinks, written originally in Greek). That the author of these canons knew C. H. is plain from a number of passages. In the first of his canons on the liturgy (no. 96) he begins with a passage which is clearly taken from C. H. can. xxix— i.e. no. (13) on p. 78 above. Then in can. 97 (Riedel p. 275) he says: 'The

The remaining paragraphs of C. H. present phenomena similar to those in nos. (3)–(7). At no. (11) the lay communicant of Eg. C. O. is replaced by the presbyters, just as at (4) he was replaced by 'clerici' and at (6) by the 'clerus.'

At no. (13) we have a combination of Eg. C. O. (7) and (10), but with the clergy again introduced. The curious and original-looking expression 'ne potiatur eo spiritus malignus' is merely a slightly softened adaptation of Eg. C. O. (10): 'ut non spiritus alienus velut te contemnente illut *delingat*.' Then in no. (14) we have the sanctuary veil[1], within which no one is permitted to speak. And again in no. (14) there is an instruction as to the decent bestowal of the dust swept from the sanctuary.

It seems unnecessary to dwell further on the contrast offered by C. H. in this passage to Eg. C. O. It remains only to observe that the derivation of Eg. C. O. from C. H. here is a moral impossibility. Further, as regards C. H. itself, there is here no room for any 'interpolation' theory. If C. H. ever had a text even approximately equivalent to that of Eg. C. O., it has been deliberately re-written from a later ecclesiastical point of view.

Achelis was sensible of the impotence of any bracketing process to restore this passage in C. H. to anything like a primitive-looking form. He says of nos. (4)–(7): 'Fragments genuine and not genuine lie here inextricably mixed up together. Without Eg. C. O. it would be quite impossible to venture to sort them out. But even so I must particularly emphasize, as regards this passage, that the brackets have the value of a suggestion only and not of an assertion' (p. 120 note). This is virtually a confession that in C. H. we have here to do with the *reduction* of an earlier document, and not with an original work merely enlarged by *interpolation*.

F. *Communion of the newly baptized.*

The next passage which I select for consideration concerns the first communion of the newly baptized. I give, besides C. H.,

deacons who have charge of the cups shall fan over the holy table with...(?) and fans.' This is evidently also based on C. H. xxix—no. (5) on p. 78 above. Hence 'Basil' interprets that passage as implying the fans.

[1] This is mentioned in C. H. at another place also, can. xxxvi § 188. Riedel has not the 'veil' in can. xxix (our passage), where he renders 'within the place.'

the Ethiopic and Latin texts of Eg. C. O. The pieces of C. H. in square brackets are rejected by Achelis as interpolations.

Eg. C. O. (Eth.) (Horner pp. 155-156)	*Eg. C. O. (Lat.)* (Hauler pp. 112-113)	*C. H.* (Can. xix §§ 142-148)
(1) And the deacons shall bring the oblation to the bishop, and he shall give thanks over the bread and the cup; and the bread that it may become the body of our Lord Christ, and the cup, the wine mixed, that it may become the blood of our Lord Christ[1], this which was shed for us and for all of us indeed who believe in him.	Et tunc iam offeratur oblatio a diaconibus episcopo et gratias agat panem quidem in exemplum, quod dicit Graecus antitypum, corporis Christi; calicem vino mixtum propter antitypum, quod dicit Graecus similitudinem, sanguinis, quod effusum est pro omnibus, qui crediderunt in eum;	Deinde diaconus [incipit sacrificare], episcopus autem defert reliquias mysteriales [corporis et sanguinis Domini nostri].
(2)		Quando autem finivit, communicat populum stans ad mensam [corporis et sanguinis Domini].
(3) And the milk and honey (shall be) mingled together, and he shall make them drink of them, because of the fulfilment of the promise which he promised to our fathers, saying: 'I will give to you the land which floweth with milk and honey': this is the Body of our Lord Christ which he gave to us who believe in him, like food of young children, who were begotten of him, those who believe in him, that he may make every bitter heart sweet by the sweetness of his word.	lac et melle mixta simul ad plenitudinem promissionis, quae ad patres fuit, quam dixit terram fluentem lac et mel, quam et dedit carnem suam Christus, per quam sicut parvuli nutriuntur, qui credunt, in suavitate verbi amara cordis dulcia efficiens;	Et presbyteri portant alios calices lactis et mellis ut doceant eos qui communicant iterum se natos esse ut parvuli, quia parvuli communicant lac et mel. [*See also* (16) *below*]
(4) All this the bishop shall go through to those who are baptized.	*See* (6) *below*	
(5) And the water also of the oblation he shall shew in the bread like the inward part of man, who is soul as well as body[3].	aquam vero in oblationem in indicium lavacri, ut et interior homo, quod est animale[2], similia consequa[n]tur sicut et corpus.	

---

[1] The Bohairic (used here by Horner to fill a gap in the Sahidic—p. 319 ll. 13-15) has this clause thus: 'because that (it is) *the form of* the flesh of the Christ; and a cup of wine because it is the blood of the Christ.' This is somewhat nearer to the Latin; and there can be no doubt that the Latin gives us here the true text, quoting as it does the Greek word 'antitype' in connexion with the bread and the cup.

[2] I.e. ψυχικόν?

[3] The Coptic (Sahidic) and Arabic omit this clause.

Eg. C. O. (Eth.)	*Eg. C. O. (Lat.)*	*C. H.*
(6) And all this explanation is what the bishop shall give to all who are baptized[1].	De universis vero his rationem reddat episcopus eis, qui percipiunt;	
(7) *See* (9) *below*	*See* (9) *below*	Presbyteris non praesentibus ad portandos illos calices, portentur a diaconis.
(8) And the bishop therefore having broken the bread of life, shall give a piece of it to each one and say: 'This is heavenly bread, the body of our Lord Christ.' And he who receives shall answer and say: 'Amen.'	frangens autem panem singulas[2] partes porrigens dicat: 'Panis caelestis in Christo Iesu.' Qui autem accipit, respondeat: 'Amen.'	Deinde porrigat illis episcopus de corpore Christi, dicens: 'Hoc est corpus Christi.' Illi vero dicant: 'Amen.'
(9) And if there are not sufficient presbyters the deacons shall take the cups and stand in order; (10) the first he who has the honey, and the second he who has the milk;	Praesbyteri vero si non fuerint sufficientes, teneant calices et diacones et cum honestate adstent et cum moderatione: primus, qui tenet aquam, secundus, qui lac,	*See* (7) *above*
(11) and he who administers the cup[3] shall say: 'In[4] God the Father almighty':	*See* (13) *below*	
(12) and the third he who has the wine.	tertius, qui vinum.	
(13) He who administers shall say: 'This is the blood of our Lord Jesus Christ.' And he who receives shall say: 'Amen and Amen.' (14)	Et gustent, qui percipient, de singulis ter dicente eo, qui dat: 'In Deo patre omnipotenti.' Dicat autem, qui accipit: 'Amen.' 'Et domino Iesu Christo et spiritu sancto et sancta ecclesia.' Et dicat: 'Amen.' Ita singulis fiat.	Et ei quibus (ille) calicem porrigit dicens: 'Hic est sanguis Christi,' dicant: 'Amen.'
(15) And when he receives the Body he shall say: 'Amen'; and at the Blood he shall say: 'Amen and Amen': a trinity. This is therefore that it shall be.		
(16) *See* (3) *above*	*See* (3) *above*	*Postea* autem sumant lac et mel in memoriam saeculi futuri et dulcedinis bonorum quae sunt studium eius qui non redit in amaritudinem, neque dissipentur.

[1] Evidently either (4) or (6) is redundant in the Ethiopic. The Sahidic and Arabic give the clause only once, omitting no. (5).
[2] The reading is doubtful; it may be 'singulis.'
[3] So all MSS except that which supplies Horner's text; this omits 'the cup.'
[4] So the best MSS; Horner's text omits 'In.'

In this passage it is to be noted that Eg. C. O.—particularly in the Latin version, which will easily be recognized as containing the better text—has certain remarkable features which quite disappear in C. H.

(a) It seems evident that at no. (1) the Ethiopic has suffered corruption under the influence of later ideas, and that the Latin must be followed as retaining the true text of Eg. C. O. This version preserves for us the original Greek terminology: the bishop 'eucharistizes' the bread ('gratias agat panem'—evidently εὐχαριστεῖν[1]) 'in exemplum, quod dicit Graecus antitypum,'[2] of the body of Christ, and the mixed cup 'propter antitypum, quod dicit Graecus similitudinem,'[3] of His blood.

These very distinctive features disappear in C. H.[4], where, be it observed, the expression 'defert reliquias mysteriales'[5] is in no way equivalent to the 'antitypus' of Eg. C. O., since 'mysteria' —as also 'corpus et sanguis Domini,' or the like—is a common expression in C. H. for the Eucharist, and is employed without any suggestion of 'figure' or 'symbol.'

(b) In C. H. the passage no. (2) anticipates no. (8), and is superfluous. Its purpose, however, is evidently to introduce no. (3) with a different sense from that which it bears in Eg. C. O.; that is, to make no. (3) refer not to the blessing of the milk and honey together with the eucharistic bread and wine (as in Eg. C. O.), but only to their distribution. Here again, in no. (2), Achelis brackets out the words 'corporis et

---

[1] Cf. Justin Martyr (1 *Apol.* c. 66) who speaks of τὴν...εὐχαριστηθεῖσαν τροφήν.

[2] Clearly εἰς ἀντίτυπον.

[3] It is not quite clear whether the meaning here is: for an antitype, which the Greek calls 'similitude' (ὁμοίωμα?); or: for an 'antitype' (εἰς ἀντίτυπον), which is what the Greek calls (is the Greek for) similitude. In the first case the Greek will have had different words for the bread (ἀντίτυπος) and the cup (ὁμοίωμα); in the second, only one for both—ἀντίτυπος. For ὁμοίωμα compare the εὐχὴ προσφόρου of Serapion at the Institution, where we find the expressions ὁμοίωμα τοῦ σώματος τοῦ μονογενοῦς and ὁμοίωμα τοῦ αἵματος (Wobbermin, *Texte u. Unters.* n. F. II 3 b p. 5; Brightman, *J. T. S.* I pp. 105, 106).

[4] We have already had—in passage E no. (9), cf. p. 78 above—the chalice spoken of in Eg. C. O. as an 'antitype of the blood of Christ'; and there too C. H. has nothing corresponding. On the eucharistic terminology of C. H. see p. 130 below.

[5] If, indeed, this gives the meaning of Haneberg's Arabic text: Riedel has simply 'completes the eucharist' (εὐχαριστία).

sanguinis Domini,' though they belong to the regular eucharistic terminology of C. H.[1]. He might have gone further and excluded the words 'stans ad mensam,' for while C. H. frequently alludes to parts of the church[2], Eg. C. O. never does so, and it is highly improbable that Eg. C. O., if derived from C. H., as Achelis supposes, should have omitted these allusions in every case.

(c) At no. (3) we find in Eg. C. O. ideas that go back to the second century. The 'land flowing with milk and honey,' promised to the fathers, is equated with 'the flesh' of Christ; and it is said that Christ, by giving us His flesh, makes sweet the 'amara cordis' by 'the sweetness of the Word.'[3]

The close connexion in thought and ideas of this passage with Clement of Alexandria's *Paed.* i 6, and less markedly with Irenaeus *Haer.* iv 38, was pointed out to me some years ago by Mr Edmund Bishop[4]. In Clement we have a mystical treatment of the 'milk' spoken of by St Paul in 1 Cor. iii. 2, which no one, I imagine, could read in connexion with nos. (3) and (5) of the above passage in Eg. C. O. without feeling that in both he was breathing nearly the same atmosphere. The whole treatment, moreover, in Clement has in view baptism, with the instruction imparted in connexion with it and the communion which follows it; and the passage of Eg. C. O. with which we are dealing concerns the first communion of the recently baptized. Clement curiously identifies the instruction given at baptism with the personal Logos. Thus the 'milk' also, of which the Apostle speaks (1 Cor. iii 2), becomes similarly identified with the Logos. But milk is both a product of blood and itself produces blood. Hence he further identifies 'milk' with 'the blood of the Word': καὶ τὸ αἷμα τοῦ λόγου πεφανέρωται ὡς γάλα (*Paed.* I vi 40, 2)[5]. But

[1] See below p. 130. [2] See below p. 131.
[3] 'Verbum' (the Coptic, Horner p. 319, has the Greek word λόγος) in the context is most naturally taken personally. Cf. in the prayer over the firstfruits: 'et offerimus tibi primitivas fructuum, quos dedisti nobis ad percipiendum, per verbum tuum enutriens ea' (Hauler p. 115); and again: 'qui memor fuit sanctorum suorum et misit verbum suum inluminantem eos' (p. 119).
[4] Cf. also Bernard, *The Odes of Solomon* (Cambridge 'Texts and Studies'), on Odes viii 17 and xix 1-3.
[5] *P. Gr.* VIII 300 A. I quote from the edition of Stählin, in the Berlin *corpus* of Greek Christian writers of the first three centuries, but add references to Migne.

he goes farther still: οὕτως πολλαχῶς ἀλληγορεῖται ὁ λόγος, καὶ βρῶμα καὶ σὰρξ καὶ τροφὴ καὶ ἄρτος καὶ αἷμα καὶ γάλα, ἃ πάντα ὁ κύριος εἰς ἀπόλαυσιν ἡμῶν τῶν εἰς αὐτὸν πεπιστευκότων. μὴ δὴ οὖν τις ξενιζέσθω λεγόντων ἡμῶν ἀλληγορεῖσθαι γάλα τὸ αἷμα τοῦ κυρίου (*Paed.* I vi 47, 2)[1].

It was seen that in Eg. C. O. at no. (3) the giving of milk and honey to the baptized stands for a fulfilment of the promise of 'a land flowing with milk and honey'; the idea evidently being that it marks their entrance into the Christian Church. This too is found in Clement, for in arguing that the milk spoken of by the Apostle does not imply any real childishness in the newly regenerated Christian—since 'the childhood which is in Christ is perfection as compared with the Law' (*Paed.* I vi 34, 2)[2]—he appeals to the promise, 'I will bring you into the good land flowing with milk and honey' (Ex. iii 8); from which he concludes: οὕτω γοῦν τελεία τροφὴ τὸ γάλα ἐστὶ τὸ τέλειον καὶ εἰς τέλος ἄγει τὸ ἀκατάπαυστον. διὸ κἂν τῇ ἀναπαύσει τὸ αὐτὸ τοῦτο ἐπήγγελται γάλα καὶ μέλι (*Paed.* I vi 36, 1)[3]. Here the 'rest' is, of course, the possession of the promised land[4]; and there can be little doubt from the context that the 'milk and honey' 'promised' in the 'rest' contains an allusion to that administered after baptism.

The argument of Irenaeus is thus summarized by Dr Bernard[5]: 'Christ came to earth in such a manner as we could receive Him. He could have come in His glory, but we could not have borne it. "And on this account, as to babes, the *perfect bread* of the Father offered Himself to us as *milk* (i.e. His Advent as man), that we being nourished by the breast as it were of His flesh, and accustomed by this lactation to eat and drink the *Logos* of God, might be able to retain in ourselves the bread of immortality which is the *Spirit* of the Father"' (*Haer.* iv 38).

Ideas connected with milk and honey similar to those in Eg. C. O. and Clement are already to be found in Barnabas.

---

[1] *P. Gr.* VIII 305 B.
[2] *Ibid.* 292 A: ἡ δὲ ἐν Χριστῷ νηπιότης τελείωσίς ἐστιν, ὡς πρὸς τὸν νόμον.
[3] *Ibid.* 292 c.
[4] As in Ps. xciv (LXX) 11; cf. Heb. iv. 1, 3.
[5] *The Odes of Solomon*, on Ode viii 17.

Having quoted Ex. xxxiii 3 in the form Εἰσέλθατε εἰς γῆν ῥέουσαν γάλα καὶ μέλι, καὶ κατακυριεύσατε αὐτῆς, he asks presently, τί οὖν τὸ γάλα καὶ τὸ μέλι; ὅτι πρῶτον τὸ παιδίον μέλιτι, εἶτα γάλακτι ζωοποιεῖται. οὕτως οὖν καὶ ἡμεῖς τῇ πίστει τῆς ἐπαγγελίας καὶ τῷ λόγῳ ζωοποιούμενοι ζήσομεν κατακυριεύοντες τῆς γῆς (vi 13, 17).

In C. H. these early conceptions vanish. Cups of milk and honey are mentioned, but the explanation of them given in nos. (3) and (16) lacks those remarkable features of the Eg. C. O. text to which attention has just been drawn. There can be no question, it seems to me, as to which of the texts at no. (3) is original and which substituted for the original[1]. And yet it is not a case of mere substitution: one of the two is based on the other in such a way that traces of their literary connexion still remain. The idea of the newly baptized as children appears in both; while the 'in *suavitate* verbi *amara* cordis *dulcia* efficiens' of Eg. C. O. at no. (3) is represented later on in C. H., at no. (16), thus: 'Postea autem sumant lac et mel in memoriam saeculi futuri[2] et *dulcedinis* bonorum quae sunt studium eius qui non redit in *amaritudinem*, neque dissipentur.' Here, then, once more, an unmistakably early and evidently original text of Eg. C. O. is found rewritten in a different sense in C. H.

(d) At no. (5) of Eg. C. O. we again find ourselves in the presence of something, to us, quite strange and unfamiliar. The water 'in oblationem' certainly refers to a separate cup of water; for at nos. (10)–(12) the Latin says of the presbyters, or deacons, who carry the *three* cups: 'primus, qui tenet aquam, secundus qui lac, tertius qui vinum.' It is true that at no. (10) the Ethiopic and Coptic have 'honey' where the Latin has 'water.' But this is only an attempted emendation on the part of some scribe or

---

[1] Dr Maclean (*The Test. of our Lord*, p. 222) says of this passage in Eg. C. O. and the parallel in Test. ii 10: 'This passage is extremely obscure both in H. [=Hauler's Latin] and Test., and is clearly original in neither.' The difficulty of the Eg. C. O. passage was evidently felt by the compiler of C. H. as well as by Dr Maclean. As regards its obscurity: is not this a necessary consequence of the fact that here, as in Clement's *Paedagogus* i 6, we are moving in a cycle of thought that is wholly unfamiliar to us?

[2] This appears to be a substitute for the Eg. C. O. 'lac et melle mixta simul ad *plenitudinem promissionis*,' at no. (3).

editor who wished to get rid of an unfamiliar feature; for at no. (3) all versions speak of the milk and honey as *mixed*[1]; and hence in making two separate cups, of honey and of milk, at no. (10) the Ethiopic contradicts what it says at no. (3). At nos. (10) and (12), then, the Ethiopic, like the Latin, speaks of *three* cups, but gets this number only by separating the milk and honey[2]. Furthermore, the Ethiopic has, with the Latin, a separate allusion to water at no. (5); and though the text there appears to be in other respects corrupt, in this particular point it testifies to the genuineness of the Latin reading. We must therefore take it as certain that the water spoken of in the Latin and Ethiopic at no. (5) is the cup of water which is expressly mentioned in the Latin at no. (10). Its purpose is to signify the cleansing of the inner, as well as the outer, man by baptism : ' ut et interior homo, quod est animale (? $\psi v \chi \iota \kappa \acute{o} v$), similia consequa[n]tur sicut et corpus.' The shifts to which the other versions have been put in order to avoid this cup of water are instructive[3].

The accusative 'aquam,' at no. (5), evidently has the same construction as 'lac et melle mixta'[4] at no. (3), and is governed by the verb 'gratias agat' in no. (1).

C. H., as by this time we should be prepared to expect, has nothing about the water at all, entirely omitting both no. (5) and no. (10).

The practice of giving the newly baptized a cup of water, as well as one of milk and honey, seems to be unknown apart from this passage of Eg. C. O. But in the chapter of his *Paedagogus*

[1] So Tertullian, *de Corona* c. 3, speaks of a 'lactis et mellis concordiam' received after baptism; and in *adv. Marc.* i 14 of a 'mellis et lactis societatem, qua (Deus) suos infantat.'

[2] The Coptic and Arabic deal with the difficulty in another way; they omit the first allusion to the water, at no. (5), altogether; and then rewrite nos. (9), (10) and (12) in such a way as to give only two cups: 'Further, if there is no [more] priest, let the deacons take hold of the cup and stand in right order ($\epsilon \dot{v} \tau a \xi \acute{\iota} q$) and give to them the Blood of the Christ Jesus our Lord; and he who has the *milk and the honey*' (Copt., Horner pp. 319–320; the Arabic similarly). Here there is no enumeration of the cups as in the Latin and Ethiopic.

[3] See the last note.

[4] This I take to mean 'milk and honey mixed.' The form 'melle' is probably intended for an accusative, and may be due to the form of the Greek word $\mu \acute{e} \lambda \iota$.

from which I have already quoted (I, vi) Clement of Alexandria has a passage which may suggest that he was acquainted with such a practice. Having, as we have seen, treated at length of certain Scripture passages which speak of milk (in particular 1 Cor. iii 1, 2), and having concluded that milk represents the Logos, the perfect nourishment of the Christian, he proceeds, towards the end of the chapter, to speak of other liquids which may be taken in conjunction with milk as wholesome food:

Ναὶ μὴν καὶ συγγένειάν τινα πρὸς τὸ ὕδωρ φυσικωτάτην ἔχει τὸ γάλα, καθάπερ ἀμέλει πρὸς τὴν πνευματικὴν τροφὴν τὸ λουτρὸν τὸ πνευματικόν[1]· οἱ γοῦν ἐπιρροφοῦντες τῷ προειρημένῳ γάλακτι ψυχροῦ ὀλίγον ὕδατος ὠφελοῦνται παραχρῆμα· οὐ γὰρ ἀποξύνεσθαι τὸ γάλα ἐᾷ ἡ πρὸς τὸ ὕδωρ κοινωνία, οὐκ ἀντιπαθείᾳ τινί, προσπεπαινομένου δὲ προσπαθείᾳ. καὶ ἦν ὁ λόγος ἔχει πρὸς τὸ βάπτισμα κοινωνίαν, ταύτην ἔχει τὸ γάλα τὴν συναλλαγὴν πρὸς τὸ ὕδωρ, δέχεται γὰρ μόνον τῶν ὑγρῶν τοῦτο καὶ τὴν πρὸς τὸ ὕδωρ μῖξιν ἐπὶ κάθαρσιν παραλαμβανόμενον[2] καθάπερ τὸ βάπτισμα ἐπὶ ἀφέσει ἁμαρτιῶν. μίγνυται δὲ καὶ μέλιτι προσφυῶς καὶ τοῦτο ἐπὶ καθάρσει πάλιν μετὰ γλυκείας τῆς τροφῆς·...ναὶ μὴν ἔτι μίγνυται τὸ γάλα καὶ οἴνῳ[3] τῷ γλυκεῖ κ.τ.λ. (Paed. I vi 50, 3–51, 1)[4].

The fact that Clement has baptism so closely in view in this passage makes it permissible to surmise that these references to the various uses of milk have a foundation in practices known to him (though possibly not all of them Alexandrian) in connexion with baptism. If so, it may further be noted that while he speaks apparently of the milk being mixed with honey and wine before it is taken, the expression οἱ γοῦν ἐπιρροφοῦντες τῷ προειρημένῳ γάλακτι ψυχροῦ ὀλίγον ὕδατος naturally means 'those who swallow a little cold water in addition to (or after) the aforesaid milk,' and so would indicate that the 'mixture' of milk with water, of which Clement goes on to speak, was one

---

[1] Cf. Eg. C.O. at no. (5): 'aquam vero...in indicium lavacri.'
[2] The context seems to require that παραλαμβανόμενον be taken with τὸ ὕδωρ; for according to the symbolism milk = the Logos, and water = baptism.
[3] St Jerome, Com. in Isai., commenting on Is. lv 1, says: 'qui mos ac typus in occidentis ecclesiis hodie usque servatur, ut renatis in Christo vinum lacque tribuatur' (P. L. xxiv 549 B).
[4] In Migne, P. Gr. VIII 309 B, C.

which took place only *after* both liquids had been swallowed. The form of the expression, 'those who swallow...are presently benefited,' suggests also that Clement is thinking of something accustomed to be done, and not merely proposing a hypothetical case. That he is speaking of a practice of drinking a little cold water after the milk (? and honey) administered at baptism, I hesitate to assert, though I think it possible, and even probable, that such is the case. If it should be so, then it is evident that the passage affords an interesting illustration, from the end of the second century, of the practice witnessed to by the Latin version of Eg. C. O.

(e) As regards the actual communion of the newly baptized, there are two points to be noted: *a*) the order of delivery for the several cups; and *β*) the formulae accompanying the delivery.

a) The order of delivery in Eg. C. O. (Latin) is very remarkable: first the Bread, second the water, third the milk (and honey), fourth the Wine. This is, so far as I can find, without parallel elsewhere. Tertullian (*de Corona* c. 3) seems to imply that the milk and honey were received immediately after baptism: 'Inde [sc. de aqua] suscepti lactis et mellis concordiam praegustamus.'[1] Since, according to the context of this passage, the baptism appears to have taken place away from the church, these words would seem to imply that the milk and honey were not given in connexion with the Eucharist at all, but before it.

In Eg. C. O. at nos. (1), (3) and (5), we find the milk and honey and the water apparently brought up to the altar and blessed by the bishop together with the bread and wine of the Eucharist. This is expressly forbidden by the second (according to Funk's numeration) of the *Apostolic Canons* (A. C. viii 47), which orders the deposition of any bishop who παρὰ τὴν τοῦ κυρίου διάταξιν τὴν ἐπὶ τῇ θυσίᾳ προσενέγκῃ ἕτερά τινα, ἢ μέλι ἐπὶ τὸ τοῦ θεοῦ θυσιαστήριον ἢ γάλα ἢ ἀντὶ οἴνου σίκερα ἐπιτηδευτὰ ἢ ὄρνεις ἢ ζῷά τινα ἢ ὄσπρια, παρὰ τὴν διάταξιν,

[1] St Jerome was able to employ this passage of Tertullian without material change: 'Nam et multa alia quae per traditionem in ecclesiis observantur, auctoritatem sibi scriptae legis usurpaverunt, velut in lavacro ter caput mergitare, deinde egressos lactis et mellis praegustare concordiam ad infantiae significationem' (*Dial. adv. Luciferianos* c. 8: *P. L.* XXIII 172 A).

καθαιρείσθω. The 24th canon of the third Council of Carthage (A.D. 397) similarly forbids anything to be offered 'in sacramentis corporis et sanguinis Domini' except bread, and wine mixed with water. It excepts, however, the 'primitiae, seu mel et lac, quod uno die solennissimo pro infantis mysterio solet offerri,' which, 'quamvis in altari offeratur, suam habent propriam benedictionem, ut a sacramento dominici corporis et sanguinis distinguantur.' At the end of the fourth century therefore the practice found in Eg. C. O. was looked upon with disfavour in some parts at least of both East and West: though the strength of the tradition in Africa is attested by the special provision for its maintenance on a single day in the year.

Now in C. H. there is nothing to indicate that the cups of milk and honey were placed on the altar; in fact the piece of text at no. (2) in C. H. seems to have been introduced for the express purpose of making no. (3) refer not to the blessing of the cups —as in Eg. C. O.—but to their distribution (see p. 86 above). Moreover in C. H. these cups are not administered until the Eucharist itself, in both kinds, has been received; see no. (16). This will doubtless appeal to us as the natural and seemly arrangement; but for that very reason it is the more difficult to suppose that a later compiler would have altered it to what we find in Eg. C. O.

β) The formulae in Eg. C. O. for administering the Eucharist and the additional cups are as remarkable as the order of delivery. That for the Bread is 'Panis caelestis in Christo Iesu.' For this C. H. has 'Hoc est corpus Christi.' Can there be a doubt as to which of these expressions is the original?

The formula for the cups of water, milk and honey, and the Wine, is 'In Deo patre omnipotenti,' to which the communicant responds 'Amen,' and 'Et domino Iesu Christo et spiritu sancto et sancta ecclesia,' followed again by 'Amen.' As I understand nos. (13) and (14), the whole formula, with the double 'Amen,' was said in delivering each of the three cups. This appears to me to be indicated by the words 'ter dicente eo, qui dat' in no. (13)[1].

---

[1] Dr Bernard (*Odes of Solomon*, p. 68) applies 'In Deo patre' to the cup of water only, and divides the rest between the cup of milk and honey and that of the Wine. The interpretation given above seems to me preferable.

This formula for the cups is something like that prescribed in Eg. C. O. for the unction which follows the imposition of the hand after baptism: 'Ungueo te sancto oleo in domino patre omnipotente et Christo Iesu et spiritu sancto' (Hauler p. 111). The mention of the Church is found in several of the doxologies of the same document (see p. 154 below).

C. H., as we have seen, places the delivery of the cups of milk and honey at the end, after that of the regular eucharistic cup. It also omits the cup of water, and gives no formula for the administration of the milk and honey. The formula for the Wine corresponds exactly to that for the Bread: 'Hic est sanguis Christi.'

Here again that which is strange to us is replaced by that which to us is familiar; and once more the later character of C. H. appears to be placed beyond reasonable doubt[1].

G. *Instruction. Hours of prayer. Sign of the Cross.*

There is a certain class of passages in Eg. C. O. which are of the first importance for the formation of a judgment as to the relation between Eg. C. O. and C. H. Of these passages nos. (3) and (5) of the text just dealt with (under F) are good examples. Their characteristic feature is a sort of catechetical explanation, accompanying certain of the practical directions, which is of a uniform and at the same time very distinctive type, and admits of illustration generally from writings of the second and third rather than from those of the fourth or succeeding centuries. In C. H. this sort of commentary frequently disappears altogether; but sometimes it is represented in a form which lacks just those features of Eg. C. O. which would incline us to assign this document to an early date. It is thus that C. H. seems clearly to

[1] The differences between the formulae for administration in the Latin and the Ethiopic need not be dwelt on here. It is sufficiently evident that the Eth., while it preserves portions of the original formulae (as in the Latin), has, under the influence of later usage, softened the formula for the Bread by substituting 'the body of our Lord Christ' for 'in Christo Iesu,' while it has quite changed the formula for the Wine. The Coptic and Arabic here go with the Ethiopic: but they further eliminate the words 'In God the Father almighty,' which the Eth. keeps in connexion with the milk, and they thus (like C. H.) suppress the formula for the additional cups altogether.

imply a knowledge of the Eg. C. O. text on the part of its author, and so betrays its secondary character. The passage next to be considered will, I think, illustrate what is here said. It is taken from the directions as to hearing instruction, times for private prayer and the making of the sign of the cross.

In C. H. the corresponding matter does not come in one continuous passage, as in Eg. C. O.; it has to be sought in four different canons, viz. xxvi, xxvii (*a*), xxv (*b*), xxvii (*b*), xxix (*b*). Apart from the rearrangement here indicated by the roman numerals, I keep the order of Haneberg's edition[1], not following Achelis in his further readjustment of some pieces of text which fall under xxvii (*b*). Achelis's further rearrangement is indicated by the insertion of his paragraph numbering, with the sign §.

Eg. C. O. (*Ethiopic*) (Horner p. 182 ff.)	*Eg. C. O.* (*Coptic*) (Horner p. 327 ff.)	*C. H.* xxvi (Achelis, §§ 226–231)
(1) And if they tell them where is the word of instruction, everyone shall choose to go thither to the place of instruction: (2)	Further, if there should be an instruction (καθήγησις) of the word of God, let everyone choose for himself to go to that place,	Si est in ecclesia conventus propter verbum Dei, singuli quique cum festinatione properent ut ad illud congregentur,
		sciantque multo magis esse illis eligendum ut audiant verbum Dei quam ut fruantur omni splendore huius mundi,
(3) and he shall know this in his heart, and consider all which he heard, that God speaks by the mouth of him who instructs, and it is He who dwells in the church, and He shall cause to pass away from him all wickedness in the day;	reckoning this in his heart, that it is God whom he hears speaking in him who gives instruction: for having prayed in the church he will be able to avoid the evil of the day.	
(4) and it shall be reckoned great loss to him who fears God, if he goes not to where is the place of instruction, (5)	Let the pious man reckon that it is a great loss, if he should not go to the place in which they instruct;	et hoc sibi magnum damnum esse numerent, si aliquando necessitas eos impediat quo minus audiant verbum Dei. Studeant vero ut saepe negotiis expediti in ecclesiam conveniant, fortiterque odium inimici expellant,
(6) and especially for him who can read.	especially if he can read:	imprimis si aliquis literas novit.

[1] That is, the order of C. H. found in Haneberg's Arabic MSS.

Eg. C. O. (Eth.)	Eg. C. O. (Copt.)	C. H.
(7) And if there is an instructor he shall not defer (from going) to the church and the place where is the instruction. Then indeed to him who speaks shall be given the word which he speaks.	or if the teacher should come, let none of you be deficient in coming to the church where they give the teaching. Then shall it be given to him who speaks	
(8) This is profit for everyone, (viz.) what he shall hear; and thou shalt hear that which thou thoughtest not there, and thou shalt profit	to utter things that are profitable to all; and thou wilt hear things which thou thinkest not; and thou wilt be profited	Tanto plus lucrabitur si audit quod non noverat;
(9)		
(10) by that which the Holy Spirit gave to thee by him who instructs:	by the things which the Holy Spirit will give thee from him who instructs:	dominus enim adest in loco ubi maiestatis memoria agitur, descenditque Spiritus in congregatos gratiamque suam effundit super omnes.
(11)		Qui autem est duplicis cordis homo inter eos, in illis requiescit, quia audisti de illorum constitutione in spiritu.
(12) and thus thy faith shall become firm because of what thou hearest.	thus thy faith will be established upon the things which thou hast heard.	
(13) And further, they shall tell thee in that place what it is proper for thee to do in thy house:	And it will be told thee also in that place the things which it is right for thee to do in thy house.	Qui autem domi commoventur a ratione, id non assequuntur quod in ecclesia audiunt.
(14) and therefore all men shall hasten to go to the church and to the place wherein the Holy Spirit rises (like the sun).	For this cause then let each one hasten to go to the church, the place in which the Holy Spirit breaks forth.	Ergo unusquisque summo studio contendat ut ecclesiam frequentet omnibus diebus quibus fiunt orationes.
(15) And if there is a day on which there is no instruction, everyone shall stay in his house, and shall take the holy Scripture and read as well as he can, for it is good.	If there is a day in which there is no instruction, let each one in his house take a holy book, and read sufficiently in it what seems to him profitable.	(xxvii (a), § 232) Quocumque die in ecclesia non orant, sumas scripturam et legas in ea.
(16)		Sol conspiciat matutino tempore scripturam super genua tua.
(17) And if thou wast in thy house, pray at the third hour and glorify God:	And if indeed thou art in thy house, pray at the third hour and bless God.	(xxv (b), §§ 233–238) Orent autem tertia hora,
(18) and if thou wast in another place, and if that hour has come to thee, pray in thy heart to God;	If however thou art in another place and thou comest by chance to that time, pray in thy heart to God.	Cf. (42) below

Eg. C. O. (Eth.)

(19) because in that hour they stripped Jesus Christ and nailed him upon the wood of the cross:

(20) and therefore the ancient law commanded to give the bread which they offer at the third hour, as a type of the body of Christ and his precious blood; and they sacrificed the lamb which was a type of the perfect Lamb, for Christ is the Shepherd, and he is the Bread which came down from the heavens.

(21) And again pray at the sixth hour;

(22) for at that hour was the hanging of our Lord Christ upon the wood of the cross, and the day was divided and darkness came: and they shall pray at that hour a strong prayer;

(23) and they shall be like the word which our Lord Christ prayed, and made all the world darkness:

(24) and the catechumens shall make a great prayer.

(25) And at the ninth hour they shall be long in prayer, and a prayer with glorifying, that ye may join in glorifying with the soul of the righteous ones, glorifying the living God who faileth not, who remembered his righteous ones, and sent to them his Son, that is, his Word, to enlighten them:

Eg. C. O. (Copt.)

For in this hour the Christ was nailed to the wood [1].

For this cause also in the old (testament) the law commanded to offer the shew bread at every hour, as a type of the body and the blood of the Christ; and the slaughter of the senseless lamb, which was a type of the perfect Lamb; for the Christ is the Shepherd; he also is the Bread which came down from heaven.

Pray also likewise at the sixth hour;

for the Christ having been nailed to the wood of the cross, that day divided, and a great darkness happened, wherefore let them pray at that hour with a prevailing prayer,

likening themselves to the voice of him who prayed, (and) caused all creation to become dark for the unbelieving Jews [2].

And let them also make a great prayer and a great blessing at the ninth hour, that thou mayest know how the soul of the righteous ones blesses the Lord the true

(*Here the Latin recommences,* Hauler p. 119) Deum, qui non mentitur, qui memor fuit sanctorum suorum et emisit verbum suum inluminantem eos.

C. H.

quia illo tempore Salvator voluntarie crucifixus est ad salvandos nos, ut nobis libertatem tribueret.

Deinde etiam hora sexta orate,

quia illa hora universa creatura perturbata est propter facinus scelestum a Judaeis perpetratum.

Hora nona iterum orent,

---

[1] Test. has (17)–(19) thus: 'Let all take care to pray at the third hour with mourning and labour, either in the church, or in the house because they cannot go (to the church). For this is the hour of the fixing of the Only-begotten on the cross' (ii 24).

[2] Test. has (21)–(23) thus: 'But at the sixth hour similarly let there be a prayer with sorrow. For then the daylight was divided by the darkness. Let there be then that voice which is like to the prophets, and to creation mourning' (ii 24).

Eg. C. O. (Eth.)

(26) because in that hour the side of Christ was pierced, and the blood and water flowed out: and then the rest of the day shone when the evening came. And therefore thou also, as thou makest beginning of another day, as a likeness of the resurrection,
(27) pray before thou restest thy body in thy bed.
(28) And at midnight

(29)

(30) having risen from thy bed, and having washed thy hand with water, pray.
(31) And if thou hast a wife, both of you pray. And if she has not yet become a believer, go aside from her and pray alone, and return again into thy bed. Because thou art bound by marriage thou shalt not leave off praying; because ye are clean, and it is not for you (to be as) unclean.

Eg. C. O. (Lat.)

Illa ergo hora in latere Christus punctus aquam et sanguem effudit et reliquum temporis diei inluminans ad vesperam deduxit. Unde incipiens dormire principium alterius diei faciens imaginem resurrectionis conplevit¹.

Ora etiam, antequam corpus cubili requiescat².
Circa mediam vero noctem³

exurgens lava manus aqua et ora.

Si autem et coniunx tua praesens est, utrique simul orate; sin vero needum est fidelis, in alio cubiculo secedens ora et iterum ad cubilem tuum revertere. Noli autem piger esse ad orandum. Qui in nuptias [con]ligatus est non est inquinatus⁴;

C. H.

quia illa hora Christus oravit et tradidit spiritum in manus Patris sui. Etiam hora qua sol occidit orent, quia est completio diei. Deinde etiam λυχνικῷ vespere orent, quia David dicit: 'Nocte loquor.'

Cf. (42) *below*

Deinde etiam media nocte orent,
quia David idem fecit. Paulus autem et Silas, famuli Christi, oraverunt media nocte et laudaverunt Deum.

(xxvii (b) §§ 241–245) Christianus lavet manus omni tempore, quo orat. Qui autem alligati sunt matrimonio, quandocumque a latere uxoris surgere velint, orent: coniugium enim non maculat.

---

¹ Test. has (25)–(26) thus: 'At the ninth hour also let prayer be protracted, as with a hymn of praise that is like to the souls of those who give praise to God that lieth not, as one who hath remembered His saints, and hath sent His Word and Wisdom to enlighten them. For in that hour life was opened to the faithful, and blood and water were shed from the side of our Lord' (ii 24).

² Test. (ii 24): 'But at evening, when it is the beginning of another day, shewing an image of the resurrection, He caused us to give praise.' See Eg. C. O. at no. (26)—prayer at the ninth hour.

³ Test. transfers most of the Eg. C. O. comments on the midnight prayer to that at dawn, but with alterations, thus: 'But at midnight let them arise with praising and lauding because of the resurrection. But at dawn with praising with psalms, because after He rose He glorified the Father while they were singing psalms. But if any have a consort or wife (not) faithful, let the husband who is faithful go and pray at these times without fail. Let those who are chaste not lessen (them). For the adornments of heaven give praise, the lights, the sun, the moon, the stars, the lightnings, the thunders, the clouds, the angels...the whole (heavenly) army, the depths, the sea, the rivers,...And all the saints also give praise and all the souls of the righteous' (ii 24).

⁴ Schwartz (*op. cit.* p. 37 n. 2) corrects the punctuation and the text, after the Coptic, thus: 'noli autem piger esse ad orandum qui in nuptiis conligatus es: non es inquinatus, qui enim' (etc.).

Eg. C. O. (Eth.)

(32) Those who have been baptized need not to be washed again, because they are clean.

(33) And if thou breathedst into thy hands and sealest thee with thy spittle which goes forth from thy mouth, thou wilt be clean all over.

(34) This is from the Holy Spirit, and the drop of the water of baptism ascends from the outgushing which is the heart of the faithful, and purifies the believers.

(35) At this hour, therefore, they shall pray carefully, because the presbyters who handed down to us thus instructed us, that at this hour all creation prays to God. The stars and the plants stand up[4], and the waters stand up[4] at that hour,

(36) and all the hosts of the heavens, the angels, ministering at that hour, with the soul of the righteous, glorify God. And therefore it is seemly for all who believe to be careful to pray at that hour.

(37) To this our Lord also is being witness, thus saying: 'Behold there was a cry at midnight, saying, Behold the bridegroom has come, rise, go forth to meet him.'

(38) *See* (40) *below*

(39) And he repeated it, saying: 'Watch, because ye know not in what hour your Lord will come.'

Eg. C. O. (Lat.)

qui enim loti sunt, non habent necessitatem lavandi iterum, quia mundi sunt.

Per consignationem cum udo flatu et per manum spiritum[1] amplectens corpus tuum usque ad pedes sanctificatum est.

Donum enim spiritus et infusio lavacri, sicuti ex fonte corde credente, cum offertur, sanctificat eum qui credidit.

Hac igitur hora necessarium est orare; nam et hi, qui tradiderunt nobis, seniores ita nos docuerunt, quia hac hora omnis creatura quiescit ad momentum quoddam, ut laudent dominum; stellas et arbusta et aquas stare in ictu,

et omne agmen angelorum ministrat ei, in hac hora una cum iustorum animabus laudare Deum. Quapropter debent ii, qui credunt, festinare hac hora orare.

Testimonium etiam habens huic rei Dominus ita ait: 'Ecce clamor factus est circa mediam noctem dicentium: Ecce sponsus venit, surgite ad occursum eius,'
See (40) *below*

et infert dicens: 'Propterea vigilate; nescitis enim, qua hora venit.'

C. H.

Neque post regenerationem opus est lavacro, excepta lotione manuum, nihil praeterea,

quia Spiritus sanctus odoratur[2] corpus fidelis, idque totum purgat.

Curet igitur quilibet ut diligenti studio oret media nocte[3], quia patres nostri dixerunt illa hora omnem creaturam ad servitium gloriae divinae parari,

ordinesque angelorum et animas iustorum benedicere Deo,

quia testatur Dominus dicitque de hoc: 'Media autem nocte clamor factus est: Ecce sponsus venit, exite obviam ei.'

Porro autem tempore, quo canit gallus, instituendae sunt orationes in ecclesiis,
quia Dominus dicit: 'Vigilate, quia nescitis qua hora filius hominis venturus sit, an galli cantu, an mane.'

---

[1] Schwartz (*op. cit.* p. 37 n. 2) expands the MS contraction 'spm' to 'sputum.' But 'spittle' in Eth. and Copt. may be due to paraphrase.

[2] Riedel, 'pervades' ('durchhaucht'), which must surely be right: 'odoratur' is meaningless in the context.

[3] This is a 'doublet' of no. (28) above.

[4] 'Stand (still)' is evidently the meaning.

Eg. C. O. (Eth.)	Eg. C. O. (Lat.)	C. H.
(40) And at the time of cock-crow, having risen, likewise pray; (41) because at this hour, cock-crow, the children of Israel denied our Lord Jesus Christ, in whom by faith we know how to trust as the eternal light, and while we hope for the resurrection of the dead. (42)	Et circa galli cantum exurgens, similiter; illa enim hora gallo cantante filii Istrahel Christum negaverunt, quem nos per fidem cognovimus, sub spe luminis aeterni in resurrectione mortuorum spectantes in diem ha⟨n⟩c.	See (38) above (§§ 239–240) Obligati sumus igitur, ut Dei recordemur omni hora.
Cf. (27) and (18) above	Cf. (27) and (18) above	Et quando quis insomnis supra lectum positus est, debet orare in corde suo, hoc modo faciens.
(43) All of you of the faithful therefore doing all this, and looking forward and remembering one another, teach ye this wisdom to the catechumens, having first built up (their faith); and ye shall not go astray or be lost while ye always remember Christ.	Itaque, omnes fideles, agentes et memoriam eorum facientes et invicem docentes et catecuminos provocantes neque temptari neque perire poteritis, cum semper Christum in memoriam habetis.	(§ 246) Nos autem una cum catechumenis invicem instruamus nosmetipsos de servitio Dei; tunc daemones non possunt contristare nos, quando in omni oratione recordamur Christi.

[*Here we come to a passage of which the Latin has preserved us a double text*[1]. *As the passage is an important one I give both these versions. I think it well also to substitute the Coptic here for the Ethiopic, since the former better illustrates the Latin, and the latter has, in the course of successive translations, developed a considerable looseness of expression.*]

Eg. C. O. (Copt.)	Eg. C. O. (Lat.)		C. H.
(44) (Horner p. 331) And make proof (πειρᾶν) at every hour of sealing (σφραγίζειν) thy forehead in fear;	(Hauler p. 118) Semper tempta modeste consignare tibi frontem.	(Hauler p. 121) Semper autem imitare cum honestate consignare tibi frontem.	(C. H. xxix (b), §§ 247–251) Signa frontem tuam signo crucis
(45) for this is the sign which is known and manifest: by this the devil is ruined. If	Hoc enim signum passionis adversum diabolum ostenditur, si ex fide faciat quis,	Hoc enim signum passionis adversum diabolum manifestum et conprobatum est, si	ad vincendum Satanam

[1] Hauler rightly observes (p. 118) that this repetition of the passage must already have been found in the Greek copy from which the Latin translation was made. This appears from the fact that the Latin gives us two independent translations. But as it also appears that some of the differences between the two Latin versions are due to variants in the underlying Greek, it would follow that the repetition must go back to an earlier Greek copy than that used by the translator.

Eg. C. O. (Copt.)	Eg. C. O. (Lat.)		C. H.
thou makest it in faith thou not only manifestest thyself before men, but in the knowledge with which thou art confident like a shield (θηρῶν): since the adversary (ἀντικείμενος), the devil, only sees the power of the heart, and if he should see the inner man that he is sensible (λογικός), sealing himself within and without with the seal of the Word (λόγος) of God, then he flies, pursued by the Holy Spirit, he who is in the man who makes place for him within him.	ut non hominibus placens, sed per scientiam sicut loricam offerens; siquidem adversarius videns virtutem spiritus ex corde in similitudine lavacri in manifestum deformatam tremens effugatur, te non illum cedente, sed inspirante.	ex fide itaque facis, non ut hominibus appareas, sed per scientiam tamquam scutum offerens; nam adversarius, cum vidit virtutem, quae ex corde est, ut homo similitudinem verbi in manifesto deformatam ostendat, infugiatur non sputante ⟨te⟩, sed flante *spiritu in te*.	et ad gloriandum propter fidem tuam.
(46) This also is what Moses the prophet taught us before by the Pascha, and the lamb which was slaughtered, he commanded that they should smear the blood on the lintel and the two door-posts, telling us of the faith which is in us now, this which was given to us by the perfect Lamb. Wherewith when we seal our foreheads with our hand, we shall be saved from those who wish to kill us. (47)	Hoc ipsut erat, de quod (*sic*) in typo Moyses in ove, quae per pascha immolabatur, sanguem asparsit in limine et duos postes unguens significat eam, quae nunc in nobis est, fidem in perfecta ove. Frontem et oculos per manum consignantes declinemus ab eo, qui exterminare temptat.	Quod deformans Moyses in ovem paschae, quae occidebatur, sanguem asparsit in limine et postes unxit, designabat eam, quae nunc in nobis est fides, quae in perfecta ove est. Frontem vero et oculos per manum consignantes declinemus eum, qui exterminare temptat.	Hoc fecit Moyses de sanguine agni, quem illevit superliminaribus et postibus ianuarum, qua re factum est ut sanarentur habitantes intra illa. Quanto magis purificabit et custodiet sanguis Christi eos qui credunt in eum et effingunt redemptionis totius orbis terrarum similitudinem, quae in sanguine agni perfecti Christi intendit[1] (condit?) omnia mysteria propter vitam et resurrectionem et sacrificium. Christiani autem soli audiunt haec, quia sigillum baptismi acceperunt; sunt enim in societatem recepti.

---

[1] Riedel (p. 219-220) gives this sentence ('Quanto magis,' etc.) in an intelligible form thus: 'How should not the blood of Christ be still more pure, and the more protect them that believe in Him? Wherefore they shall openly bear the mark

This continuous passage well illustrates what has been said above (at p. 94), viz. that Eg. C. O. is in places characterized by a sort of catechetical instruction accompanying the practical directions, and that this catechesis is of a uniform and at the same time distinctive type; and further, to employ words already used (*ibid.*), that in C. H. 'this sort of commentary frequently disappears altogether; but sometimes it is represented in a form which lacks just those features of Eg. C. O. which would incline us to assign this document to an early date.' If we read through the Eg. C. O. columns of this passage we can hardly fail to recognize in them a sustained and self-consistent instruction on hearing the Christian teaching, on the times for prayer, and on the meaning and use of the sign of the cross. This instruction reads like the expression of an original train of thought in the mind of one who has worked out for himself the meanings of the things he wishes to explain; and its essential unity appears not only from the consistent and uniform character of the explanations given, but also from the recurrence, quite naturally and spontaneously, of certain distinctive ideas in different parts of the passage[1]. These marks of unity, together with nearly everything that is striking and distinctive in Eg. C. O., vanish almost entirely in C. H.

of the redemption of the world (τῆς οἰκουμένης) which was accomplished by the blood of the perfect Lamb, Christ. All mysteries of the life and the resurrection the Christians alone shall hear, because they have received the seal of baptism and are thus become partakers.' The passage 'All mysteries,' etc., answers to one in Eg. C. O. that comes in a different context, viz. after the communion of the newly baptized (see p. 122 below).

[1] Thus, (*a*) all the hours for prayer, from the third hour to cock-crow inclusive, are explained with reference to events of our Lord's passion. (*b*) In nos. (20) and (46) we have Old Testament types of 'the perfect Lamb.' (*c*) In no. (22) it is said that at the sixth hour, when our Lord was nailed to the cross, the day 'divided'; and at no. (26) that at the ninth hour, when the sun again shone forth, Christ made 'the beginning of another day.' (*d*) At no. (26) the beginning of a new day (at the ninth hour) is taken as a type of the resurrection, and at no. (41) this idea occurs again. (*e*) In both no. (25) and no. (36) it is said that 'the souls of the righteous' praise God. (*f*) In nos. (33) and (44) we have allusions to a very remarkable manner of making the sign of the cross, and some equally remarkable ideas connected therewith. All these points are considered in what follows; but it seems well to have them brought together beforehand under one comprehensive view.

I will first draw attention to some of the more distinctive features in the Eg. C. O. text, and then consider a number of subordinate points in which C. H. appears to be inferior and secondary.

(*a*) At (22) C. H. has nothing, and at (26) little, corresponding to Eg. C. O. At (22) Eg. C. O. says that at the sixth hour, when Christ was nailed to the wood, 'the day divided.' At (26) we see more exactly what is the idea connected with this remark; for it is there said that our Lord, when at the ninth hour His side was pierced, 'reliquum tempus diei inluminans ad vesperam deduxit,' and then is added: 'Unde incipiens dormire *principium alterius diei* faciens imaginem resurrectionis conplevit.' The Ethiopic takes this last sentence differently, thus: 'And therefore thou also, as thou makest *beginning of another day*, as a likeness of the resurrection, [this is then joined with the next paragraph, as to praying at bedtime] pray before thou restest thy body in thy bed.' But here the Ethiopic has misunderstood the symbolical allusion, and really makes no sense, since the ninth hour is not bedtime. The 'incipiens dormire' of the Latin clearly refers to our Lord's death; and the fact that at His death the day, as it were, began again, with the reappearance of the light, is taken as a figure of the resurrection. The same interpretation of the beginning of the day as a symbol of the resurrection meets us again in no. (41), where the hour of cock-crow is connected with the 'spe luminis aeterni in resurrectione mortuorum.'[1]

This idea of the day having been divided into two days by the three hours of darkness goes back at least to the third century; the *Didascalia* has it (v 14; Funk I pp. 274-6), and uses it for the purpose of reckoning three clear days between our Lord's death and His resurrection, in accord with Matth. xii 40. The same use of the idea (though with a somewhat different method of application) is found in the first of the Syriac Fathers, Aphraates (*Hom.* xii § 7), a writer in whom we look for early

---

[1] From Dionysius of Alexandria, *Epist. Canonica* (Routh, *Rel. Sacr.* III p. 224), we learn that at Rome the paschal fast ended at cock-crow on Easter Sunday morning because that was regarded as the hour of our Lord's resurrection (Οἱ μὲν γὰρ ἐν Ῥώμῃ ἀδελφοί, ὥς φασι, περιμένουσι τὸν ἀλέκτορα).

ideas[1]; and it is reproduced by St Ephraim in his Commentary on the *Diatessaron* (Moesinger p. 222); and in his Hymns *de Crucifixione* (ed. Lamy, vol. I col. 695). It was not, however, unknown to Greek and Latin writers of the fourth and fifth centuries[2].

(*b*) At nos. (31) and (32) Eg. C. O. insists that conjugal relations should not be held as constituting an obstacle to prayer, 'qui enim loti sunt (sc. in baptism), non habent necessitatem lavandi iterum, quia mundi sunt.' This appears to be directed against some practice of ceremonial washings on the part of married persons, such as is condemned in the *Didascalia*[3].

Thus far C. H. is in substantial agreement. But then in nos. (33) and (34) is added in Eg. C. O. a passage which in the Latin is somewhat obscure, but of which the Ethiopic (as also the Coptic) seems to reproduce the correct general sense. The idea of this passage must strike us as strange: instead of any ceremonial washing, as a sort of re-baptism, it is enough to breathe upon the hand and thus sign oneself with the cross; for this moist breath, coming from the heart of the believer, is in some sense an integral part of the one and original baptism, and therewith the Holy Spirit, received in baptism, is brought forth from the heart and sanctifies the whole body.

If we now turn to no. (45) we meet with this idea (or part of it) again in the section on the sign of the cross. This 'signum passionis' is an armour against the adversary, who

[1] It is possible that Aphraates got the idea from the *Didascalia*, which he seems to have known (cf. *Liturgical Homilies of Narsai*, p. xlviii: 'Texts and Studies,' VIII 1).

[2] Funk (II p. 14) cites St Augustine and St Gregory of Nyssa.

[3] Compare *Didasc.* vi 21 (Funk p. 368), and *ib.* p. 372-4; and particularly vi 22 p. 378: 'Et mulier ergo, cum in menstruis est, et vir, cum in cursu seminis, et vir et mulier legibus ad nuptias convenientes et *ab alterutrum exsurgentes*, sine observatione et *non loti orent, et mundi sunt*.' Hippolytus, *Philos.* ix 13, 14, states that a system of expiatory baptisms was introduced in some circles at Rome by a certain Alcibiades, of the Elchasaite sect, in the time of Pope Callistus.

Tertullian, though he condemns the practice of washing the hands before prayer, witnesses to its general currency (*de Orat.* c. 13, al. 11). He says it sometimes went to the extent of bathing the whole body: 'etiam cum lavacro totius corporis.' Eg. C. O. permits, even prescribes, washing of the hands before prayer; but apparently condemns ceremonial baths taken on occasions such as are described in the *Didascalia*.

'videns virtutem spiritus ex corde in similitudine lavacri[1] in manifestum deformatam tremens effugatur, te non illum cedente[2] sed inspirante.'
Neither at nos. (33)–(34) nor at no. (45) has C. H. anything corresponding to this[3]; yet we seem to be here in the midst of very early ideas and practices. For an illustration we may turn to a passage of Tertullian, part of which has already been quoted (cf. p. 80, note 1):

'Latebisne tu, cum lectulum, cum corpusculum tuum signas, *cum aliquid immundum flatu expuis*, cum etiam per noctem exsurgis oratum, et non magiae aliquid videberis operari?' (*ad Uxorem* ii 5).

And again in *de Idol.* 11 we read:
'Quo ore Christianus turarius, si per templa transibit, quo ore fumantes aras *despuet et exsufflabit*, quibus ipse prospexit? qua constantia exorcizabit alumnos suos (the demons), quibus domum suam cellarium praestat? ille quidem si *excluserit daemonium*, non sibi placeat de fide; neque enim inimicum exclusit.'

These texts of Tertullian give us an insight into the probable ideas underlying the passages in Eg. C. O. The idols of the heathen stand for, if they are not actually identified with, evil spirits[4], with which the very air is infested, so that there is danger of the Christian breathing them in[5]; and they are to be puffed

---

[1] This is the text of Hauler p. 118. The duplicate text on p. 121 reads 'verbi' for 'lavacri.' These readings seem to go back to a Greek variant λόγου, λουτροῦ. The passage at no. (34) which speaks of the moist breath as 'infusio lavacri, sicuti ex corde credente,' seems to shew that here also 'lavacri' is the correct reading.

[2] The duplicate passage on p. 121 has 'non sputante ⟨te⟩ sed flante.' But 'sputante' and 'flante' convey much the same idea [cf. the expressions in Tertullian, quoted just after in the text above], and hence we do not expect to find these two verbs set in opposition to each other. If we might treat 'cedente' as 'caedente,' then this and the 'sputante' of p. 121 might be referred to a Greek variant τύπτοντος and πτύοντος.

[3] We shall see that C. H. has traces of (45), but without the curious ideas found in Eg. C. O.—see (*n*) below.

[4] Cf. [Cyprian] *Quod idola dii non sint* c. 7: 'Hi ergo spiritus sub statuis atque imaginibus consecratis delitescunt,...inrepentes etiam spiritus in corporibus occulte mentes terrent.' Similarly Minucius Felix, *Octav.* c. 27.

[5] Cf. Tertullian *Apol.* c. 22: 'Suppetit illis ad utramque substantiam hominis adeundam mira subtilitas et tenuitas sua.'

away or even expelled with the breath. The parallel is not complete, but it is enough to shew that we are in the same region of ideas[1].

I notice that no trace of these ideas is preserved in A. C. viii 34 and Test. ii 24, where the compilers are using the Eg. C. O. prescriptions as to the times of prayer; and when I find that the same ideas are absent from C. H. as well, I am the more inclined to conclude that they were either unacceptable or unintelligible at the date when C. H. was compiled. But in the case under consideration C. H. has sufficient trace of what we find in Eg. C. O. to warrant the belief that the compiler had the whole before him; for at no. (34) we read: 'quia Spiritus sanctus odoratur corpus fidelis, idque totum purgat.' For 'odoratur' Riedel translates 'pervades' ('durchhaucht'), which seems obviously to be the sense required by the context. Again, at nos. (44)-(45) 'Signa frontem tuam signo crucis ad vincendum Satanam' of C. H. answers to 'Semper autem imitare cum honestate consignare tibi frontem. Hoc enim signum passionis adversum diabolum manifestum et conprobatum est' (Hauler p. 121); while at (46) C. H. clearly stands in close literary relation to Eg. C. O.

[1] It may be observed that the same idea of the obtrusive ubiquity of evil spirits throws some light on another passage of Eg. C. O., already considered, in which the reason assigned for being careful not to spill the chalice is ' ut non spiritus alienus velut te contemnente illut delingat.' As to this idea of the demons ' licking up' the sacred contents of the Christian cup when spilt through the (culpable) carelessness of the receivers, cf. Tertullian *Apol.* c. 22: 'quorum (sc. wiles of the devil) iste potissimus, quo deos istos captis et circumscriptis hominum mentibus commendat, ut et *sibi pabula propria nidoris et sanguinis procuret* simulacris et imaginibus oblata.' Similarly Justin, *Apol.* i 12: οἱ καὶ παρὰ τῶν ἀλόγως βιούντων αἰτοῦσι θύματα καὶ θεραπείας. Similar ideas are to be found in Origen: as in *contra Celsum* iii 37, vii 5, 6. Compare Minucius Felix, *Octav.* c. 27: ' ut nidore altarium vel hostiis pecudum saginati remissis quae constrinxerant curasse videantur.' Earlier, in c. 26, Minucius describes the demons as being not wholly spiritual, but ' insinceri, vagi, a caelesti vigore terrenis labibus et cupiditatibus degravati,' who ' posteaquam simplicitatem substantiae suae onusti et immersi vitiis perdiderunt... non desinunt perditi iam perdere'; and he quotes with apparent approval Plato's opinion, that they are 'substantiam inter mortalem immortalemque, id est, inter corpus et spiritum mediam.' Thus it was part of the early Christian conception of the demons that they could devour sacrifices and libations put in their way. The thought in the Eg. C. O. passage appears to be, that by carelessly and disrespectfully spilling the cup the Christian puts it in the way of evil spirits, who will be apt to avail themselves of it as for their own sustenance.

EG. C. O. IN RELATION TO C. H. 107

(c) The reason assigned in Eg. C. O. at no. (25) for praying at the ninth hour is, according to the Ethiopic (similarly Copt.), 'that ye may join in glorifying with the soul of the righteous ones, glorifying the living God[1] who faileth not, who remembered his righteous ones, and sent to them his Son, that is[2], his Word, to enlighten them.' This clearly refers to our Lord's descent to Hades[3] and the light that shone there when He visited the souls of the just, and the praises they uttered. 'How wide a range these ideas attained,' says Dr Swete[4], 'will be seen when we add that in one form or another they occur in Ignatius, Hermas, Justin, Irenaeus, the Petrine Gospel, Clement of Alexandria, Hippolytus, Origen, the Edessan document cited by Eusebius (*H. E.* i 13), and the Teaching of Addai.' To this list we can now add the forty-second of the recently discovered (probably second-century) *Odes of Solomon*[5]. Already in St Justin's time the following words had found their way into copies of the prophet Jeremiah: 'The Lord God, the Holy One of Israel, remembered His dead[6], which slept in the dust of the earth, and descended to them, to preach unto them His salvation' (*Dial.* 72). Justin accuses the Jews of having removed these words from their copies of Jeremiah. They are also quoted a number of times by Irenaeus (*Haer.* iii 20. 4; iv 22. 1; iv 33. 1, 12; v 31. 1)[7].

These ideas are not, of course, peculiar to the second and third centuries; so that there would be no difficulty, absolutely speaking, in supposing that in Eg. C. O. they represent a later addition to an earlier form of these instructions on the times of prayer. But the slightness and unobtrusiveness of the allusion to the *Descensus* in this document does not suggest interpolation. Moreover the

---
[1] Here the Latin recommences, thus: '...Deum, qui non mentitur, qui memor fuit sanctorum suorum et emisit verbum suum inluminantem eos.' We find the same thought and expression in the eucharistic prayer of Eg. C. O. (Hauler p. 106-7): 'ut mortem solvat et vincula diaboli dirumpat et infernum calcet *et iustos inluminet*,' etc.
[2] The words 'his Son, that is' are probably a gloss in the Eth. and Copt., the Latin has simply 'verbum suum.'
[3] Cf. 1 Pet. iii. 19; cp. Matt. xxvii. 52, 53, and Eph. iv. 9.
[4] *The Apostles' Creed* (Cambridge, 1899) p. 57-8.
[5] Ed. Rendel Harris (Cambridge, 1911, 2nd ed., p. 136).
[6] Cf. the 'memor fuit sanctorum suorum' of Eg. C. O.
[7] Cf. Swete, *op. cit.* p. 58-9.

idea of the 'souls of the righteous' praising God occurs again at no. (36)[1]; and there it appears in C. H. also, but with omission of a curious feature with which the idea is coupled in Eg. C. O.

(*d*) The feature in no. (36) just referred to is a certain tradition 'of the elders,' that at midnight all creation stands still for a moment's space to praise God. C. H. there also cites as a tradition (of 'our fathers') the praising of God by all creation at midnight, but without just that feature which in Eg. C. O. constitutes the whole point of the appeal to a tradition, viz. *the standing still*[2].

I now proceed to indicate some further points in the passage under discussion, in which C. H. appears to me to betray signs of a secondary character as compared with Eg. C. O.

(*e*) No. (6) of C. H. seems to be rendered pointless by the insertion of no. (5) between it and no. (4); while no. (8) is similarly meaningless through the omission of what Eg. C. O. has at no. (7).

(*f*) As regards the whole section (1)–(15), Eg. C. O. gives a set of directions and explanations which are uniform in character and develop naturally and self-consistently. They could not conceivably have been built up on the disjointed and incoherent clauses of C. H.; while the latter have the appearance of resulting from a hurried and unskilful redaction and condensation of Eg. C. O.

(*g*) At no. (19) observe the difference between 'for in this hour the Christ was nailed to the wood' (Eg. C. O.), and '*quia illo tempore Salvator* voluntarie crucifixus est ad salvandos nos, ut *nobis libertatem tribueret*.' With the italicized words compare a passage of C. H. which Achelis brackets out as an interpolation (can. xxxviii § 257): 'illa enim nocte (sc. resurrectionis) *Salvator* omni creaturae *libertatem comparavit*.'

(*h*) Out of the Eg. C. O. clause 'et reliquum temporis diei *inluminans* ad *vesperam* deduxit,' at no. (26), C. H. appears to have made the two further hours for prayer which it has in

---

[1] These are evidently the same as the souls mentioned in (25) (see below, p. 167), and therefore those in Hades. But as C. H. omits the allusion to them at (25), there is nothing in this document to indicate that the souls in question in (36) are also those of the just in Hades.

[2] The only parallel to this that I know (and it is but partial) is in the *Apocalypse of Adam*. See M. R. James, *Apocrypha Anecdota* p. 143, nos. vi and vii (' Texts and Studies,' II 3).

addition to those mentioned in Eg. C. O., viz. 'Etiam *hora qua sol occidit* orent, quia est completio diei,' and 'Deinde λυχνικῷ vespere orent, quia David dicit: Nocte loquor.' It is to be remembered that all the prayers spoken of in this context are meant to be *private* prayers, said at home : cf. Eg. C. O. at no. (17). But C. H. has introduced the public service of the lamp-lighting[1] among these prayers, building no doubt on the words '*inluminans ad vesperam deduxit*' of Eg. C. O.

(*i*) At no. (28) C. H. is not supported by Eg. C. O. in citing David, and Paul and Silas (Acts xvi 25), as authorities for praying at midnight. Achelis brackets out this passage of C. H. as an interpolation. It certainly has no standing room in Eg. C. O., which gives reasons of an entirely different kind for praying at midnight[2], reasons based, as in the case of most of the other prayers, on considerations connected with our Lord's passion.

That the prayer of Paul and Silas in prison at Philippi offers any scriptural 'authority' for praying at midnight seems a conceit little in keeping with all that is said in Eg. C. O. about times for prayer. But it was evidently familiar to the compiler of C. H. We find it in the second half of the fourth century in St Basil's *Regulae fusius tractatae* (*P. Gr.* XXXI 1016 B), coupled, as in C. H., with an appeal to David: τὸ δὲ μεσονύκτιον Παῦλος καὶ Σίλας ἡμῖν ἀναγκαῖον εἰς προσευχὴν παραδεδώκασιν, ὡς ἡ τῶν πράξεων ἱστορία παρίστησι λέγουσα...καὶ ὁ ψαλμῳδὸς λέγων· μεσονύκτιον ἐξεγειρόμην, κτλ.

(*j*) At no. (31) C. H. eliminates the regulation, found in Eg. C. O., regarding a case where inconvenience may arise from the heathen wife, viz. as to rising to pray at midnight[3]. C. H. seems not to contemplate this possibility.

(*k*) At no. (37) Eg. C. O., in adducing additional reasons for praying at midnight, cites Matth. xxv 6 in a very unfamiliar form: '*Ecce* clamor factus est *circa* mediam noctem *dicentium*:

---

[1] On this see below p. 111 ff. This service included a supper at which psalms were sung by the people and prayers recited by the bishop.

[2] At nos. (35) and (36). These reasons are also reproduced in part by C. H., as we have seen at (*d*) above.

[3] Cf. Tertullian *ad Uxorem* ii 5: 'Latebisne tu...cum etiam per noctem exsurgis oratum...', referring to the case of a Christian wife who has a heathen husband.

Ecce sponsus venit, surgite ad occursum eius.' This may well be a memory quotation; but in C. H. we have the text in its usual form: 'Media autem nocte clamor factus est: Ecce sponsus venit, exite obviam ei.' It seems unlikely that the quotation in Eg. C. O. was made by a writer who had under his eyes the form of text found in C. H.

(*l*) Nos. (44)–(46) deal with the method of making the sign of the cross. Of these no. (45) has already been considered in connexion with the singular manner of making the sign prescribed in Eg. C. O.[1]; but the whole passage deserves to be examined again from the point of view of its general structure in Eg. C. O. and C. H. respectively.

As regards no. (45), it is to be noticed that there is here an evident literary connexion between the two documents: the 'ad vincendum Satanam' of C. H. clearly answers to the 'signum passionis *adversum diabolum*' of Eg. C. O. The equivalent of 'signum passionis' is found in C. H. at no. (46) in 'redemptionis totius orbis terrarum similitudinem'; while the 'ad gloriandum propter fidem tuam' of C. H. seems to answer to 'si ex fide itaque facis, non ut hominibus appareas' of Eg. C. O.

Which, then, of the two texts at no. (45) is more likely to have been derived from the other? Was the remarkable passage of Eg. C. O., echoing ideas found in Tertullian[2], built up round the nine words in C. H., or are these words the residue of the Eg. C. O. text after its peculiar ideas have been excluded? I notice in the first place that the 'ad gloriandum propter fidem tuam' of C. H. seems to have an echo of the 'edification' ideas so often found in this document[3] where they do not occur in Eg. C. O. The thought appears to be, that the Christian should openly proclaim his faith before the heathen by making the sign of the cross,—which does not seem a natural piece of advice for times of persecution.

Next, the words which immediately follow in C. H. at no. (46), 'hoc fecit Moyses de sanguine agni,' etc., form no logical sequel to no. (45): there is no obvious connexion in thought between the two passages. In Eg. C. O. on the other hand no. (46) carries on and develops the idea of no. (45) naturally and consistently: in no. (45) *the Devil is driven away* by the sign of the cross made

[1] See (*b*), p. 104 ff. above.   [2] See p. 105 above.   [3] See p. 55 ff.

after *moistening the hand with breath or spittle*[1], and similarly in no. (46) Moses *smears the lintel and door posts with the blood* of the lamb, thereby doing in type what Christians do when they make the sign of the cross in the manner prescribed, viz. *warding off* '*eum qui exterminare temptat*,' the destroying angel (cf. Ex. xii 23). Here there is a double correspondence between nos. (46) and (45): the smearing of the door posts answers to the moistening of the hand, and the destroying angel answers to the Devil, or 'the adversary.' But C. H. spoils both these parallels. The moistening of the hand does not appear in this document at no. (45), and in (46) the destroying angel is not mentioned.

The last sentence of C. H. at no. (46)—'Quanto magis,' etc., as far as 'condit'—differs completely in conception from anything in the corresponding Eg. C. O. text; yet its literary connexion with the latter is unmistakable: the words 'in sanguine *agni perfecti*[2] Christi' answer to 'fides quae in *perfecta ove* est' of Eg. C. O.; while 'qui *credunt* in eum' appears to correspond to 'quae nunc in nobis est *fides*.'

As regards the whole passage on the sign of the cross, nos. (44)-(46), I cannot think it possible that Eg. C. O. is derived from C. H., whereas the reverse dependence appears to me to lie on the face of the parallel texts[3].

H. *Service of the evening lamp.*

I next call attention to a passage in which C. H. appears to me to be intelligible only by reference to the corresponding text of Eg. C. O.: a passage in fact which alludes to something that has been omitted, but is to be found in Eg. C. O.

[1] See nos. (33) and (34) preceding.

[2] It is curious that Achelis brackets out the context in which these words occur, though he recognizes, by underlining them, that they belong to the original stock of C. H. This is only one more indication that, if C. H. ever stood in a different form from that in which we have it, its present form is due not to mere interpolation but to redaction.

[3] Schwartz (*op. cit.* p. 37, note 2) regards both no. (33) and nos. (45)-(46) as early interpolations into Eg. C. O., due to one and the same interpolator. My reasons for thinking that he is mistaken in this are stated in Additional Note II at p. 155 below. His view, whether it be right or wrong, does not affect the conclusions drawn above.

It has been pointed out (see above p. 37, note 1 (*d*)) that until the full text of the Ethiopic version of Eg. C. O. was published by Mr Horner, in 1904, it was not known that Eg. C. O. contained a passage on the service for the lighting of the evening lamp. C. H. and Test. both speak of this service, but the Latin, Coptic and Arabic versions of Eg. C. O. omit it. Here are the texts of the Ethiopic, C. H. and Test. (ii 11)[1].

Eg. C. O. (Eth.) (Horner pp. 159-161)	*C. H.* (can. xxxii, §§ 164-168)	*Test.* (Cooper-Maclean p. 129)
(1) Concerning the bringing in of lamps at the supper of the congregation.		
(2) When the evening has come, the bishop being there, the deacon shall bring in a lamp, and standing in the midst of the faithful, being about to give thanks, the bishop shall first give the salutation, saying:	Si agape fit vel cena ab aliquo pauperibus paratur κυριακῇ tempore accensus lucernae, praesente episcopo surgat diaconus ad accendendum. Episcopus autem oret super eos et eum qui invitavit illos.	Let the lamp be offered in the temple by the deacon, saying:
(3) 'The Lord (be) with you.' And the people also shall say: 'With thy spirit.'		'The grace of our Lord (be) with you all.' And let all the people say: 'And with thy spirit.'
(4) 'Let us give thanks to the Lord.' And they shall say: 'Right and just, both greatness and exaltation with glory are due to him.' And they shall not say: 'Lift up your hearts,' because that shall be said at the oblation.	Et necessaria est pauperibus εὐχαριστία, quae est in initio missae.	

(5) And he prays thus, saying: 'We give thee thanks, God, through thy Son Jesus Christ our Lord, because thou hast enlightened us by revealing the incorruptible light: we having therefore finished the length of a day and having come to the beginning of the night, and having been satiated with the light of the day, which thou hast created for our satisfaction, and now since we have not been deficient of the light of the evening by thy grace, we sanctify thee and we glorify thee through thy Son Jesus Christ our Lord, through whom to thee (be) glory and might and honour with the Holy Spirit now, etc.'

(6) And they shall say: 'Amen.' And having risen up therefore after supper, the children having prayed, they shall say the psalms, and the virgins:	Missos autem faciat eos, ut separatim recedant, antequam tenebrae oboriantur. Psalmos recitent antequam recedant.	And let the little boys say spiritual psalms and hymns of praise by the light of the lamp.

[1] In a few cases I have substituted readings from Mr Horner's collation for those in his text.

(7) and afterwards the deacon, holding the mingled cup of the Presphora, shall say the psalm from that in which (is) written Hālē luyā, [and]¹ after that the presbyter has commanded: 'And likewise from those psalms.' And afterwards the bishop having offered the cup, as is proper for the cup, he shall say the psalm Hālē luyā;

(8) and all of them as he recites the psalms shall say Hālē luyā, which is to say: 'We praise him who is God²: glorified and praised is he who founded all the world with one word.'

Let all the people respond Hallelujah to the psalm and to the chant sung together, with one accord, and with voices in harmony.

(9) And likewise, the psalm having been completed, he shall give thanks over the cup, and shall give of the fragments to all the faithful. And as they are eating their supper those who are the believers shall take a little bread from the hand of the bishop before they partake of their own bread, for it is eulogia and not eucharist as the body of our Lord.

When we remember that Eg. C. O. is the immediate source of Test. for that matter which the latter has in common with other documents of this group, we can have no reason to doubt that Test. gives us here an abbreviated version of Eg. C. O. That the compiler of A. C. viii also had before him a copy of Eg. C. O. which contained the passage on the lamp, seems certain. In the course of the evening service, prescribed to follow τὸν ἐπιλύχνιον ψαλμόν (viii 35-37), the bishop says a prayer in which occur these words, ὁ διαγαγὼν ἡμᾶς τὸ μῆκος τῆς ἡμέρας καὶ ἀγαγὼν ἐπὶ τὰς ἀρχὰς τῆς νυκτός (viii 37), and in the Eg. C. O. prayer at no. (5) we have the nearly identical words: 'we having therefore finished the length of a day and come to the beginning of the night.'³

---

¹ Horner brackets out this word as redundant; but the MS b, one of the best and oldest, has the words 'and...commanded' in red ink, so that they form a rubric and stand apart from the regular construction. There seems nevertheless to be some confusion in the text.

² A couple of MSS (a, d) add 'most high.'

³ It is possible that the compiler of A. C. kept just these words of the Eg. C. O. prayer because they contain an echo of the evening hymn (ancient already in St Basil's day) Φῶς ἱλαρόν (see below, p. 115, n. 1).

Thus it is probable that the passage preserved by the Ethiopic is a genuine part of Eg. C. O., having been found in this document by the compilers of Test. and A. C.

C. H. has also, at no. (2), a verbal coincidence (slight, indeed, but I think sufficient) with Eg. C. O. which marks the literary connexion, 'praesente episcopo' answering to 'the bishop being there.' But C. H. then goes straight on to mention the bishop's prayer ('Episcopus autem oret super eos et eum qui invitavit illos'), without speaking of the preliminary salutations found in Eg. C. O. and Test. at nos. (3) and (4). At no. (4), however, C. H. interjects this remark: 'Et necessaria est pauperibus εὐχαριστία, quae est in initio missae.'

Achelis, who had neither Test. nor the Ethiopic of Eg. C. O. before him, could make nothing of these words, and he bracketed them out as an interpolation, saying in a note (p. 105): 'The passage is interpolated; it is unknown to Eg. C. O., and already for this reason suspect. Moreover the εὐχαριστία, according to C. H., does not come at the beginning of the liturgy.'

His last remark is quite just, if we understand εὐχαριστία here to mean 'the Eucharist,' Holy Communion. But does it mean that? The term is not elsewhere found in C. H. in that sense; for 'the Eucharist,' the consecrated elements, this document regularly uses either 'mysteria,'[1] or 'corpus (et sanguis) Christi (*or* Domini),' or the like[2]. On the other hand, we find (at § 134) 'chrisma εὐχαριστίας' in the sense of 'oil of thanksgiving,' oil over which a thanksgiving has been pronounced. The probability is therefore that 'εὐχαριστία quae est in initio missae' refers to a formula of 'thanksgiving' said at the beginning of the mass[3] (*ḳiddās*). This could only be either the thanksgiving dialogue before the eucharistic prayer, εὐχαριστήσωμεν τῷ κυρίῳ (cf. C. H. § 25), or the beginning of the eucharistic prayer itself. When we actually find part of this dialogue in Eg. C. O. and Test. the otherwise unintelligible allusion in C. H. receives a perfectly natural explanation. But again, if we look at Eg. C. O. no. (2),

[1] See §§ 169, 201, 205, 206, 215.
[2] See §§ 142, 143, 146, 149, 150, 153, 258.
[3] This is the sense in which Haneberg, the original editor of C. H., understood the clause, for he translated it: 'Pauperes autem adsint quando *in initio missae Eucharistia agitur.*'

we find the dialogue introduced in these words: 'being about to give *thanks*, the bishop shall first give the salutation'; and the first words of his prayer are, at no. (5), 'We give thee thanks.' Thus, even if the 'thanksgiving at the beginning of the ķiddās' ('sacrum,' 'mass') in C. H. refer not to the portion of the dialogue which says 'Let us give thanks,' etc., but to the opening of the eucharistic prayer itself, we have in Eg. C. O. a natural point of reference for the expression[1]. I have no doubt, however, that the 'thanksgiving' in question is really that in the dialogue ('Let us give thanks to the Lord'); for in Eg. C. O. at no. (4) it is particularly ordered that the clause of the dialogue 'Lift up

[1] In his *de Spiritu sancto* (c. xxix) St Basil cites a formula used by the people at this service as something ἀναγκαῖον εἰς μαρτυρίαν (to the form of doxology he is defending) διὰ τοῦ χρόνου τὴν ἀρχαιότητα, thus:

"Ἔδοξε τοῖς πατράσιν ἡμῶν μὴ σιωπῇ τὴν χάριν τοῦ ἑσπερινοῦ φωτὸς δέχεσθαι, ἀλλ' εὐθὺς φανέντος **εὐχαριστεῖν.** Καὶ ὅστις μὲν ὁ πατὴρ τῶν ῥημάτων ἐκείνων **τῆς ἐπι-λυχνίου εὐχαριστίας,** εἰπεῖν οὐκ ἔχομεν· ὁ μέντοι λαὸς ἀρχαίαν ἀφίησι τὴν φωνήν, καὶ οὐδενὶ πώποτε ἀσεβεῖν ἐνομίσθησαν οἱ λέγοντες· **Αἰνοῦμεν πατέρα καὶ υἱὸν καὶ ἅγιον πνεῦμα θεοῦ.**

Besides the emphasis laid on the antiquity of the people's formula, we may notice two other points about this passage: (1) St Basil's use of the words εὐχαριστεῖν and εὐχαριστία to describe the people's part, even though this does not contain those words; and (2) that the people's formula referred to is evidently the ancient evening hymn Φῶς ἱλαρόν, which may here be quoted in full from Routh *Rel. Sacr.* iii p. 515:

Φῶς ἱλαρὸν ἁγίας δόξης ἀθανάτου πατρός, οὐρανίου, ἁγίου, μάκαρος, Ἰησοῦ Χριστέ· ἐλθόντες ἐπὶ τοῦ ἡλίου δύσιν, ἰδόντες φῶς ἑσπερινόν, ὑμνοῦμεν πατέρα καὶ υἱὸν καὶ ἅγιον πνεῦμα θεοῦ. Ἄξιος εἶ ἐν πᾶσι καιροῖς ὑμνεῖσθαι φωναῖς ὁσίαις, υἱὲ θεοῦ, ζωὴν ὁ διδούς· διὸ ὁ κόσμος σε δοξάζει.

It will be observed that the words quoted by St Basil are found in the Hymn, with the only difference that the latter has ὑμνοῦμεν instead of αἰνοῦμεν. But further, ἐλθόντες ἐπὶ τοῦ ἡλίου δύσιν, ἰδόντες φῶς ἑσπερινόν of the Hymn has evidently a literary connexion with the words 'having therefore finished the length of a day and come to the beginning of the night,...and now since we have not been deficient of the light of the evening,' in Eg. C. O. at (5). It is possible that these words in the prayer were inserted by the person who composed it as an intentional echo of the phrase in the Hymn; and their partial retention in A. C. viii 37 (ὁ διαγαγὼν ἡμᾶς τὸ μῆκος τῆς ἡμέρας καὶ ἀγαγὼν ἐπὶ τὰς ἀρχὰς τῆς νυκτός), where the Eg. C. O. prayer is otherwise completely re-written, may also be due to their recognition by the A. C. compiler as an echo of the Φῶς ἱλαρόν.

This point of connexion between the Eg. C. O. prayer and the Φῶς ἱλαρόν, the origin of which was already lost in antiquity in St Basil's day, affords additional ground for regarding the service here preserved by the Ethiopic as a genuine portion of the original Eg. C. O.

your hearts' is *not* to be said in the service of the lamp, because it is (only) said 'at the oblation' (i.e. at mass). Here, I am much inclined to believe, we have the origin of the C. H. expression 'in initio missae.'

It may be asked, If εὐχαριστία in the C. H. passage means 'thanksgiving' and not 'the Eucharist,' why is it said to be necessary for *the poor*? The answer to this seems to me to lie in the fact that C. H. makes the service of the lamp-lighting take place at a supper held specifically for the poor—see no. (2). Consequently the poor form the congregation, and it is they who, on the explanation given above, are exhorted to 'give thanks to the Lord.'

J. Burial of the dead.

There is one passage of C. H. in which Achelis is constrained to recognize that his 'interpolators' have re-written in a different sense a prescription which originally stood as in Eg. C. O., in other words, have edited instead of merely interpolating the original C. H.

Eg. C. O. (Copt.)[1]

(Horner p. 327) Let not men overcharge (βαρεῖν) for burying men in the cemetery (κοιμητήριον); for it is the property of all the poor; or else (πλήν) let them give the wages of the workman (ἐργάτης) to him who digs, and the price of the earthen vessels (κέραμος). But those who are at that place who take care (of it), let the bishop support, lest any of those who go to that place (τόπος) should be burdened.

C. H.[2]

(Can. xxiv §§ 220-221) They shall not cause the sick to sleep in the κοιμητήριον, except the poor. Wherefore he who has a house shall not be brought in to the house of God, except only to pray; and then he shall return to his house. (Can. xxv § 222) The economus, who has the care of the sick, let the bishop bear the charges of them (*sic*), even to the earthen vessels, because the sick require it: the bishop gives it to the economus.

The literary connexion between these two passages is plain and unmistakable; one is a deliberate alteration of the other.

In Eg. C. O. we have κοιμητήριον used in its regular Christian sense of 'cemetery,' 'graveyard'; in C. H. the word would seem at first sight to have the non-Christian sense of 'sleeping place,'

---

[1] I give Eg. C. O. according to the Coptic, as it retains a number of Greek words and appears to preserve the sense better than the Ethiopic (the Latin is not extant).

[2] I translate from Riedel's German, which is more intelligible than Achelis's Latin.

and to denote either the church itself or some building closely associated with it. But it is possible that what is meant is a cemetery chapel, in which the sick may be healed by sleeping near the remains of the holy dead. Achelis is of opinion that the original text of C. H., like the present text of Eg. C. O., dealt with burial and not with the sick; though he can offer no explanation of κέραμος in connexion with burial (*op. cit.* p. 124, note). Already in Tertullian's day the Christians had separate burial grounds of their own, called *areae*[1] (*ad Scap.* c. 3); and Hippolytus tells us (*Philosophum.* ix 12) that Pope Zephyrinus 'set Callistus over the cemetery' (εἰς τὸ κοιμητήριον καθέστησεν).

. Christian 'hospitals' in the strict sense appear not to be mentioned before the middle of the fourth century, and to have come into existence only after the freedom granted to the Church by Constantine. St Jerome seems to say that the first hospital for the sick in Rome was built in his time by Fabiola: 'prima omnium νοσοκομεῖον instituit, in quo aegrotantes colligeret de plateis, et consumpta languoribus atque inedia miserorum membra foveret' (Ep. 77 § 6, *ad Oceanum*).

Let us now consider our parallel texts. The expression in C. H., 'let the bishop bear the charges of them (? the sick who sleep in the κοιμητήριον), *even to the earthen vessels,*' is very unobvious, and seems without point in its context. There is no evident reason why the utensils required for the sick should be mentioned here, or why *earthen* ones should be specified. If we turn to Eg. C. O. we find it said, as I understand the passage, that the relatives or friends of those who are buried in the cemetery are not to be burdened with payment for this, as for a privilege; save only (πλήν) that they are to give 'the wages of the workman' and 'the price of the κέραμοι.' What are these κέραμοι which deserve to be legislated for in connexion with burial?

If there were independent grounds for thinking Eg. C. O. to be a Roman document of, let us say, the third century, the κέραμοι would admit of explanation in reference to the tiles used for closing the *loculi* in the catacombs after the insertion of the

[1] In another passage (*de Anima* c. 51) Tertullian uses the word 'coemeterium' in connexion with burial: 'Est et alia relatio apud nostros, in coemeterio corpus corpori iuxta collocando spatium recessu communicasse.'

bodies. De Rossi (*Bullettino di Archeologia Cristiana* III pp. 38, 39; May, 1865) describes such tiles ('tegole') found in the cemeteries of Saints Domitilla and Priscilla. Some of the earliest are inscribed with the makers' names, with some such formula as 'ex figlinis' (N. N.). Evidently they would require to be purchased from the regular *figuli* by the persons defraying the cost of a burial. The present is not the occasion on which to pursue this subject; but it seems worth while to throw out a suggestion in regard to it here in view of certain facts, bearing upon the date and *provenance* of Eg. C. O., which will be stated in the following chapter.

In the *Canons of Athanasius*, edited by Riedel and Crum[1], there is a passage which throws some light upon the text of C. H., printed above, and its relation to the parallel text of Eg. C. O. No. 80 of the 'Athanasian' canons begins thus: 'As for *the sick which are in the holy place, if they have wherewithal to live*, they shall not be a burden upon the church. But *if they be poor, the steward of the church shall care for them which sleep therein* like his children; he shall watch over them as it were the vessels of the church.'

When the words which I have italicized in this passage are compared with the above text of C. H., it is difficult to resist drawing the conclusion that there is a literary connexion of some sort between the two canons. In his Introduction to the *Canons of Athanasius* (p. xxiii), Riedel observes the resemblance and concludes that the C. H. text is the later. That borrowing, on one side or the other, has here taken place between C. H. and 'Athanasius,' is rendered probable by the fact that the two documents shew other points of coincidence. The following may be noticed: (*a*) the bells on Aaron's garment ('Ath.' Proem and c. 7; C. H. c. xxix); (*b*) white garments of the clergy ('Ath.' c. 28; C. H. c. xxxvii); (*c*) silence to be observed in the sanctuary ('Ath.' c. 32; C. H. c. xxix); (*d*) *one* (deacon) to stand by with a fan during the 'anaphora' ('Ath.' c. 39; cf. C. H. c. xxix); (*e*) double measures not to be used ('Ath.' c. 9; C. H. c. xxx Haneberg, c. xxxviii Riedel). It will be observed that in the passage under

[1] In the publications of the 'Text and Translation Society,' 1904. Riedel thinks these Canons are really by St Athanasius; but this view is open to serious doubt.

consideration the C. H. text presents a combination of features found separately in Eg. C. O. and 'Athanasius.'

Schwartz (op. cit. p. 35) regards the passage on burial as part of an early ('nicht jungen Datums') interpolation in Eg. C. O. His objection to it lay in its position. It constitutes *Statute* 61 in the Coptic of Horner's edition, and is preceded by *Statutes* 58, 59, 60^a (on care in receiving the Eucharist), and 60^b (on the duty of deacons and presbyters assembling daily at a place appointed by the bishop). The whole passage (58–61) lies between two others (*Statutes* 57 and 62^a), of which one is merely a repetition of the other. This arrangement is found also in the Ethiopic (*Statutes* 43–48^a) and Arabic (*Statutes* 42–47^a), and, so far as it goes, in the Latin (Hauler p. 117 l. 2 ff.).

Schwartz would explain the repetition in *Statutes* 57 and 62^a (of the Coptic) as the result of a later insertion, from the margin, of *Statutes* 58–61. But the indication of Roman origin which the passage on burial contains, combined with the fact that its parallels both in C. H. and Test. (ii 23) occur in precisely the same position as in Eg. C. O. (viz. just before the prescriptions as to daily prayers), suggests that the repetition is due merely to an early clerical error. From the somewhat promiscuous contents of *Statutes* 58–60^a, 60^b and 61, nothing adverse to them can be concluded; for they are immediately preceded by four prescriptions of an equally varied character, viz. *Stat.* 52 (supper of widows), 53–4 (firstfruits), 55 (the paschal fast), 56 (deacons and subdeacons to inform the bishop of the sick).

K. *Prayer over firstfruits.*

I would now invite the student of these Church Orders to pass judgment on the relative merits of the prayers over firstfruits found in Eg. C. O. and C. H. respectively. And by 'merits' I mean features suggestive of antiquity or priority.

Eg. C. O.	*C. H.*
(Hauler p. 115)	(can. xxxvi §§ 189–193)
(a) Gratias tibi agimus, Deus, et offerimus tibi primitivas fructuum, quos dedisti nobis ad percipiendum, per verbum tuum enutriens ea, iubens terrae omnes fructus adferre	Gratias agimus tibi, omnipotens Domine Deus, qui nos fecisti dignos qui hos fructus videamus, quos terra hoc anno produxit.

Eg. C. O.	C. H.
(b)	Benedic eos, o Domine, sicut coronam anni tui, secundum benignitatem tuam[1],
(c) ad laetitiam et nutrimentum hominum et omnibus animalibus.	sintque ad satietatem pauperibus populi tui.
(d) Super his omnibus laudamus te, Deus, et in omnibus, quibus nos iuvasti, adornans nobis omnem creaturam variis fructibus	
(e)	Et servum tuum N., qui haec obtulit ex opibus tuis[2], quia timet te, benedic eum de caelo sacro tuo una cum domo et filiis eius, et effunde super eos misericordiam et gratiam tuam sacram, ut sciat voluntatem tuam in omnibus rebus; et fac ut haereditate accipiat id quod est in caelis,
(f) per puerum tuum Iesum Christum, dominum nostrum, per quem tibi gloria in saecula saeculorum. Amen.	per dominum nostrum Iesum Christum filium tuum dilectum et Spiritum sanctum in saecula saeculorum. Amen.

I can hardly imagine that anyone should entertain a doubt as to which of these two forms of prayer is primary and which secondary. The citation of Ps. lxiv 12 (LXX) in C. H. is a familiar feature in the liturgical Intercession prayers for weather and crops; it is found in St James (Greek and Syriac), St Mark (Greek and Coptic), St Basil, and in all the East-Syrian liturgies, including the sixth-century fragment in the British Museum (MS *Add.* 14669 fols. 20, 21). Its combination also with the phrase 'the poor of thy people' is found in St Mark, and the coincidence is hardly accidental:

St Mark[3]	C. H.
εὐλόγησον καὶ νῦν κύριε τὸν στέφανον τοῦ ἐνιαυτοῦ τῆς χρηστότητός σου διὰ τοὺς πτωχοὺς τοῦ λαοῦ σου.	Benedic eos, o Domine, sicut coronam anni tui, secundum benignitatem tuam, sintque in satietatem pauperibus populi tui.

[1] Riedel: 'Bless, O Lord, the crown of the year of thy goodness,' which is Ps. lxiv 12 exactly.

[2] Riedel: 'who hath brought this of thine own.'

[3] Brightman *L. E. W.* I p 127 ll. 31-32. So in the Coptic (*op. cit.* p. 167 ll. 34-35): 'Bless the crown of the year with thy goodness for the sake of the poor of thy people.'

EG. C. O. IN RELATION TO C. H. 121

That this double coincidence with the Intercession prayer is to be explained as a reminiscence, on the part of the C. H. compiler, of the Greek or Coptic liturgy of St Mark, is rendered more than probable by the fact that what immediately follows in the C. H. prayer has a similar double coincidence with the Invocation prayer in the same liturgy:

St Mark	C. H.
σοὶ ἐκ τῶν σῶν [cf. 1 Chr. xxix 14] δώρων προεθήκαμεν ἐνώπιόν σου καὶ δεόμεθα...ἐξαπόστειλον ἐξ ὕψους ἁγίου σου [cf. Ps. xix (xx) 7]...τὸν παράκλητον, τὸ πνεῦμα τῆς ἀληθείας τὸ ἅγιον... (Brightman L. E. W. 1 133 l. 30 ff.).	Et servum tuum N., qui *haec obtulit ex* opibus *tuis* [Riedel: '*who hath brought this of thine own*'], quia timet te, benedic eum *de caelo sacro tuo* una cum domo et filiis eius, et effunde super eos misericordiam et gratiam tuam sacram.

There is no trace of any of these coincidences with the liturgy of St Mark in the corresponding prayer in Eg. C. O. They would seem to afford a definite indication that C. H. was compiled in Egypt.

L. C. H. canon xxx.

If we look at Riedel's translation of C. H., at the top of p. 220, we find the following passage (can. xxix *fin*.-xxx):

'All mysteries of the life and the resurrection and the oblation the Christians alone shall hear, because they have received the seal of baptism and are thus become partakers. (Can. xxx) But the catechumens hear only the preaching on the faith and the instruction. That is the purity ('Reinheit') of which John says that no one knows it except him that receives it' (Apoc. ii 17).

If we turn now to Haneberg's translation, p. 85-90, we find that it has between the words 'instruction' and 'That is' (in can. xxx) a long passage which reads like a piece of a sermon, beginning: '(Catechumenus)[1] propinquos consanguineos suos a se avertat' (p. 85), and ending: 'Communiones, orationem multam cum ieiunio amet' (p. 90). To this passage there is nothing corresponding in any of the other Church Orders. I shall refer to it in what follows as S (= 'Sermon').

[1] The bracketed word is supplied by Haneberg in translating, it is not in his Arabic text.

The piece quoted above from Riedel, into the middle of which Haneberg's text introduces the long passage S, comes in C. H. just after the directions as to the sign of the cross (can. xxix); but from Eg. C. O. we can see that it ought properly to follow can. xix § 149, and so come immediately after the sections on baptism and the first communion of the newly baptized. That this is so is evident when the piece is placed opposite its parallel in Eg. C. O., which has that position. The Latin of Eg. C. O. is wanting here, so I give the Ethiopic and Coptic. For C. H. I follow Riedel, since Haneberg's version is for the first part quite unintelligible.

Eg. C. O. (Eth.)	Eg. C. O. (Copt.)	C. H.
(a) (Horner p. 156-7) This we have taught you to be said openly concerning baptism and the ordinance of *the oblation*; and behold, we have finished the instruction which we give you concerning *the resurrection* of the body, and the rest as it was written. And if there is anything else which is right to be told, then the bishop shall tell it and give it to those who are *communicated*. And they shall accept (it), and none shall know it except the believers, but only after they have *communicated*. (b) (c) (d) And they shall first receive *this* holy blessing[1], which Yuhannes speaks of that there was written upon it a new name (which) no one knows except him who receives the blessing.	(Horner p. 320) Now we have delivered these things to you in brief concerning the holy baptism and *the* holy *oblation*, since they have already instructed ($\kappa\alpha\theta\eta\gamma\epsilon\tilde{\iota}\sigma\theta\alpha\iota$) you concerning *the resurrection* of the flesh and all other things according as it is written. But if there is any other thing which is right to be told, let the bishop say it quietly to those who shall be *baptized*; and let not the unbelievers know (it), except they are first *baptized*. *This is the* white *stone* ($\psi\tilde{\eta}\phi o s$) *of which Johannes said,* that there is a new name written on it *which no one knows except him who will receive* the stone ($\psi\tilde{\eta}\phi o s$).	(Can. xxix fin.) All mysteries of the life and *the resurrection* and *the oblation* the Christians alone shall hear, because they have *received* the seal of *baptism* and are thus become *partakers*. But the catechumens hear only the preaching on the faith and the instruction. [Here in Haneberg comes passage S.] *That is the purity* ('Reinheit') *of which John says that no one knows it except him that receives it*.

Achelis saw that there is no place for S between the passages marked (b) and (d), where it stands in Haneberg. Its opening

---

[1] $\psi\tilde{\eta}\phi o s$ has evidently caused the translators some trouble; but there can be no reasonable doubt that it ultimately stands behind both the 'blessing' of Eth. and the 'purity' of C. H. The reference is to the $\psi\tilde{\eta}\phi o\nu$ $\lambda\epsilon\nu\kappa\acute{\eta}\nu$ of Apoc. ii 17.

words (in Haneberg), 'propinquos...a se avertat,' cannot originally have followed (b); nor can its last words, 'Communiones... amet,' have stood just before (d); whereas (d) itself evidently stood originally in close connexion with (a) and (b). Yet an examination of its contents convinced Achelis that the passage (S) came from the same hand as the rest of C. H. There can be no doubt that here he was right. Among the parallels with the rest of C. H. which he cites (p. 288–290) some are of little or no significance; but there are others which cannot be accidental. The passage is certainly by the compiler of C. H.; but how are we to explain it in view of the fact that it plainly does not belong to the context in which it is found in Haneberg?

Achelis attempted to solve this difficulty by seeing in S two sermon fragments by Hippolytus, which had somehow found their way into C. H. He divided it in two after the words 'quae est superbia' (Haneberg p. 87), and printed it separately from C. H. in Appendix II to his *Canones Hippolyti* (p. 281 ff.), under the title *Zwei Fragmente Hippolyteischer Predigten*[1]. For Achelis the proof that the passage is by the compiler of C. H. constitutes the proof that it is by Hippolytus, since he has already drawn the confident conclusion that C. H. itself is the work of Hippolytus.

Amongst other valuable additions to our understanding of C. H. which have come with Riedel's better text and generally (I understand) more accurate translation, not the least in importance is the true solution of the puzzle presented in Haneberg's text by the passage we are considering.

Riedel's MSS have the passage *not in can. xxx, but near the end of the last canon of all*, viz. xxxviii (after the words 'ut simus ferventes spiritu omni tempore,' or § 260 of Achelis's paragraphs). They shew us, moreover, that in Haneberg's text the passage has been bisected and the second part placed before the first: a circumstance which led Achelis to conclude, from the lack of sequence thus brought about, that in S we have to do with two separate *Predigt* fragments. The construction of the passage, as restored by Riedel's text, is as follows:

[1] Achelis wrongly includes as part of S (and so omits from his text of C. H. itself) the two pieces (b) and (d) above, the one at the beginning, the other at the end (see *Die Canones Hippolyti* p. 281 and p. 285).

i. 'Cuius autem opus et studium' (Haneberg p. 87; Achelis p. 283 § 7) to 'Communiones, orationem multam cum ieiunio amet' (Haneberg p. 90; Achelis p. 285—in the bracketed piece, just before 'Hic est,' etc.).

ii. 'propinquos consanguineos suos a se avertat' (Haneberg p. 85; Achelis p. 281 § 2) to 'hoc mihi fecistis' (Haneberg p. 87; Achelis p. 283 § 6).

When the last words in Haneberg are thus read before the first, there can be no possible doubt that Riedel's text has restored S to its original form. But further, when the whole passage, thus restored, is read where Riedel has it (i.e. immediately after can. xxxviii § 260), it is as little open to doubt that this is its correct and original place. To satisfy ourselves of this we need only to have before us the contexts in which occur (*a*) the juncture of the whole passage with can. xxxviii § 260, and (*β*) the juncture of Haneberg's opening passage with his concluding one. These two contexts are for the reader's convenience printed out here at some length in the Latin translation found in Achelis. I mark the points of juncture by a dagger (†).

(*a*) Can. xxxviii (Achelis p. 137) § 258. Debemus igitur vigiles esse omni tempore, non indulgentes oculis nostris somnum. Cavendum est, ne somnolentia nos opprimat, donec inveniamus locum domino, neve quis dicat: Equidem et baptizatus et corpore Christi pastus sum—et fretus dicat: Sum christianus, et inveniatur talis amator deliciarum, aversus a mandatis Christi. (§ 259) Talis similis est homini sordibus pleno, qui in balneum quidem intravit, sed prius inde exivit, quam bene defricatus esset, ita ut sordes in eo etiam postea inveniantur. (§ 260) Ille enim non adhibuit exustionem spiritus, de qua loquitur beatus Paulus apostolus monens, ut simus ferventes spiritu omni tempore (Rom. xii 11). † Cuius[1] autem opus et studium vigilantia non custoditur, id incendio delebitur, quia vitam non habet in virtute, sed est mortuus in perversitate. Illique ipsi furno destinati sunt, id est, ludibrio erunt diabolo, qui primo ore suo dixerunt: Renuntio tibi, o satana; iam vero operibus suis malis ad eum recurrunt. Revera autem diabolus non valde gaudere videtur de iis, qui cum ipso sunt et ad eum pertinent, sicut illi, qui corpore quidem nobiscum sunt, animabus autem cum illo. De his dixit apostolus: Confitentur se nosse Deum, factis autem negant (Tit. i 16). De iisdemque in proverbiis dicitur (Prov. xxvi 11): Est sicut canis, qui revertitur ad vomitum suum, sic imprudens, qui iterat peccata sua. Beatus autem Petrus de iis dicit: Esse similes porco, qui postquam lotus est, volutatur in coeno suo (2 Pet. ii 22). Et huius quidem generis non pauci sunt, ut dicat quis coram Deo: Equidem omnem voluntatem tuam faciam, sed simul malis suis intentionibus etiam ad servitutem diaboli convertitur. Similis est militi, qui accipit quidem vestitum militarem,

[1] Here begins passage S according to Riedel (=Haneberg p. 87, or about the middle of the passage according to his text).

EG. C. O. IN RELATION TO C. H. 125

neque tamen ipsi curae est res militaris, sed ignominia afficitur detectis criminibus, et quamvis se ipsum solus nominet militem, nihil nisi externam formam militiae habet, qua indutus est, quaque fit, ut sibi arrogare possit. Sic quidam ipsi gloriantur, se christianos esse, neque tamen operibus induti sunt....

(β) ...Si autem christianus ad gradum regni[1] aspirat, a mulieribus longe omnino recedat et firmiter in corde suo sibi proponat, se non aspecturum esse illas neque cibum cum illis sumturum. Sine cunctatione omnes thesauros suos distribuat pauperibus sibique assumat angelicam benignitatem, cum humilitate cordis et corporis, sufficiatque sibi ipse solus, similis sit aviculae, quae armis caret, largiatur indigentibus de labore suo; communiones, orationem multam cum ieiunio amet[2]; † propinquos, consanguineos suos a se avertat omniaque incommoda toleret, quae ipsum invadunt propter religionem; et tollat crucem suam sequens salvatorem, sitque paratus ad perpetiendam mortem propter professionem Christi. Effugium enim non relinquitur, quominus homo, qui perfectionem quaerit, tentetur, sicut tentatus est dominus noster his tribus tentationibus, scilicet cupiditate, superbia et amore auri....

In (a) the organic connexion of the beginning of the passage which I have called S with can. xxxviii §§ 258–260 appears from the close correspondence in argument and ideas:

1. The canon says: 'Debemus igitur *vigiles* esse omni tempore'; S says: 'Cuius autem opus et studium *vigilantia* non custoditur,' etc.

2. In both there is the contrast between the profession of Christianity and a life unworthy of a Christian: 'Neve *quis dicat*: Equidem et baptizatus et corpore Christi pastus sum—et fretus *dicat*: Sum *christianus*, et inveniatur talis amator deliciarum' (can. xxxviii § 258); 'ut *dicat quis* coram Deo: Equidem omnem voluntatem tuam faciam, sed simul malis suis intentionibus (etc.)... Sic quidam ipsi gloriantur *se christianos esse*, neque tamen,' etc. (S).

3. In both canon xxxviii and S this contrast is illustrated by examples: in the canon there is the simile of the man who leaves his bath before he is washed clean; in S there is the dog that returns to his vomit, the sow that was washed and goes back to her wallowing in the mire, and the counterfeit soldier.

In (β) the first words (in Haneberg) of S actually take up the last words in the middle of a sentence; they continue and

[1] Riedel (p. 226 *fin.*) 'to the rank of the *angels*,' rightly: cf. 'angelicam benignitatem,' just below. Haneberg's mistake rests on the similarity in Arabic (as in Hebrew and Syriac) of the roots underlying the words for 'king,' 'kingdom,' and 'angel.'

[2] This is the end of the whole passage S in Haneberg, and what follows is Haneberg's beginning.

complete the list of qualifications required in one who aspires to the 'condition of the angels.'

Riedel's text, then, both restores S to its original form and establishes beyond all doubt its organic connexion with can. xxxviii §§ 258–260, a passage pronounced by Achelis to be a genuine part of C. H. in its original and authentic form.

We can now go beyond this, and assert that both can. xxxviii §§ 258–260 and S are by the same hand as the rest of C. H.[1]. This, of course, Achelis holds to be the case; but we shall do well not to accept the statement on his bare authority, and so I adduce here some of the more satisfying of the parallels which he has collected.

C. H.

(Can. xix §§ 108–9) *orans ut malignum spiritum ab omnibus membris eorum expellat*[2]. Ipsi vero caveant, ne abhinc *operibus et actibus ad illos*[3] *revertantur*.

(Can. xix § 149) Iam vero facti sunt *christiani* perfecti, qui *fruuntur corpore Christi*.

(Can. xvii § 84) *omni tempore Dei recordatione* fruatur.

(Can. xvii § 86) *cogitetque de pauperibus, quasi sint propinqui ipsius* et curam habeat oblationum.

(Can. xv § 76) *iniuriosus* vel *amator mundi*.

Can. xxxviii and S

(S) qui primo ore suo dixerunt: Renuntio tibi, o satana; iam vero *operibus suis malis ad eum recurrunt*......ut dicat quis coram Deo: Equidem omnem voluntatem tuam faciam, sed simul *malis suis intentionibus etiam ad servitutem diaboli convertitur* (printed above).

(Can. xxxviii § 258) Neve quis dicat: Equidem et baptizatus et *corpore Christi pastus sum*—et fretus dicat: *Sum christianus*.

(S) *omnique hora* perseverat in continua *recordatione Dei* (Achel. p. 282 § 25).

(S) *non obliviscantur indigentium*... sed potius amatores peregrinorum...*sed in numero filiorum suorum eos habent*... neque cunctanter et negligenter agunt in perceptione *s. communionis* et in adorationibus[4]......*largiatur indigentibus* de labore suo; *communiones*[5], orationem multam cum ieiunio amet (Achel. p. 284 § 24 seqq.).

(S) neque *amatores mundi*...ab *iniuriis* abstinent (Achel. p. 284 §§ 23, 24).

---

[1] It is necessary to have this point brought out clearly and established, because it may conceivably be said that Riedel's text merely shews that can. xxxviii §§ 258–260 is a part of the 'Predigt' passage, and that the whole piece, thus restored, may still be detached from the body of C. H. and regarded as a late addition.

[2] This refers to the exorcism of those about to be baptized.

[3] Sc. the evil spirits.

[4] Riedel (p. 226) 'vernachlässige die *Opfer* und Erstlinge nicht.'

[5] Riedel (p. 227) 'sowie den *Opfern*.'

I do not see how we can avoid concluding with Achelis that the passage S is by the same hand as the rest of C. H.; and further (this time against Achelis), that it is an integral part of C. H. And I think it will readily be conceded that the correct deduction from these facts is, not that S is therefore by Hippolytus, but that its date is the date of the whole compilation. If we wish to know whether this could possibly fall in the third century we shall do well to study C. H. in the light of S.

Riedel rightly observes (p. 197 *fin.*) that S deals with two clearly distinct classes of Christians, a lower and a higher. The first are those who are content to remain just Christian *men*, the second are those who aspire to the condition of the *angels*. Let us place the beginning of the passage, in which the latter class are dealt with, opposite can. vii §§ 48–50. I follow the translation of Riedel for both passages.

Can. vii	S (Riedel, p. 226–7)
He who is celibate and has no wife is not ordained unless testimony is borne to him, and he is declared to be chaste by (his) neighbours: to wit, that in the time of his maturity he has kept himself apart from women. A celibate receives no imposition of hand ('Handauflegung') until he has reached maturity and goes(?) into a treasury(?)[1]; he shall be considered worthy if testimony is borne to him.	If a Christian aspires to the condition of the angels, let him keep himself for ever apart from women and be determined in his heart not to look at them and not to eat with them. Let him speedily dispose of all his treasures for the poor and take upon himself the law of the angels in lowliness of heart and body. Let him be content with his solitary estate ('Einsamkeit'), and be like the birds which have no tools. Let him give to the poor of the labour of

his hands, and likewise to the oblations, and devote himself much to prayer and fasting. Let him put away from him those who are near to him according to the flesh, and accept all sufferings that come to him for God's sake; let him take up his cross and follow the Saviour; yea, let him be ready at any time for Christ's sake to die in the faith, since he cannot escape from that whereby those are tempted who seek after perfection, even as our Lord Christ was tempted with these three things, lust, pride, and love of gold. Whence the tempter presented himself to our Saviour while He was fasting and said to Him: 'If thou be the Son of God, speak that these stones be made bread.' So thou also, o ascetic, must fast: that is thy mystery.

Riedel remarks (p. 198) that in C. H. there is nothing about

[1] Riedel: 'und in eine Schatzkammer (?) eingeht (?).' Though Riedel adds the two queries in the text he gives no note in explanation of them.

monasticism; though he adds in a note: 'Except perhaps in canon vii?' This does not seem a very well grounded assertion in view of the passages just quoted. The class of persons in question in can. vii are obviously bound to strict and perpetual celibacy; and in S they are forbidden to eat with women, or so much as look at them. Further (in S) they are to bestow all their possessions on the poor; they are to 'aspire to the condition of the angels,' to 'seek perfection,' to be solitary, to forsake kith and kin, to be 'like the birds,' and without care for the morrow. Finally they are styled 'ascetics'; and further on we find that they are bound by some sort of religious vow: 'Igitur ea hora, qua *foedere quodam coram Deo se obstringit* homo [Riedel: 'In the hour, then, when any one *makes a covenant before God*'], atque etiam postea caveat summo studio, ne decidat in id, quod scriptum est: Ne tentes Dominum Deum tuum.'[1]

It appears to me that the formal division of Christians, found in S, into two distinct classes—the ordinary baptized folk and professing 'ascetics,' or seekers after a higher 'perfection' and the 'angelic' life—could hardly have been made by an ecclesiastical writer, even in Egypt, before the regularization of monasticism at the beginning of the fourth century. That the above language could have been employed by Hippolytus at the beginning of the third century, and at Rome, would seem to be devoid of probability.

Turning from historical to purely literary considerations, I would point out that in can. vii the passage on male celibates who ask for ordination occupies the place of one in Eg. C. O. on (female) virgins—an institution as to the early date of which there is no question. To this we must add that in Eg. C. O. there is not only no trace of the passage S itself, but none of any of the parallels which have been adduced to establish the organic connexion of S with the rest of C. H.

---

[1] As Riedel queries his translation 'enters a treasury' in can. vii, I do not venture to attach any special significance to it. But in view of the above it would not be surprising to find that it meant 'enters a cenobium,' or '*laura*,' and that the canon contemplates the case of monks who ask for clerical ordination—unless indeed the ordination in question refers to a formal institution of monks such as we find in the *de eccl. Hier.* of Ps.-Dionysius Areop.

M. Baptismal features in C. H.

A point which deserves notice is the occurrence in C. H. of three prescriptions connected with baptism that are not found in Eg. C. O. (1) In can. xix § 108 it is directed that those who are to be baptized should turn their faces to the East while they are being exorcized by the bishop. (2) In the same canon, § 119, the candidate is said to turn his face to the West for his renunciation of Satan. (3) And in § 121 he again turns to the East for the baptism and confession of faith.

The turning to the East for the exorcism seems peculiar; but the turning to the West for the renunciation, and to the East for the confession of faith, are fairly common features from the fourth century onward. They are found in St Cyril of Jerusalem (*Cat. Myst.* i), in Pseudo-Dionysius (*Eccles. Hier.* iii), in the *Testament of our Lord* (ii 8). St Ambrose (*de Mysteriis* c. ii) mentions the turning to the East after the renunciation; and St Jerome (*in Amos* vi 14) mentions both.

Whether it is more probable that such features should have been omitted by the compiler of Eg. C. O. in using C. H., or added by the compiler of C. H. in using Eg. C. O., is a point on which I should hesitate to decide apart from other evidence; but in view of the indications already considered, it seems to me that we may allow its full weight here to the *a priori* probability that familiar features of this sort would be added rather than omitted by a later compiler.

Yet another feature of the C. H. baptismal rite, absent from Eg. C. O. but common from the fourth century onward, is the act of submission to God after the renunciation of Satan : 'Ego credo et me inclino coram te et coram tota pompa (*lit.* 'retinue,' or 'service') tua, o Pater et Fili et Spiritus sancte' (§ 122). Compare A. C. vii 41 : μετὰ δὲ τὴν ἀποταγὴν συντασσόμενος λεγέτω, ὅτι καὶ συντάσσομαι τῷ Χριστῷ· καὶ πιστεύω καὶ βαπτίζομαι εἰς ἕνα...θεὸν κ.τ.λ.

N. *Terminology, etc., in C. H.*

As a conclusion to this investigation into the relation of Eg. C. O. to C. H. it may be instructive to bring together in one view a number of texts in C. H. which either illustrate the characteristic terminology of this document, as compared with Eg. C. O., or reveal allusions to ecclesiastical institutions not found in Eg. C. O. I mark with an asterisk (*) passages which Achelis regards as interpolations; where only a part of the text cited is 'interpolated' this part is placed in square brackets.

i. *Eucharistic terminology.*

'mysteria.'

§ 75   a participatione mysteriorum abstineant (c. xiv).
§ 81   quando vult participare mysteriis sacris (c. xvii).
§ 90   neve tunc ad mysteria admittatur (c. xvii).
§ 93   non participentur mysteriis (c. xvii; in Riedel xviii).
§ 103 qui fruatur mysteriis (c. xix).
§ 169 mysteria sumant (c. xxxiii).
§ 201 quotiescumque episcopus mysteriis frui vult (c. xxxvii).
§ 205 nisi antea de mysteriis sumserit (c. xxviii).
§ 206 ad sumenda sacra mysteria (c. xxviii).
§ 209 qui autem distribuit mysterium (c. xxix).
§ 215 offerat ei mysteria (c. xxx).

'corpus Christi' (or the like).

*§ 142 defert reliquias mysteriales (Riedel: 'completes the εὐχαριστία of') [corporis et sanguinis Domini] (c. xix).
*§ 143 communicat populum stans ad mensam [corporis et sanguinis Domini] (c. xix).
§ 146 deinde porrigat illis episcopus de corpore Christi (c. xix).
§ 146 Hoc est corpus Christi (c. xix).
§ 147 Hic est sanguis Christi (c. xix).
§ 149 qui fruuntur corpore Christi (c. xix).
*§ 150 antequam sumserint de corpore Christi (c. xix).
*§ 151 ante communionem corporis (c. xix).

*§ 153 antequam...communionem corporis et sanguinis finierint (c. xix).
§ 258 et baptizatus et corpore Christi pastus sum (c. xxxviii)¹.

ii. *Parts of the church.*

§ 30 nisi quod cathedrae non insideat (sc. presbyter) (c. iv).
*§ 52 ὑποδιάκονος et ἀναγνώστης, quando soli orant, consistant in posteriore parte (Riedel: 'shall stand behind') (c. vii).
*§ 100 mulier quae peperit stet extra locum sacrum (c. xviii).
*§ 143 stans ad mensam [corporis et sanguinis Domini] (c. xix).
*§ 188 extra velum adstante eo, qui illa attulit (c. xxxvi).
*§ 203 et stent in loco lectionis (c. xxxvii).
*§ 207 stet clerus vacans altari (c. xxix).
*§ 208 ideo unus custodiat locum sacrum (c. xxix).
*§ 210 nemo intra velum² aliquid loquatur (c. xxix).
*§ 212 propter potestates loci sacri (c. xxix).
*§ 212 prosternentur ante altare (c. xxix).
*§ 213 pulverem autem qui scopis converritur de loco sacro (c. xxix).

¹ The citation of these passages is not meant to imply that there is anything novel, or specifically late, about such expressions as 'corpus Christi,' 'corpus et sanguis Domini': of course there is not. Nevertheless I think it is true to say that in the first two or three centuries there was a certain limitation to their range of use: they would be employed rather by way of asserting or emphasizing the nature of the Sacrament than as regular current terms of reference to the Eucharist. For the latter purpose I imagine the term 'Eucharist' itself was by far the most common. I doubt, for instance, if the absolute use of 'corpus' or 'corpus et sanguis' (without a following genitive 'Christi' or 'Domini') which we find in §§ 151 and 153, could be paralleled from the second or third century. The difference between such a use and an expression like 'corpus enim est Christi edendum credentibus et non contemnendum' (Hauler p. 117) seems obvious. It is the *manner* in which these terms are employed in C. H. that seems to me to savour of the fifth rather than of the third century. Of course this does not apply to all the C. H. passages, and especially not to the formulae for giving communion (at §§ 146, 147); but even these latter have a significance when set beside the Eg. C. O. formulae—'Panis caelestis in Christo Jesu,' etc.
² Riedel has only: 'within the place.'

iii. *Vestments.*

§§ 201-3 Quotiescumque episcopus mysteriis frui vult, congregentur diaconi et presbyteri apud eum, induti vestimentis albis pulchrioribus toto populo, potissimum autem splendidis. Bona autem opera omnibus vestimentis praestant. Etiam ἀναγνῶσται habeant festiva indumenta[1] (c. xxxvii).

iv. *Excommunication*[2].

§ 5 separavimus illos quoniam non consentiunt ecclesiae in Deo (c. i).
§ 5 ideoque separavimus illos ab ecclesia (c. i).
*§ 55 presbyter cuius uxor peperit ne segregetur (c. viii).
§ 66 si quis autem artifex post baptismum...excommunicetur donec poenitentiam agat (c. xi).
§ 75 a participatione mysteriorum abstineat, nisi forte singulari conversione morum cum lacrimis et planctu correctus erit (c. xiv).
§ 79 quodsi post baptismum in illa quae significavimus criminosa flagitia relapsi inveniuntur, ex ecclesia expellantur, donec poenitentiam egerint cum fletu, ieiunio et operibus misericordiae[3] (c. xv).
§ 156 qui autem huic adversatur...extra canonem versatur (Riedel: 'transgresses the canon') (c. xx).
§ 218 de κλήρῳ autem qui convenire negligunt,...separentur (c. xxi).

Conclusions.

In regard to the question of the relations subsisting between the 'Egyptian Church Order' and the 'Canons of Hippolytus,' my conclusion is that C. H. is a comparatively late and very unskilful redaction of Eg. C. O., made not earlier than the middle

[1] Cf. A. C. viii 12 (Funk I p. 496 l. 6 ff.) εὐξάμενος οὖν καθ' ἑαυτὸν ὁ ἀρχιερεὺς ἅμα τοῖς ἱερεῦσιν καὶ λαμπρὰν ἐσθῆτα μετενδύς, κ.τ.λ.
[2] Eg. C. O. nowhere speaks of excommunication or deprivation.
[3] This and the two preceding clauses occur in a context which deals solely with qualifications for reception into the catechumenate, where rules about admission to or exclusion from communion are entirely out of place.

of the fourth century, and perhaps dating from the fifth or sixth century. We are now in a position to complete the table given on p. 54 above. I should express the relation of the five kindred documents with which we have been dealing as follows[1].

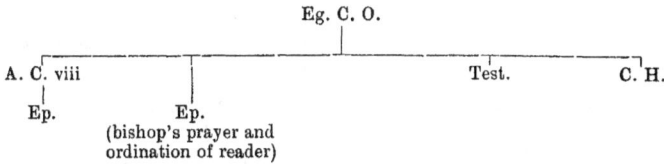

The results summarised in this table, though they have been arrived at quite independently from a close study of the documents, do not represent an entirely new discovery. They were all previously reached by Professor Eduard Schwartz, and set down by him in 1910 in his study *Ueber die pseudoapostolischen Kirchenordnungen*. But most of them were merely asserted by Schwartz as obvious conclusions from the literary evidence; and this notwithstanding the considerable measure of acceptance enjoyed by the views of Funk, on the one side, and Achelis on the other. Only as regards two points, the true explanation of which had hitherto been suggested by no one, did Schwartz enter upon any detailed statement of the evidence. The first of these—the key, in reality, to the whole problem of the interrelation of these documents—was the case of the Ep. texts of the bishop's ordination prayer and the passage on the reader. These he shewed to be mere substitutions (by the Epitomist of A. C. viii) of the Eg. C. O. texts for the corresponding passages in A. C. The second point was one which will be considered in the following chapter[2]. As

[1] I do not hereby intend to express any opinion as to the relative dates of A. C. viii, Ep., Test. and C. H., beyond what seems to me the evident fact that Ep. is later than A. C. viii.

[2] As regards the other results indicated in the table above, it is to be remembered that it is the grouping of them that is new in Schwartz's work. That A. C. viii and Test. are derived from Eg. C. O. was held by Achelis and others; that C. H. is derived from Eg. C. O., and that Ep. is an excerpt from A. C. viii was maintained by Funk. These two sets of conclusions have commonly been regarded as mutually exclusive; and Schwartz was the first, to my knowledge, to combine them and recognize Eg. C. O. as the direct source of A. C. viii, Test. and C. H. and the ultimate source of Ep.

regards the immediate and separate dependence of A. C., Test. and C. H. upon Eg. C. O., and the relation of Ep. as a whole to A. C. viii, the foregoing pages may serve to indicate some of the critical reasons which probably led Schwartz to what I must regard as the first satisfactory solution, and indeed the only true solution, of the whole group of problems presented by our cycle of 'Church Orders.' In the case of C. H. it was particularly desirable that the nature of the evidence should be fully discussed. This document has very widely, and now for many years, usurped a place in early Christian literature which, I am convinced, does not belong to it, and has been credited with an antiquity and accorded an authority to which it has no just claim; and it seems time that we should cease from attempting to illustrate remote Christian antiquity by citing from it passages due entirely to the late compiler, or such as give only distorted versions of texts found in an earlier work, which work we have in our hands.

CHAPTER III

HIPPOLYTUS AND THE CHURCH ORDERS

How did Hippolytus come to be mentioned in the 'Constitutiones per Hippolytum,' otherwise called the 'Epitome' of A. C. viii, as the author of a part of that work? Let me repeat what I have said in the introductory remarks on this document (p. 7 above), as to the name 'Constitutiones per Hippolytum.' It is given to the *whole* document only by modern writers. In the Greek MSS the book is divided into five parts, of which the first (identical with A. C. viii 1–2) is entitled Διδασκαλία τῶν ἁγίων ἀποστόλων περὶ χαρισμάτων, and only the second Διατάξεις τῶν ἁγίων ἀποστόλων περὶ χειροτονιῶν διὰ Ἱππολύτου[1]. For our purposes it may be left an open question whether this second title applies to the second part only, or to all except the first part.

From the fact that the name of Hippolytus is actually found attached to two of the documents of our cycle (C. H. and Ep.) it is a not unnatural inference, and one which has often been drawn, that the opening passage περὶ χαρισμάτων in A. C. viii 1–2 and Ep. §§ 1–2 has some sort of connexion with the Hippolytean work Περὶ χαρισμάτων. But it is troublesome that in neither A. C. nor Ep. is Hippolytus claimed as the author of this particular passage. A. C. does not contain his name at all, and Ep. makes him the author of a different part. Moreover, the point at which

[1] See Funk, *Didasc. et Const. Apost.* II p. xi. In his *apparatus* (II p. 77) Funk says: 'διὰ Ἱππολύτου habet etiam f' (f being the Florence MS). The meaning of this note is found by turning to Funk's earlier book *Die apostolischen Konstitutionen* p. 143, where he says erroneously: 'The Florentine MS above...does not contain the name of Hippolytus.'

Hippolytus is brought in in Ep. is just that at which Ep. begins to run parallel to Eg. C. O.[1].

How then came the name of Hippolytus to be attached to any part of Ep., and how to this part in particular? No one, so far as I know, maintains that either A. C. viii or Ep. was directly based on C. H., the only other of our documents which now claims Hippolytus for its author. Nor is there any ground for supposing that either of those two documents (A. C. and Ep.) owes anything directly to C. H. Achelis, after having written out in parallel columns the whole contents of C. H., Eg. C. O. (in the Sahidic version) and the relative parts of Ep. and A. C. viii, could declare (*op. cit.* p. 27) that 'there is not a word common to C. H. and A. C. viii that is not also to be found in Eg. C. O.'. He derives A. C. viii (in an earlier form, which he postulates) from Eg. C. O., and considers Ep. an excerpt from the earlier form of A. C. viii. It cannot be, therefore, that the ascription of a part of Ep. to Hippolytus comes from C. H. Achelis's solution of the problem is, in bare outline, as follows:

The title of Eg. C. O. (the document which is the immediate source of A. C. viii) is lost[2]; but when it existed *it must have contained the name of Hippolytus and have described him as the author of the work*. From Eg. C. O. the name passed over to A. C. viii, in its original form, and is now preserved in an excerpt from the original A. C. viii, namely Ep. (*op. cit.* p. 242-5, 271).

So Achelis in brief; but his case requires to be stated more fully. I venture to summarise his argument thus:

The ancient catalogue of the works of Hippolytus, found inscribed on the chair in which his statue is seated, contains these four consecutive words:

π]εριχαρισματων
α]ποστολικηπαραδο
cιc

These words form not the title of a single work, but the titles of two separate works. One was called Περὶ χαρισμάτων, the other

---

[1] Namely, at the beginning of the first of the practical prescriptions—that concerned with the ordination of a bishop. This corresponds to A. C. viii 4. Ep. omits A. C. viii 3, which forms the connecting link between A. C. viii 1-2 and 4.

[2] On this see p. 3 f. above.

Ἀποστολικὴ παράδοσις. The passage A. C. viii 1–2 (= Ep. §§ 1–2), dealing with the subject of charismatic gifts, and in Ep. entitled Διδασκαλία τῶν ἁγίων ἀποστόλων περὶ χαρισμάτων[1], is based on the lost work of Hippolytus Περὶ χαρισμάτων; and C. H. is itself his other book, Ἀποστολικὴ παράδοσις, but has suffered a good deal through later interpolation and (after can. xix) derangement of its original order. Eg. C. O. is derived immediately from C. H. (in its genuine form), and it not only enables us in many cases to detect interpolations in the present C. H., but preserves the original order throughout. The title of Eg. C. O. is lost; but, like C. H., it must have borne Hippolytus's name. A. C. viii c. 4 seqq. (but in an earlier form than the existing one) is based immediately on Eg. C. O.; and thus the Ἀποστολικὴ παράδοσις of Hippolytus (= C. H.) becomes, through Eg. C. O., the ultimate source of A. C. viii c. 4 seqq. in its earlier form. From that earlier form of A. C. viii Ep. is an excerpt. Originally in A. C. viii both cc. 1–2 and 4 seqq. were ascribed to Hippolytus as author; the ascription being derived in the case of cc. 1–2 directly from Hippolytus's work Περὶ χαρισμάτων, on which these two chapters were based, and in the case of c. 4 seqq. from Eg. C. O. The ascription to Hippolytus of cc. 4 seqq. is still preserved in Ep. It is by a mere freak of accident ('durch das Spiel des Zufalls,' p. 252) that in the present headings of A. C. viii 1–2 and Ep. §§ 1–2 *the title of the work* (Περὶ χαρισμάτων) *is preserved without the name of the author*, while in the heading of Ep. § 3 (= A. C. viii 4) *the name of the author is kept without the original title of the work* (sc. Ἀποστολικὴ παράδοσις). Thus far Achelis.

I have maintained (1) that Eg. C. O. is not derived from C. H., but *vice versa*, and (2) that Ep. is excerpted from the present A. C. viii; though the excerptor also had a first-hand acquaintance with Eg. C. O. and drew thence his text of the bishop's ordination prayer and his passage on the appointment of a reader. But these conclusions, if correct, would only render more probable Achelis's judgment that the name of Hippolytus stood in the lost title of Eg. C. O. For (1), if Eg. C. O. is the source of C. H., it

[1] The words περὶ χαρισμάτων, describing this passage, are also found in the general title to the whole of A. C. viii.

will be an almost certain inference that the compiler of C. H. derived the ascription of his Canons to Hippolytus from the title of Eg. C. O.; and (2), if the epitomist of A. C. viii had an independent acquaintance with Eg. C. O., this would supply an easy and obvious explanation of the fact that, while Hippolytus's name is attached to Ep. at the very point where Ep. begins to run parallel to Eg. C. O. (viz. at § 3 = A. C. viii 4), it is not connected with the passage περὶ χαρισμάτων (§§ 1–2 = A. C. viii 1–2), and is not found at all in A. C.

Bearing these points in mind, let us now consider whether Achelis's conjecture as to the sometime existence of an earlier text of A. C. viii would, if adopted, offer any satisfactory explanation of the appearance of Hippolytus's name in Ep. and of its entire absence from the present text of A. C. viii.

As already noticed, Achelis makes the passage of the name from Eg. C. O. to Ep. thus: A. C. viii, in its original form, took over the name (at c. 4) from the title of Eg. C. O.; and Ep. is merely an excerpt from that lost original form (*op. cit.* p. 245, 271).

Now there is a difficulty in the way of this solution which, while it appears to me to be insurmountable, seems not to have occurred to Achelis. This is the fiction of Clementine authorship which runs through the 'Apostolic Constitutions.' What are the facts in regard to this?

1. For the ascription to Clement in the title of bk. i the manuscript authority may perhaps appear insufficient, so that it will be safer not to build any argument upon it.

2. In bk. vi 9 (Funk I p. 319 l. 17) Nicetas and Aquila are referred to, in a speech by St Peter, as ἀδελφῶν Κλήμεντος τοῦ Ῥωμαίων ἐπισκόπου τε καὶ πολίτου. Such a bare allusion to Clement of course proves nothing of itself as to his supposed authorship. It is, however, worth noting in view of other passages; and it may also be observed that 'Ῥωμαίων πολίτης is Clement's proper pseudo-Clementine description (see Achelis *op. cit.* p. 243 n. 1).

3. In vi 18 (Funk *ib.* p. 347 l. 1 ff.) the apostles are made to speak of themselves as καταλιπόντες ὑμῖν τοῖς ἐπισκόποις...τήνδε τὴν καθολικὴν διδασκαλίαν...διὰ τοῦ συλλειτουργοῦ ἡμῶν Κλήμεντος...ἅμα καὶ Βαρνάβᾳ καὶ Τιμοθέῳ κ.τ.λ. Here Clement is

definitely the chief medium of transmission of the καθολικὴ διδασκαλία, though not the only one.

4. In viii 46 (Funk *ib.* p. 560 l. 25 ff.) the apostles are represented as saying ὑπὸ δὲ τοῦ σωτῆρος ἡμῶν ἡμεῖς οἱ δεκατρεῖς ἀπόστολοι (κατεστάθημεν), and then is added ὑπὸ δὲ τῶν ἀποστόλων ἐγὼ Ἰάκωβος καὶ ἐγὼ Κλήμης (*al. l.* ἐγὼ Κ. καὶ ἐγὼ Ἰ.) καὶ σὺν ἡμῖν ἕτεροι. Here it would hardly seem that James and Clement are represented as speaking together with, and on the same occasion as, the thirteen apostles. Rather the pretence is that they first give the words of the thirteen, which were to be delivered by them to the Church, and then add, in delivering those words: 'And we ourselves were appointed by the apostles.'

5. Finally in viii 47 (Funk *ib.* p. 592 l. 6 ff.—this is no. 85 of the *Apostolic Canons*) in a list of the O. T. and N. T. books we find Κλήμεντος (ἐπιστολαὶ) δύο, καὶ αἱ Διαταγαὶ ὑμῖν τοῖς ἐπισκόποις δι' ἐμοῦ Κλήμεντος ἐν ὀκτὼ βιβλίοις προσπεφωνημέναι.

Clement, then, in bk. viii even more clearly than elsewhere, appears as the editor, or redactor, of the whole work. Now I do not find that Achelis questions the generally accepted idea that Clement of Rome is, for the compiler of A. C., the medium of transmission of the 'apostolic' ordinances contained in the eight books, nor that he anywhere suggests that this feature was not found in the 'original form' of A. C. viii. He says, for example (*op. cit.* p. 278), that it is improbable that the tractate of Hippolytus on *charismata* was more extensive than the 'pseudo-Clementine' piece περὶ χαρισμάτων (i.e. than A. C. viii 1–2); and he adds as a reason for this opinion, that we may rather surmise that the Hippolytean tract was even shorter, since 'some parts of the chapters [A. C. viii 1–2] *bear too clearly the stamp of the Pseudo-Clement* to permit of our ascribing them (those parts) to Hippolytus.' But as cc. 1–2 are also in Ep. (an extract, *ex hypothesi*, from the original A. C. viii), it is clear that Achelis recognized the Clementine pretence as an original feature of A. C. viii. And even in Ep. itself we find Clement speaking; for it contains the passage cited above (at no. 4) from A. C. viii 46: only in Ep. the order ἐγὼ Κλήμης καὶ ἐγὼ Ἰάκωβος appears to have the better manuscript attestation (see Funk II p. 95 l. 6).

But if the Clementine authorship of the 'Apostolic Constitutions' is part and parcel of the original pretence, is there any room for Hippolytus as well in the capacity of author? I cannot see that there is[1], nor can I understand how this difficulty escaped the notice of Achelis. If bk. viii is διὰ Κλήμεντος it cannot also have been διὰ Ἱππολύτου. As then, from the nature of the case, Hippolytus's name could never have stood in any title of A. C., Achelis's hypothesis of an earlier text of bk. viii offers no explanation whatever of the appearance of the name in connexion with Ep.; and the epitomist *must* have got it from elsewhere. It is my conviction that he took the name from the same source from which he took his text of the bishop's ordination prayer and his passage on the reader[2], that is, direct from Eg. C. O.

I have already had occasion to say something about a short preface, or prologue, to Eg. C. O. which appears in the Latin version. As this passage has an important bearing on the present question and must now be considered again, and as I find that what I have already said about it will form a suitable introduction to what needs to be said here, I may begin by repeating some of my former remarks[3].

'A. C. viii 1-2, on *charismata*, is not found in Eg. C. O., the principal source of A. C. bk. viii; so that this passage was either wholly composed by the A. C. compiler himself, or based by him on some document other than Eg. C. O. Nor was it known until comparatively recently that viii 3 (the link passage between cc. 1-2 and 4) had any basis in Eg. C. O. It was thought by Achelis, for instance, to be merely an artificial device of the A. C. compiler for connecting cc. 1-2 with c. 4 seqq. But with the publication, in 1900, of the Verona Latin fragments came the discovery that Eg. C. O. opened with a short preface, not found in the Coptic versions, in which alone the complete document was previously known, and not occurring among the extracts from the

---

[1] Funk uses the same argument against Achelis (*Das Test. unseres Herrn* p. 210).
[2] See pp. 45 ff., and 49 ff. above.
[3] See p. 43 ff. above. I omit the notes on certain points there added.

HIPPOLYTUS AND THE CHURCH ORDERS 141

Ethiopic version published by Ludolf. But again, with the publication of the full text of the Ethiopic by Mr Horner, in 1904, this prefatory passage appeared in that version also—not, however, at the beginning, but about the middle of the document (Horner p. 162)[1].

'When this preface of Eg. C. O. is compared with A. C. viii 3 it is seen that the latter passage is based upon it[2].

Eg. C. O. (Eth.) (Horner p. 162)	*Eg. C. O. (Lat.)* (Hauler p. 101–3)	*A. C.* viii 3 (Funk ɪ, p. 470)
(a) We have written CONCERNING GRACES so far as God [our Lord] has granted to us of his own counsel. Formerly he gave it (grace) to man, while bringing near to him that which had gone astray in type; (b)	Ea quidem, quae verba[3] fuerunt, digne posuimus DE DONATIONIBUS, quanta quidem Deus a principio secundum propriam voluntatem praestitit hominibus offerens sibi eam imaginem, quae aberraverat.	Τὰ μὲν οὖν πρῶτα τοῦ λόγου ἐξεθέμεθα περὶ τῶν χαρισμάτων, ὅσαπερ ὁ θεὸς κατ' ἰδίαν βούλησιν πάρεσχεν ἀνθρώποις, καὶ ὅπως τῶν ψευδῆ ἐπιχειρούντων λέγειν ἢ ἀλλοτρίῳ πνεύματι κινουμένων ἤλεγξε τὸν τρόπον, καὶ ὅτι πονηροῖς πολλάκις ἀπεχρήσατο ὁ θεὸς πρός τε προφητείαν καὶ τερατοποιίαν[4].
(c) and now (he gave) the beloved [Son] who is in all the holy ones. Having come to the source of the proper tradition in the churches, we have attained that (men) should learn well what has been (received) until now; they handed them on and kept them as our ordinances:	Nunc autem ex caritate, quam in omnes sanctos habuit, producti ad verticem traditionis, quae catecizat, ad ecclesias perreximus, ut ii, qui bene ducti (v. l. docti) sunt, eam, quae permansit usque nunc, traditionem exponentibus nobis custodiant	νυνὶ δὲ ἐπὶ τὸ κορυφαιότατον τῆς ἐκκλησιαστικῆς διατυπώσεως ὁ λόγος ἡμᾶς ἐπείγει, ὅπως καὶ ταύτην μαθόντες παρ' ἡμῶν τὴν διάταξιν, οἱ ταχθέντες δι' ἡμῶν γνώμῃ Χριστοῦ ἐπίσκοποι, πάντα κατὰ τὰς παραδοθείσας ἡμῖν ἐντολὰς ποιῆσθε,
(d) yet, though they knew that they were quite firm concerning that which had been found for them, now unawares they slipped away. And those indeed who knew not, (to them)	etagnoscentes firmiores maneant, propter eum, qui nuper inventus est per ignorantiam lapsus vel error, et hos, qui ignorant, praestante sancto spiritu perfectam gratiam eis, qui	

[1] There attached to some interpolated matter on baptism.
[2] I give here the full texts of the Latin and Greek, which at p. 44 were abbreviated, and add the Ethiopic in the first column. Words in [ ] should be omitted on the evidence of the MSS.
[3] Hauler says of the last letter: '(a *vix* i).'
[4] It may be noticed that this passage—absent from Eg. C. O.—has direct reference to, and sums up the argument of, A. C. viii 1–2 (περὶ χαρισμάτων).

Eg. C. O. (Eth.)	*Eg. C. O. (Lat.)*	*A. C.* viii 3
the Holy Spirit is giving the perfection of grace. For them who believe rightly as they know, how seemly it is that they should hand on and keep those things which are established in the church. (e)	recte credunt, ut cognoscant, quomodo oportet tradi et custodiri¹ omnia eos, qui ecclesiae praesunt.	εἰδότες, ὅτι ὁ ἡμῶν ἀκούων Χριστοῦ ἀκούει, ὁ δὲ Χριστοῦ ἀκούων τοῦ θεοῦ αὐτοῦ καὶ πατρὸς ἀκούει, ᾧ ἡ δόξα εἰς τοὺς αἰῶνας· ἀμήν.

'Knowing, as we do, that A. C. viii is directly based on Eg. C. O., it is plain from the above texts that the compiler of A. C. had before him a copy of Eg. C. O. which, like our Latin version, opened with a prefatory passage containing an allusion to a previous treatise "de donationibus."'

Let us now examine this Eg. C. O. preface somewhat more closely.

(1) The differences between the Ethiopic and the Latin need not detain us; they are evidently differences resulting from translation. Much of the Ethiopic, as it comes to hand after successive translations, is barely intelligible, and for our present purpose may be neglected.

(2) That the passage is a real preface, or prologue, is evident from the nature of its contents, quite apart from the position it occupies in the Latin and the position of the derived passage in A. C.

(3) We may also, I think, take it as certain that in this preface the author of Eg. C. O. refers his readers back not to a mere *passage*, standing just before in the same document (as is the case in A. C.), but to a separate (though related) *treatise*, purporting to be by himself, on the subject of 'gifts' or 'graces'— 'de donationibus,' Lat.; 'concerning graces,' Eth. None of the versions we possess of Eg. C. O. give any indication that it once opened with a passage on charismatic gifts, such as we find in

---

¹ Schwartz would emend the text by reading '<circa> eos' (*op. cit.* p. 38); but this is not countenanced by the Ethiopic. But the 'eos' probably results from the Greek construction, πρὸς τὸ ἐπιγνῶναι πῶς χρὴ παραδίδοσθαί τε καὶ φυλάσσεσθαι τὰ πάντα τοὺς τῆς ἐκκλησίας προεστῶτας.

A. C. viii 1–2 and Ep. §§ 1–2. Moreover the wording of the preface seems itself to mark a very formal and decided transition, as if from one comprehensive treatise to another. Such a balancing of the whole subsequent contents of Eg. C. O. against a mere introductory passage on *charismata* does not seem natural or probable.

(4) The secondary character of the A. C. passage is manifest from the apostolic pretence which runs through it. That the use of the first person plural in Eg. C. O. is not to be interpreted as implying a similar pretence is, I think, apparent from the epilogue of this document. This epilogue stands in close relation to the prologue, or preface; and the author there, in a passage which the Latin has in duplicate, uses the first person singular: 'Custodiri haec *consilium do*' (Hauler p. 121); 'Quae custodiri *moneo*' (Hauler p. 118).

(5) Whether or no the compiler of A. C. viii actually based his cc. 1–2 on the lost work of Hippolytus Περὶ χαρισμάτων, it seems hardly doubtful that it was from the opening words of the Eg. C. O. preface that he drew the idea, the inspiration, of inserting those chapters at the beginning of his eighth book—just before he began to adapt the contents of Eg. C. O. itself. Had he not had that preface before him, with its reference to a previous tract 'de donationibus,' it is safe to say that his passage περὶ χαρισμάτων would never have been written.

My personal opinion is that the compiler of A. C. had not Hippolytus's work, or any other source, before him when he penned cc. 1–2. If he had had in his hands a complete treatise Περὶ χαρισμάτων, such as is referred to in the preface of Eg. C. O., it is antecedently probable that he would have treated it as he treated every other early document that he worked over: he would have altered much and interpolated freely, but would not have produced a treatise appreciably shorter than the original one. Achelis felt so sure that he would 'omit as little as possible,' that he was driven to conclude that the Περὶ χαρισμάτων of Hippolytus, which he supposed the A. C. compiler to be using, must have been quite brief—even shorter than A. C. viii 1–2, since 'some parts of these chapters bear too clearly the stamp of the Pseudo-Clement to admit of our ascribing them to Hippolytus' (*op. cit.* p. 278). To the last sentence I agree; but I cannot believe that the previous work 'de donationibus,' which is referred to in the preface of Eg. C. O., and which the compiler of A. C. clearly intended his own passage on *charismata* to represent, was a minute tract, shorter even than the A. C. passage itself[1].

(6) What are the probabilities that the work 'de donationibus,' to which the author of Eg. C. O. refers, was or purported to be the Hippolytean Περὶ χαρισμάτων? Here we must recall some facts already dwelt upon: (*a*) that Hippolytus's name stands in the title of C. H., a work manifestly based upon Eg. C. O.; (*b*) that Ep., just at the point where its contents begin to answer to those of Eg. C. O., introduces Hippolytus as author; (*c*) that the ascription to Hippolytus of this part of Ep. was not derived from A. C., the document 'epitomized,' nor yet from C. H.; (*d*) that there is good independent evidence that the epitomist of A. C. viii was directly acquainted with Eg. C. O.—because he certainly drew thence his text of the bishop's ordination prayer and his passage on the reader.

These indications leave little doubt in my mind that the epitomist of A. C. viii found Hippolytus's name in the title of Eg. C. O. That it stood there is also the belief of Achelis[2], Funk[3] and Bardenhewer[4].

If this be a sound conclusion, then the previous work 'de donationibus' (i.e. περὶ χαρισμάτων), referred to in the preface of Eg. C. O., can only have been the Περὶ χαρισμάτων of Hippolytus. On the other hand, the very fact that Eg. C. O. professes to be the sequel to a work with that title would seem to give us assurance that we were right in concluding (on independent grounds) that Eg. C. O. was itself ascribed in its title to Hippolytus. What work of Hippolytus would be more likely to form a sequel to his Περὶ χαρισμάτων than his Ἀποστολικὴ παράδοσις, which immediately follows it in the ancient catalogue of his works? Let us look again at the Eg. C. O. preface:

[1] I am reassured to find that the view expressed in the text coincides with that of Schwartz, though arrived at quite independently. He writes (*op. cit.* p. 38): 'Out of the title which he found in the introduction to Eg. C. O. the author of A. C. has spun a chapter of his own device (viii 1, 2) and placed it in front of his treatment of Eg. C. O., at the beginning of the (eighth) book.'

[2] *Op. cit.* p. 245.   [3] *Das Test. unseres Herrn* p. 275.
[4] *Patrology* (English trans.; Herder, 1908) p. 354.

Ea quidem, *quae verba* [possibly *verbi*] *fuerunt, digne posuimus de donationibus*.... Nunc autem...producti ad verticem *traditionis*, quae catecizat, ad ecclesias perreximus, ut ii...*traditionem* exponentibus nobis custodiant...praestante sancto spiritu perfectam gratiam eis, qui recte credunt, ut cognoscant, quomodo oportet *tradi* et custodiri omnia eos, qui ecclesiae praesunt. Eg. C. O. then is, in the mind of the author, very definitely a work on *tradition*. Let us now turn from the prologue to the epilogue of the document. The last words of the last extant Latin fragment are as follows (Hauler p. 121):

Haec itaque si cum gratia et fide recta accipiuntur, praestant aedificationem in ecclesia et vitam aeternam credentibus. Custodiri haec consilium do ab omnibus bene sapientibus. Universis enim audientibus *apostolicam tra⟨ditionem⟩*[1]....

This passage forms the latter part of a piece of text which the Latin version has in duplicate (see above p. 100). The text first occurs, out of its place, at Hauler p. 118, and is repeated in its proper position on p. 121. Nor was this duplication of the passage due merely to the Latin translator or to a subsequent Latin scribe; it must have stood already in the Greek copy used by the translator. The evidence of this is (1) that the two Latin texts are plainly two separate translations, though by the same hand, and (2) that some of the differences between these two translations arise out of variants already developed in the Greek. The above extract from the text on p. 121 appears on p. 118 as follows:

Haec itaque cum gratia et fide recta gloriosae[2] cum audiantur, aedificationem praestant ecclesiae et vitam aeternam credentibus.

---

[1] Here the fragment breaks off.

[2] Hauler prints 'glorios[a]e,' the brackets indicating that he discards the 'a' as superfluous. He took the word to be 'gloriose,' and says in a note: '*quod adverb. fort. ex marg. irrepsit.*' But the original reading was doubtless that of the MS (or perhaps 'gloriosa'). The 'recta gloriosae' is simply ὀρθοδόξου turned quite baldly into Latin. The Greek was probably μετὰ χάριτος καὶ πίστεως ὀρθοδόξου; and hence possibly the genitive ending. For a similar phenomenon cf. Loofs' *Nestoriana* p. 300 (Marius Mercator's translation of a sermon of Nestorius): 'nemo enim, aiunt, *rectam fidei gloriam* sequens vocem hanc (sc. θεοτόκος) aliquando declinavit.' So in Syriac, 'the orthodox faith' is often rendered quite baldly 'the faith right (*or* straight) of glory,' and 'orthodoxy' is 'rightness (*or* straightness) of glory.'

Quae custodiri moneo ab eis, qui bene sapiunt. Universis enim audientibus apos(tolicam traditionem)....

The Sahidic completes the last sentence for us thus: ['For if all should follow] the tradition (παράδοσις) of the apostles (ἀπόστολος), these things which they have heard, and keep them, no heretics will prevail to lead them astray, nor any man at all' (Horner p. 331).

As, then, the author of Eg. C. O. opens by describing a previous treatise of his as one περὶ χαρισμάτων, and by speaking of his present work as one concerned with *tradition*, so he ends by describing the scope of the latter by the words ἀποστολικὴ παράδοσις: and thus we have at the beginning and end of Eg. C. O. the exact titles of the two works of Hippolytus found together in the ancient catalogue. When we add to this the fact that there are good independent grounds for believing that the original title of Eg. C. O. bore the name of Hippolytus, it is not easy to resist the conclusion that Eg. C. O. itself purported to be that writer's work on *Apostolic Tradition*.

A further point may be noted in connexion with the Latin versions of this epilogue passage. One contains the words 'Custodiri haec *consilium do*,' the other 'Quae custodiri *moneo*.' Thus the first person singular has a double attestation, and we may be sure that it stood in both places in the Greek manuscript from which the Latin translations were made. This first person singular supports what has been said earlier, namely, that there is no sign of any apostolic pretence in Eg. C. O. It is the work of one person[1], who 'counsels,' but does not 'command,' those who are 'bene sapientes' to keep the 'apostolic tradition' as he has essayed to set it before them. Nowhere in Eg. C. O. is there any question of διατάξεις or ἐντολαί coming directly from the mouth of the Apostles. The author appeals to the 'apostolic tradition' in the same sense as do Irenaeus and Tertullian; and he speaks of it as 'eam quae *permansit usque nunc* traditionem.'[2] He also appeals to a tradition of the 'elders': 'nam et hi qui

---

[1] The use of the first person plural in the preface is, of course, not incompatible with singularity of authorship: the first person singular at the end asserts it.

[2] Contrast with this the A. C. adaptation: ὅπως καὶ ταύτην μαθόντες παρ' ἡμῶν τὴν διάταξιν, οἱ ταχθέντες δι' ἡμῶν γνώμῃ Χριστοῦ ἐπίσκοποι.

tradiderunt nobis seniores (Copt. πρεσβύτεροι) ita nos docuerunt' (Hauler p. 120).

Conclusions.

As regards the connexion of Hippolytus's name with our cycle of documents, my reading of the evidence is as follows:
1. Eg. C. O., the direct source of A. C. viii, C. H. and Test., was in its original title ascribed to Hippolytus. The earlier work περὶ χαρισμάτων, to which its preface refers, was the actual Περὶ χαρισμάτων of Hippolytus. Eg. C. O. itself purports to be the Ἀποστολικὴ παράδοσις of Hippolytus. That it not only purports to be so, but is so in fact, I see no reason whatever to doubt.
2. The compiler of C. H. took over from the title of Eg. C. O. the attribution to Hippolytus, though he altered the title in other ways. He omitted the Eg. C. O. preface, containing the allusion to the Περὶ χαρισμάτων (of which work he knew nothing), and substituted for it an entirely different one.
3. The presence of Hippolytus's name in the title to the second part of Ep. cannot be explained by regarding Ep. as a *first draft* of A. C. viii; for the evidence against that hypothesis is conclusive. No more can it be explained by the supposition that Ep. is an excerpt from *an earlier form* of A. C. viii which contained the attribution to Hippolytus; because the fiction of Clementine authorship is an original and essential feature of A. C., and is even found in Ep. itself; so that Hippolytus's name could never have been attached to A. C. viii as that of author. Nor did the name come into Ep. directly from C. H.; for there is no evidence of any literary dependence on C. H. on the part of A. C. or Ep. It must have been taken by the 'Epitomist' of A. C. viii straight from Eg. C. O., with which he had an independent acquaintance, and from which he drew his text of the bishop's ordination prayer and his ordinance on the appointment of the reader.
4. The passage on *charismata* with which A. C. viii and Ep. open, and to which there is nothing corresponding in Eg. C. O., C. H. or Test., is no part of the original stock of this group of

documents: it is not a survival from any 'lost Church Order' which may be supposed to have stood behind all of our documents. Nor do I see any reason to believe that it was based on the Περὶ χαρισμάτων of Hippolytus; the motive for its insertion (at a point just before the A. C. compiler began to make use of Eg. C. O.) is to be found in the preface of Eg. C. O. The compiler adapted that preface; and, finding in it an allusion to a previous work Περὶ χαρισμάτων, he inserted at the beginning of his eighth book a passage of his own composition on this subject to satisfy the allusion. No one, I am inclined to think, who is familiar with the compiler's other literary efforts will pronounce him unequal to the creation *ex nihilo* of A. C. viii cc. 1-2.

The whole of this chapter, with the exception of two notes, was already written before I had read Professor E. Schwartz *über die pseudoapostolischen Kirchenordnungen*. On reading his tract I found that in each of the four conclusions drawn above I had been forestalled by him, as also in those others (as to the relations of Eg. C. O., A. C. viii, Ep., Test. and C. H.) set forth on p. 54 and p. 133 of this volume. In this I find no cause for surprise. The results thus reached independently appear to me to follow inevitably from the evidence of the documents. The most important of these results—that Eg. C. O. is substantially the Ἀποστολικὴ παράδοσις—would, I am inclined to think, almost certainly have been arrived at by Achelis but for his unfortunate prepossession in favour of C. H. But even as it was, it was he who in reality discovered the key to the problem, though he did not find the lock into which it fitted. The arguments he adduced to prove that C. H. was the Ἀποστολικὴ παράδοσις were bound to suggest that Eg. C. O. was in fact that work, when once the dependence of C. H. on Eg. C. O. was established. It was from him that I derived this suggestion, and the evidence which has come to light since he wrote his *Canones Hippolyti* has produced in me the conviction that it is correct.

This conclusion Schwartz, writing in 1915, regards as now generally accepted in Germany. In a review of Th. Schermann's *Weiherituale der römischen Kirche* he says: 'In my tract *über die pseudoapostolischen Kirchenordnungen* I put forward the hypothesis that KO [= Eg. C. O.] is substantially, and apart from isolated interpolations, nothing else than the 'Ἀποστολικὴ παράδοσις of Hippolytus. Moreover the hypothesis has been accepted by the critics: at least no opposition of importance has come to my notice.'[1]

It is to be hoped that the so-called 'Egyptian Church Order,' and not the so-called 'Canons of Hippolytus,' will yet find its place in an edition of the *Quae supersunt omnia* of Hippolytus, under the title 'Ἀποστολικὴ παράδοσις. With a view to this all the versions will need to be critically dealt with, with due regard not only to the evidence of the manuscripts but also to that supplied by the related documents, A. C., Ep., Test. and C. H. An adequate edition of this deeply interesting and important document will be produced only at the cost of very great labour and research, and will call for exceptional qualifications on the part of its editor or editors. But the result would be a contribution of the very first importance for the study of early Christian institutions. 'Eg. C. O.,' in the fulness and precision of its information as to the worship and regulated working of a Christian Church, is unique in the first three centuries; it supplements in this respect the *Didascalia*, unique on its side as a presentment of the religious life and ideas of an early Christian Community.

[1] *Oriens Christianus*: new series IV 2, p. 350 (1915).

ADDITIONAL NOTES

I. *Some Ep. readings in the Bishop's Ordination Prayer*

At p. 21 of this volume the reader was referred to 'Additional Notes' for some further observations on certain passages in the Ep. text of the bishop's ordination prayer. Those passages were such as presented differences from the Eg. C. O. text of a kind that could not readily be explained as merely clerical, mere 'variae lectiones,' but seemed to imply some degree of 'editing' on the part of the Epitomist of A. C., who substituted the Eg. C. O. prayer for that in A. C. I proceed now to consider the bearing of these passages upon the conclusions which have been drawn in the body of this essay.

(i)

One of Funk's palmary arguments for the dependence of Ep. upon A. C. viii is drawn from the passage in the bishop's ordination prayer which comes under nos. (33)–(40) of the table given at p. 12 ff. The parallel texts of Eg. C. O., Ep. and A. C. may for convenience be repeated here.

Eg. C. O.	*Ep.*	*A. C.*
(a) nunc effunde eam virtutem, quae a te est, principalis spiritus,	καὶ νῦν ἐπίχεε τὴν παρὰ σοῦ δύναμιν τοῦ ἡγεμονικοῦ πνεύματος,	αὐτὸς καὶ νῦν μεσιτείᾳ τοῦ Χριστοῦ σου δι' ἡμῶν ἐπίχεε τὴν δύναμιν τοῦ ἡγεμονικοῦ πνεύματος,
(b) quem *dedisti* dilecto filio tuo Iesu Christo, quod donavit sanctis apostolis.	ὅπερ **διὰ** τοῦ ἠγαπημένου σου παιδὸς Ἰησοῦ Χριστοῦ δεδώρησαι τοῖς ἁγίοις σου ἀποστόλοις.	ὅπερ **διακονεῖται** τῷ ἠγαπημένῳ σου παιδὶ Ἰησοῦ Χριστῷ, ὅπερ ἐδωρήσατο γνώμῃ σου τοῖς ἁγίοις ἀποστόλοις σου τοῦ αἰωνίου θεοῦ.

The crucial clause is (b). Funk lays all the weight of his argument on the verb διακονεῖται—the 'ministering' of the Holy Spirit to the Son. This, he thinks, must have been the original reading in the passage. He maintains, indeed, that the expression is not to be understood as 'pneumatomachian,' but is to be regarded as a survival of earlier theological language. Nevertheless, he says, a later reader of A. C. 'might take exception to the archaic expression.'[1] So again in *Didasc. et Const. Apost.* (II p. xiv), after quoting the texts of A. C. and Ep., he says : 'Rursus clarum est, quae verba priora

[1] *Das Test. u. Herrn*, p. 184.

ADDITIONAL NOTES 151

sint. Ne opponas, formulam secundam [that of Ep.] iam in Canonibus Hippolyti et *Constitutionibus aegyptiacis* [=Eg. C. O.] *legi*. Formula revera demonstrat, has quoque scripturas aetatis recentioris esse.' The italics are mine.

Now Funk has here committed a very strange oversight. Owing, it would appear, to his preoccupation with the verb διακονεῖται in A. C., he has forgotten to look with an attentive eye at some other features of these parallel texts. Had he done so he could hardly have stated, as he does, that the Ep. formula is found in Eg. C. O. Not only is this not the case, but in fact Eg. C. O. and A. C. have a fundamental element of agreement against Ep., and one which excludes the possibility of Ep. having stood (as Funk supposed) between A. C. and Eg. C. O.

A. C. says : ὅπερ διακονεῖται τῷ ἠγαπημένῳ σου παιδὶ ᾽Ιησοῦ Χριστῷ, ὅπερ ἐδωρήσατο, κ.τ.λ.

Eg. C. O. says : 'quem *dedisti* dilecto filio tuo Iesu Christo, quod (*sic*) donavit,' etc.

Thus, when we neglect the amplifications γνώμη σου and τοῦ αἰωνίου θεοῦ in A. C., the only difference between A. C. and Eg. C. O. is involved in the verbs διακονεῖται and 'dedisti.'

Ep., on the contrary, radically alters the whole construction, saying : ὅπερ διὰ τοῦ ἠγαπημένου σου παιδὸς ᾽Ιησοῦ Χριστοῦ δεδώρησαι, κ.τ.λ.

It is plain that neither the A. C. nor the Eg. C. O. text has passed from one of these documents to the other *through* Ep. ; and the only explanation of the phenomena, which can be reconciled with the facts already set forth in this volume, is that the compiler of A. C. and the Epitomist have both, in different ways, modified the text of Eg. C. O. The former has, besides expanding somewhat, introduced an idea which is characteristic of him, in substituting διακονεῖται for ἔδωκας ('dedisti')[1]; the latter has removed the statement that the Father gave the Spirit to the Son. This, doubtless, was done with a theological purpose : lest such an expression should be regarded as countenancing the heresy that the Divinity of our Lord dated only from some occasion on which He received the divine Spirit (as on that of His baptism)[2].

We must conclude that though Funk was right in regarding Ep. as merely an excerpt from A. C. viii, yet this particular argument of his for

[1] On the conception of the Holy Spirit as 'minister' of the Son in A. C. see Schwartz *op. cit.* p. 16. The actual expression τὸν διάκονον τοῦ μονογενοῦς occurs in a passage which there are at least strong grounds for ascribing to the compiler of A. C. (cf. C. H. Turner in *J. T. S.* XVI 526—July, 1915).

[2] It will be seen by looking at the table of the bishop's prayer that C. H. has given this passage the same turn that it has in Ep.: 'quem *tribuisti* sanctis apostolis *per* dominum nostrum,' etc. As I know of no ground for supposing that there is any direct literary connexion between C. H. and Ep., this coincidence must probably be attributed to a common motive cause—the desire to be strictly orthodox.

1 1 *

so concluding is fallacious. That it should prove to be so was inevitable; since it is based on a passage—in the bishop's prayer—which the Epitomist did not derive from A. C., but took directly from Eg. C. O. A further inference from the points of agreement between A. C. and Eg. C. O. against Ep. in this passage is this: that the present Ep. text of the bishop's ordination prayer could not have stood, as Achelis supposed, in an earlier edition of A. C. viii than the existing one. The opposite view would require us to believe that the A. C. compiler first corrected the Eg. C. O. text to the form it now has in Ep., and afterwards undid his work, reverting to a closer agreement with Eg. C. O. Such a proceeding is, in the present case, extremely improbable.

(ii)

At nos. (47), (49), (51), (52), (54)[1] we have the following texts in Eg. C. O., Ep. and A. C.:

Eg. C. O.	Ep.	A. C.
...in gloriam et laudem indeficientem nomini tuo. Da, cordis cognitor pater, super hunc servum tuum, quem elegisti ad episcopatum, pascere gregem sanctam tuam...	...εἰς δόξαν καὶ αἶνον ἀδιάλειπτον τοῦ ὀνόματός σου. καρδιογνῶστα πάντων, δὸς ἐπὶ τὸν δοῦλόν σου τοῦτον, ὃν ἐξελέξω εἰς ἐπισκοπήν σου τὴν ἁγίαν,...	δὸς ἐν τῷ ὀνόματί σου, καρδιογνῶστα θεέ, ἐπὶ τὸν δοῦλόν σου τόνδε, ὃν ἐξελέξω εἰς ἐπίσκοπον, ποιμαίνειν τὴν ἁγίαν σου ποίμνην...

Here there are four points to notice: (a) the readings 'cordis cognitor pater,' καρδιογνῶστα πάντων, and καρδιογνῶστα θεέ; (b) the positions of the imperative 'da,' δός; (c) the omission in A. C. of εἰς δόξαν καὶ αἶνον ἀδιάλειπτον; and (d) the omission in Ep. of the equivalent of 'pascere gregem.'

(a) It has been shewn (at p. 25 above) that 'pater' is the true reading of Eg. C. O. (since it is found in the Ethiopic as well as in the Latin, and occurs also in Test.)[2], and that πάντων of Ep. is probably an accommodation to Acts i 24. It remains only to observe that θεέ of A. C. is more likely to have resulted from πάτερ, or ὁ πατήρ, than from πάντων.

(b) A. C. agrees with Eg. C. O. in placing the imperative δός before the vocative, whereas Ep. has it after.

(c) Ep. is here in agreement with Eg. C. O. against A. C.

(d) If the omission of 'pascere gregem' in Ep. is not the result of a mere accident, then A. C. is here again—as in (b)—in agreement with Eg. C. O. against Ep. If the omission is only accidental, the most obvious restoration would be εἰς ἐπισκοπὴν <ποιμαίνειν τὴν ποίμνην> σου τὴν ἁγίαν. But this

---

[1] No. (48) is occupied by a piece of text peculiar to Test., (50) by an incorrect reading of the Ethiopic of Eg. C. O. (see p. 25 above), and (53) by a piece peculiar to C. H.

[2] Schwartz has failed to note the reading in Ludolf's version of Eth., and thinks that πάντων of Ep. preserves the original reading of Eg. C. O. (op. cit. p. 30 n. 5).

ADDITIONAL NOTES   153

does not give us the order found in A. C.; and the omission may well be original and intentional in Ep.

Here again it is seen, from the evidence of (b) at least, that Ep. cannot have stood between A. C. and Eg. C. O., as Funk thought. And Achelis's view is also excluded; for if we suppose that Ep. gives us a part of the text of an earlier edition of A. C. viii, we must necessarily conclude that, in making his second edition (=A. C.), the compiler went back for some trifling corrections to his original source (=Eg. C. O.)—though, in the case of the bishop's prayer, his 'second edition' is characterized generally by a much freer departure from that source.

(iii)

A comparison of the doxologies of the bishop's ordination prayer in Eg. C. O., Ep. and A. C. is instructive.

Eg. C. O.	*Ep.*	*A. C.*
per puerum tuum Iesum Christum, per quem tibi gloria et potentia et honor, patri et filio cum spiritu sancto[1]...	διὰ τοῦ παιδός σου Ἰησοῦ Χριστοῦ τοῦ κυρίου ἡμῶν, μεθ' οὗ σοι δόξα, κράτος, τιμὴ σὺν ἁγίῳ πνεύματι...	διὰ τοῦ ἁγίου παιδός σου Ἰησοῦ Χριστοῦ τοῦ θεοῦ καὶ σωτῆρος ἡμῶν, δι' οὗ σοι δόξα, τιμὴ καὶ σέβας ἐν ἁγίῳ πνεύματι...

If the forms of doxology in A. C. are examined with reference to the manuscript readings recorded by Funk, it will be seen that the form at the end of the bishop's prayer is characteristic as regards the prepositions and the ascriptions.

As to the prepositions, the evidence of the manuscripts points to the conclusion that δι' οὗ...ἐν ἁγίῳ πν. were used almost always by the compiler: though Funk often follows the reading μετὰ...καὶ[2].

If we next consult the doxologies of Ep., at the end of the various ordination prayers taken from A. C. viii (exclusive, therefore, of the bishop's prayer), we find that the Epitomist too had a fixed practice in regard to prepositions. He everywhere alters the δι' οὗ...ἐν of A. C. into μεθ' οὗ...σύν. As this is a consciously orthodox correction of a formula which by the end of the fourth century had fallen into disrepute, it is quite fatal to Achelis's hypothesis, that Ep. as a whole is earlier than A. C. viii—unless, indeed, we are prepared to maintain that all the doxologies in Ep. have been subjected to revision by a still later hand.

But the presence of μετὰ...σύν in the Ep. doxology of the bishop's prayer, as well as in the doxologies of the prayers taken over from A. C., does not necessarily imply that διὰ...ἐν stood in the original doxology of Eg. C. O. It is not improbable that the Epitomist would substitute his own fixed formula for other expressions as well[3].

[1] The Ethiopic adds 'in the holy Church.'
[2] Cf. C. H. Turner in *J. T. S.* xv 54 (Oct. 1913).
[3] Schwartz's restoration (*op. cit.* p. 30 n. 9) of the Greek of the Eg. C. O. doxology (δι' οὗ σοι δόξα, κράτος, τιμὴ ἐν ἁγίῳ πνεύματι) seems therefore to lack authority.

On the ascriptions δόξα, τιμὴ καὶ σέβας in the A. C. doxology something has already been said at p. 32 above. It was there pointed out that the same formula occurs seven times elsewhere in A. C. viii, and that σέβας, in particular, is found in a large majority of the doxologies of A. C. Here it may be added that this word occurs in the doxologies of all the remaining ordination prayers, excepting only that for a deaconess, where its place is taken by προσκύνησις.

Now in this matter Ep. follows A. C. closely. It has σέβας in these prayers where A. C. has it; and it has προσκύνησις in the prayer for a deaconess. In the bishop's prayer alone it has not the σέβας of A. C., but the κράτος of Eg. C. O. I cannot see that the views of Funk and Achelis as to the relation of Eg. C. O., A. C. and Ep. offer any satisfactory explanation of this phenomenon. On the other hand, it is readily explained if the A. C. and Ep. doxologies were both based on that of Eg. C. O. The compiler of A. C. had a fixed practice as to the prepositions, and a more or less fixed practice as to the ascriptions. Hence his departure from Eg. C. O. in both these points. The Epitomist is particular only about the prepositions; and so he keeps the ascriptions of Eg. C. O.

Into the question of the Eg. C. O. doxologies there is no need to enter here. Whether the 'per quem tibi...patri et filio cum spiritu sancto' of the Latin is old and original, or the alteration of some earlier form, I am unable to say. But there are two features, of frequent occurrence in the Eg. C. O. doxologies, which are certainly early and genuine. These are 'per *puerum* tuum' (= διὰ τοῦ παιδός σου), and 'in sancta ecclesia.'

As to παῖς, the use of 'this old Messianic title "the Servant" of Jehovah' in the earliest forms of Christian prayer is well illustrated by the Dean of Wells, Dr Armitage Robinson, in an article in *The Expositor* of Jan. 1899 (pp. 66–69). It is found in Acts iii 13, 26, iv 27, 30, in Clement of Rome i 59, in the *Didache* cc. 9, 10, in the doxology of Polycarp's prayer, and in the *Epistle to Diognetus* c. 8.

As regards 'in sancta ecclesia,' this does not appear in the Latin text of the bishop's prayer; but the Ethiopic has it there, and no doubt rightly. It occurs several times elsewhere in the Latin in doxologies (Hauler pp. 107, 108, 109, 111), and appears also in the formula for administering the cups at the communion of the newly baptized (p. 113). I know of only one doxology, outside of Eg. C. O., in which the same expression occurs[1]; and it is not a little significant that this is found at the end of a work of Hippolytus (*contra haer. Noëti*). The text is as follows:

οὗτος ὁ θεὸς, ὁ ἄνθρωπος δι' ἡμᾶς γεγονώς, ᾧ πάντα ὑπέταξεν ὁ πατήρ. αὐτῷ ἡ δόξα καὶ τὸ κράτος ἅμα πατρὶ καὶ ἁγίῳ πνεύματι ἐν τῇ ἁγίᾳ ἐκκλησίᾳ καὶ νῦν καὶ ἀεὶ καὶ εἰς τοὺς αἰῶνας τῶν αἰώνων· ἀμήν (*P. Gr.* x 829 B).

[1] Though we must compare Eph. iii 21, αὐτῷ ἡ δόξα ἐν τῇ ἐκκλησίᾳ καὶ ἐν Χριστῷ Ἰησοῦ εἰς πάντας τὰς γενεὰς τοῦ αἰῶνος τῶν αἰώνων· ἀμήν. [See also the Index below, s.v. 'Church.']

II. *Two suggested interpolations in Eg. C. O.*

Schwartz (*op. cit.* p. 37 n. 2) regards as early interpolations into Eg. C. O. (and both by the same hand) no. (33) and nos. (45)–(46) of the text printed out under G at pp. 99, 101 above. It is in any case clear that these two passages express the same ideas in connexion with the same subject (a particular method of making the sign of the cross), and so evidently come from the same hand.

My reasons for thinking that Schwartz is mistaken in regarding these pieces as interpolations are as follows. He appears not to have observed that the piece of text which immediately follows no. (33), namely, no. (34), and which he keeps as part of the original document, is closely bound up in thought and expression with no. (45)—a part of his second 'interpolated' piece—and is also organically connected with no. (33). That this close connexion really exists will, I think, be seen, when the texts are set side by side. I place in square brackets the pieces which Schwartz takes to be interpolations:

(33) [Per consignationem cum udo flatu et per manum $\overline{\text{spm}}$[1] amplectens corpus tuum usque ad pedes sanctificatum est.]

(34) *Donum* enim *spiritus* et infusio *lavacri*, sicuti *ex fonte corde credente*, cum *offertur*, sanctificat eum qui credidit (Hauler p. 119-120).

(45) [Hoc enim signum passionis adversum diabolum manifestum et comprobatum est, si *ex fide* itaque facis, non ut hominibus appareas, sed per scientiam tamquam scutum *offerens*; nam adversarius, cum vidit *virtutem*[2], quae *ex corde* est, ut homo similitudinem verbi[3] in manifesto deformatam ostendat, infugiatur...] (Hauler p. 121).

Here no. (34) explains no. (33), by saying in effect just what is said in no. (45): viz. that the moisture produced by breathing on the hand, preparatory to signing oneself with the cross, represents in some way the 'gift,' or the 'power,' 'of the Spirit' brought forth ('offerens,' 'cum offertur') from 'the heart': since this moisture stands for the original 'laver' of baptism.

It is also to be observed that the words 'corpus tuum *usque ad pedes* sanctificatum est,' in no. (33), evidently form part of an allusion to John xiii 10 which has come in the previous sentence: 'qui enim loti sunt, non habent necessitatem lavandi iterum, quia mundi sunt.' Otherwise the mention of the 'feet' is unexplained.

[1] Schwartz would expand 'sputum' on the authority of the Coptic, 'spittle,' which is read also in the Ethiopic (but see above, p. 99 n. 1).

[2] In the duplicate text of this passage, which the Latin has at p. 118 (Hauler), we find 'virtutem spiritus'; cf. the 'donum spiritus' of no. (34).

[3] At p. 118 (Hauler) we have, no doubt correctly, 'lavacri' for 'verbi': so no. (34) opposite.

III. C. H. and Pseudo-Athanasius 'de Virginitate'

There are some parallels between C. H. and the pseudo-Athanasian treatise *de Virginitate* which deserve notice.

de Virg. c. 12.

(a) Ἤτω δὲ τὸ ἔργον σου διὰ παντὸς μελέτη τῶν θείων γραφῶν· ψαλτήριον ἔχε, καὶ τοὺς ψαλμοὺς μάνθανε.

(b) ἀνατέλλων ὁ ἥλιος βλεπέτω τὸ βιβλίον ἐν ταῖς χερσί σου,

(c) καὶ μετὰ τρίτην ὥραν συνάξεις ἐπιτέλει,

(d) ὅτι ταύτῃ τῇ ὥρᾳ ἐπάγη τὸ ξύλον τοῦ σταυροῦ.

(e) See (g) below.

(f) ἕκτῃ ὥρᾳ ὁμοίως ἐπιτέλει σου τὰς προσευχὰς μετὰ ψαλμῶν καὶ κλαυθμοῦ καὶ δεήσεως·

(g) ὅτι αὐτῇ τῇ ὥρᾳ ἐκρεμάσθη ὁ υἱὸς τοῦ θεοῦ ἐπὶ τοῦ σταυροῦ.

(h)

(i) ἐνάτῃ ὥρᾳ πάλιν ἐν ὕμνοις καὶ δοξολογίαις, μετὰ δακρύων ἐξομολογουμένη τὰ παραπτώματά σου, τὸν θεὸν ἱκέτευε, ὅτι ἐν αὐτῇ τῇ ὥρᾳ ὁ κύριος κρεμάμενος ἐπὶ σταυροῦ ἀπέδωκε τὸ πνεῦμα.

C. H.

(Can. xxvii a) Quocumque die in ecclesia non orant sumas scripturam ut legas in ea.

Sol conspiciat matutino tempore scripturam super genua tua[1].

(Can. xxv b) Orent autem tertia hora,

quia illo tempore Salvator voluntarie crucifixus est ad salvandos nos, ut nobis libertatem tribueret.

Deinde etiam hora sexta orate,

See (e) above.

quia illa hora universa creatura perturbata est propter facinus scelestum a Iudaeis perpetratum.

Hora nona iterum orent, quia illa hora Christus oravit et *tradidit spiritum* in manus patris sui.

The directions in C. H. as to prayer at the third, sixth and ninth hours have already been considered in relation to the parallel texts of Eg. C. O. (see p. 94 ff.); and the conclusion was drawn that the compiler of C. H. must have had Eg. C. O. before him.

In view of the parallels just set out, we must now ask ourselves whether the compiler of C. H. may not have been influenced by the *de Virginitate* as well. As regards the reasons for praying at the third and sixth hours, C. H. agrees in the main with Eg. C. O. against *de Virg.*; for it connects the first of these two prayers with our Lord's crucifixion, and the second with the

---

[1] In C. H. this piece from can. xxvii comes in connexion with the hours for prayer; but it precedes the directions as to prayer at midnight. The first sentence —(a)—however is parallel to a passage in Eg. C. O. which, like *de Virg.* here, introduces the prayer of the *third* hour (Horner p. 182 l. 27, Eth.; p. 328 l. 21, Copt.).

ADDITIONAL NOTES 157

disturbance of nature; while *de Virg.* connects the first with the setting up of the cross, and the second with the actual crucifying of Christ. But at (*i*), on prayer at the ninth hour, C. H. has a noteworthy coincidence with *de Virg.* against Eg. C. O. In connexion with the ninth hour Eg. C. O. makes no direct mention of our Lord's death, but only of the piercing of His side and the return of the light. But C. H. and *de Virg.* both say that at the ninth hour He 'gave up His spirit.' This coincidence can of course be explained by reference to the synoptic Gospels. But there is one item common to C. H. and *de Virg.* which cannot be so explained. The saying at (*b*), 'let the sun in the morning (ἀνατέλλων, *de Virg.*) see the Scripture on thy knees' (ἐν ταῖς χερσί σου, *de Virg.*), is surely the result of literary borrowing on one side or the other.

On which side the borrowing took place there is not much to shew. But it may be remarked that the graphic touch in (*b*), though it comes naturally enough in *de Virg.* (which is of a lively and personal character), seems less at home in a dull and unoriginal compilation like C. H. It is also to be observed that in *de Virg.* the saying precedes the mention of the third-hour prayer, while in C. H. it is placed inappropriately before the direction as to midnight prayer. My impressions of both documents would lead me to think that it was the author of *de Virg.*, and not the compiler of C. H., who was the originator of the saying.

Besides C. H., Test. also appears to have a point of contact with the *de Virginibus* in the matter of the hours for prayer.

de Virg. c. 20.

Μεσονύκτιον ἐγερθήσῃ καὶ ὑμνήσεις κύριον τὸν θεόν σου· ἐν αὐτῇ γὰρ τῇ ὥρᾳ ἀνέστη ὁ κύριος ἡμῶν ἐκ νεκρῶν, καὶ ὕμνησε τὸν πατέρα· διὰ τοῦτο αὐτῇ τῇ ὥρᾳ προσετάγη ἡμῖν ὑμνεῖν τὸν θεόν......

πρὸς ὄρθρον δὲ τὸν ψαλμὸν τοῦτον λέγετε· "'Ο θεὸς ὁ θεός μου, πρὸς σὲ ὀρθρίζω...." διάφαυμα δέ· "Εὐλογεῖτε, πάντα τὰ ἔργα κυρίου, τὸν κύριον. δόξα ἐν ὑψίστοις θεῷ," κτλ.

Test. ii 24.

But at midnight let them arise praising and lauding *because of the resurrection.*

But at dawn praising with psalms, because *after He rose He glorified the Father while they were singing psalms.*

Though Test. is clearly based on Eg. C. O. in the chapter on the hours for prayer (ii 24), yet it here departs from its main source in three respects: (1) Eg. C. O. connects the resurrection with the hour of cock-crow, not with that of midnight; (2) it does not (as do *de Virg.* and Test.) speak of Christ praising the Father after His resurrection; (3) it speaks of the early morning prayer as that of 'cock-crow,' not that of 'dawn.' It appears to me not improbable that the compilers of both C. H. and Test. have drawn upon the *de Virginitate* (or some closely related document) as a subsidiary source in their treatment of the hours for prayer.

IV. *The custom of giving Apophoreta*

It has been observed (under J, p. 117 above) that the Roman origin of Eg. C. O. would, if it could be regarded as probable on other grounds, offer a simple and satisfactory explanation of a feature in this document which seems otherwise inexplicable, namely, an allusion to certain κέραμοι as an essential item of burial.

Another feature in Eg. C. O. which is characteristically, if not exclusively, Roman, deserves to be noticed here. Attention was first drawn to it by Schwartz, who describes it as 'a specially Roman trait' (*op. cit.* p. 40). In Hauler's Latin we read (p. 114): 'Si communiter vero omnibus oblatum fuerit quod dicitur Graece apoforetum, accipite ab eo ; si autem ut omnes gustent, sufficienter gustate, ut et superet et quibuscumque voluerit, qui vocavit vos, mittat tamquam de reliquiis sanctorum.' The context, as well as the name, indicates that the *apophoretum* was something to be carried away, while the other viands were to be partaken of at table. Now, with one doubtful exception, all other known allusions to *apophoreta* occur in Roman, or at least western, writers and refer to Roman usage. Most of these references may be found in the *Thesaurus Linguae Latinae*. The custom, it will be seen, had a special connexion with the Roman festival of the Saturnalia. Thus, Suetonius says of Vespasian: 'dabat sicut Saturnalibus viris apophoreta ita per Kal. Mart. feminis' (*Vesp.* 19). *Apophoreta* is the title of the 14th book of Martial's Epigrams ; and in his introductory lines he mentions the Saturnalia as the occasion on which the verses were written : 'sed quid agam potius madidis, Saturne, diebus?' These particular epigrams, written in couplets, were evidently intended to accompany the gifts bestowed as *apophoreta*, and each has the name of the gift prefixed.

That the word and the custom it denoted were thoroughly familiar to early western ecclesiastical writers, the following passages will suffice to shew :

1. Ambrosiaster.

   (*a*) *In Rom.* i 1 : 'Evangelium autem Dei est, per quod mysterium Dei manifestatur, quod latuit a saeculis in Deo : quod est Christus. Ad quod omnes invitati apophoreta duplicia consequuntur ; remissionem enim peccatorum accipiunt, et filii Dei fiunt' (*P. L.* xvii 50-51 A).

   (*b*) *In Eph.* iii 9 : 'Sicut enim in magna vota maxima dantur apophoreta' (*P. L.* xvii 404 B).

   (*c*) *In Eph.* iii 11, 12 : 'ut quasi dedicatio regni Christi hanc gratiam credentibus pro apophoretis largiretur' (*P. L.* xvii 405 B).

2. *Quaestiones vet. et nov. test.* ; qu. 123 : 'cum id elaborare soleant divites, ut in die festo natalis sui exquisita invitatis dent apophoreta' (*P. L.* xxxv 2371 *vers. fin.* For the reading see Souter, *A Study of Ambrosiaster* p. 83 : 'Texts and Studies' vii no. 4).

ADDITIONAL NOTES 159

3. Ambrose, *Exhort. Virg.* 1 (*init.*): 'Qui ad convivium magnum invitantur, apophoreta secum referre consueverunt. Ego ad Bononiense invitatus convivium, ubi sancti martyris celebrata translatio est, apophoreta vobis plena sanctitatis et gratiae reservavi. Apophoreta autem solent habere triumphos principum: et haec apophoreta triumphalia sunt; Christi enim nostri principis triumphi sunt martyrum palmae' (*P. L.* XVI 351 A).

4. Augustine, *Ep.* 150 (Probae et Iulianae): 'Velationis apophoretum gratissime accepimus' (*P. L.* XXXIII 645 *fin.*). Here the word appears to mean simply 'gift,' but yet a gift connected with an occasion which is compared to a banquet (cf. Ambrose above).

5. Hermas, *Pastor*, Sim. v 2, 5. Here the gifts are *sent* from the master's table to a faithful servant; also they are not called ἀποφόρητα but ἐδέσματα. But the passage is worth quoting in illustration of Eg. C. O.: the gifts are really *apophoreta*, though not brought away by the recipient himself; in v 5 they are referred to as τὰ ἐδέσματα ἃ ἔπεμψεν αὐτῷ ἐκ τοῦ δείπνου.

From the Christian East we have nothing parallel. In his Lexicon of later Greek (from B.C. 146 to A.D. 1100) Sophocles has not produced a single Greek patristic reference to *apophoreta*.

Apart from the author of Eg. C. O., the one Greek writer who mentions *apophoreta* is Athenaeus. But even he wrote in Rome (after A.D. 230). Moreover, in the passage in which he alludes to the custom he is describing a banquet given by Cleopatra to Antony and his suite; and he mentions that in that banquet she imitated the Roman extravagance of using vessels of silver and gold. He goes on to say that she gave this plate to the guests for 'the *apophoreta*'; and he adds that in this she went to the limit of extravagance. It is true that he does not say, or appear to imply, that the actual giving of *apophoreta* was part of her imitation of the Romans, though (if the occasion described was really historical) we might be inclined to suspect that she had copied them in this also. The allusion is in any case an isolated one; and it does not seem to afford sufficient grounds for doubting that the custom was characteristically Roman. The absence of any Greek patristic evidence is very remarkable in view of the ample allusions found in Latin Fathers. The following is the immediate context in which Athenaeus mentions *apophoreta*:

Μέχρι γὰρ τῶν Μακεδονικῶν χρόνων κεραμεοῖς σκεύεσιν οἱ δειπνοῦντες διηκονοῦντο, ὥς φησιν ὁ ἐμὸς Ἰόβας· μεταβαλόντων δ' ἐπὶ τὸ πολυτελέστερον Ῥωμαίων τὴν δίαιταν, κατὰ μίμησιν ἐκδιαιτηθεῖσα Κλεοπάτρα, ἡ τῶν Αἰγύπτου καταλύσασα βασιλείαν, τοὔνομα οὐ δυναμένη ἀλλάξαι, ἀργυροῦν καὶ χρυσοῦν ἀπεκάλει κέραμον αὐτό, κεράμα τ' ἀπεδίδοτο τὰ ἀποφόρητα τοῖς δειπνοῦσι· καὶ τοῦτ' ἦν τὸ πολυτελέστατον (*Deipnosoph.* bk vi ch. 15 p. 229 c).

V. *Some parallels to Eg. C. O. from Hippolytus*

I indicate here a few parallels to Eg. C. O. occurring in the genuine remains of Hippolytus. No doubt a more thorough examination would reveal others.

(i) The prologue, or preface, of Eg. C. O. has already been printed out at p. 141. It is printed again in Appendix B. With it may be compared the following passages :

(a) *Philos.* vi 6. Ὅσα μὲν οὖν ἐδόκει τοῖς ἀπὸ τοῦ ὄφεως τὰς ἀρχὰς παρειληφόσι...**ἐν τῇ πρὸ ταύτης βίβλῳ οὔσῃ πέμπτῃ τοῦ ἐλέγχου τῶν αἱρέσεων ἐξεθέμην**· νυνὶ δὲ καὶ τῶν ἀκολούθων τὰς γνώμας οὐ σιωπήσω.

(b) *Ib.* ix 31. Δοκεῖ μὲν ἡμῖν ἱκανῶς τὰ πάντων...δόγματα **ἐκτεθεῖσθαι**...διὰ πάντων οὖν διαδραμόντες...εὔλογον ἡγούμεθα ὥσπερ **κορυφὴν** τοῦ παντὸς <τὸν> περὶ ἀληθείας λόγον ἐπενέγκαι.

(c) *Ib.* x 5. Ἀλλά γε καὶ νῦν οὐκ ἄλογον ἐκρίναμεν ἐπὶ πᾶσι τοῖς Ἕλλησι δεδοκημένοις καὶ αἱρετικοῖς ὡσεὶ **κορωνίδα** τῶν βίβλων ἐπενέγκαι ταύτην τὴν ἀπόδειξιν διὰ τῆς δεκάτης βίβλου.

Throughout the *Philosophumena* Hippolytus is constantly inserting short retrospective passages of the kind just cited under (a), (b) and (c); and he frequently specifies the book in which he has treated of such and such a matter. These retrospects serve as transitional pieces, preparatory to the taking up of some new theme. The prologue to Eg. C. O. is just such a transitional retrospect: it refers back to a previous book which treated of χαρίσματα, and thereby introduces the matter of Eg. C. O. itself. If we compare passage (a) above with that prologue, we find further resemblances in the form in which the two passages are cast: Eg. C. O. begins : 'Ea quidem, quae verba fuerunt, digne posuimus de donationibus, quanta quidem,' etc.; and of this A. C. preserves the Greek fairly closely : τὰ **μὲν οὖν πρῶτα** τοῦ λόγου **ἐξεθέμεθα** περὶ τῶν χαρισμάτων, ὅσαπερ, κ.τ.λ. Then the transition is made, as in (a), by νυνὶ δέ. That in ἐξεθέμεθα A. C. gives the original of 'posuimus,' there can be little doubt. But the verb ἐκτίθεσθαι occurs over and over again in the transition passages of the *Philosophumena*. Here are some examples :

i *Proem.* ὧν καὶ πάλαι μετρίως τὰ δόγματα **ἐξεθέμεθα**...ὅπως δι' αἰνιγμάτων ἡμῶν **ἐκθεμένων** τὰ δόξαντα αὐτοῖς, αἰσχυνθέντες...παύσωνται τι τῆς ἀλογίστου γνώμης.

i 26. Οὗτοι μὲν οὖν πάντες...ταῦτα καθὼς **ἐξεθέμεθα** τῇ αὐτῶν δόξῃ ἐξεῖπον... Τὰς μὲν οὖν...δόξας ἱκανῶς **ἐκτεθεῖσθαι** νομίζω...δοκεῖ δὲ πρότερον **ἐκτεθειμένους** τὰ μυστικά, κ.τ.λ.

iv 51. Ἐπεὶ οὖν καὶ ταῦτα δοκεῖ ἱκανῶς ἡμᾶς **ἐκτεθεῖσθαι**.

v 6. Πάνυ νομίζω πεπονημένως τὰ δόξαντα...**ἐκτεθεῖσθαι** ἐν ταῖς πρὸ ταύτης τέσσαρσι βίβλοις...περιλείπεται τοίνυν ἐπὶ τὸν τῶν αἱρέσεων ἔλεγχον ὁρμᾶν, οὗ χάριν καὶ τὰ προειρημένα ἡμῖν **ἐκτεθείμεθα**.

ADDITIONAL NOTES 161

v 28. Ἐπεὶ γοῦν...ἐξεθέμεθα, δοκεῖ καὶ...ἐν ταῖς ἑξῆς βίβλοις ἐκθέσθαι.
vi 7. Δοκεῖ οὖν καὶ τὰ Σίμωνος...νῦν ἐκθέσθαι.
vi 55. Ἀλλ' ἐπεὶ ἱκανῶς νομίζω...ἐκτεθεῖσθαι[1].

In passages (b) and (c) we have the words κορυφή and κορωνίς denoting the finishing stroke which will be given to the whole work against the heresies by the exposition of the true teaching in bk. x. In the prologue of Eg. C. O. the author says he has now come 'ad *verticem* traditionis quae catecizat.' There A. C. viii 3 has ἐπὶ τὸ κορυφαιότατον; but the original word may have been simply κορυφήν. The Ethiopic is rendered by Mr Horner (p. 162) 'source.' What meaning is to be attached to the expression is not clear. I am inclined to think that the author regarded the matter of his previous treatise, 'de donationibus,' as forming part of the tradition, and that of Eg. C. O. itself as its completion[2].

(d) In the first part of the prologue of Eg. C. O. there is a clause for misinterpreting which Schwartz has severely criticized Schermann, but of which his own explanation is far from satisfactory.

'Ea quidem, quae verba fuerunt, digne posuimus de donationibus, quanta quidem Deus a principio secundum propriam voluntatem praestitit hominibus *offerens sibi eam imaginem, quae aberraverat*.'

Of this Schwartz says that *sibi*, in this class of Latin, 'can stand for the non-reflexive αὐτῷ and αὐτοῖς.' He accordingly takes *sibi* for αὐτοῖς, and 'offerens' in the sense of 'hold up before' (as an example to be avoided). But he does not, apparently, make this αὐτοῖς refer to 'hominibus,' nor 'offerens' to 'Deus.' He says: 'In the first part of his discourse' the writer 'has spoken of the charismata, and has made use of the occasion to hold up before his *Publikum* the "false *Typus*" which went astray" (imaginem quae aberraverat = τὸν τύπον τὸν πεπλανημένον), that is, to warn them against the false prophets who claimed a charisma which they did not possess.'[3]

There are, however, grave objections to this interpretation; and 'sibi' for αὐτοῖς must, in my judgment, be counted among them. In the first place, the Ethiopic (Horner p. 162) has 'bringing near *to him* [God] that which had gone astray in type.' Next, there is no antecedent for αὐτοῖς (since it is not even made to refer to 'hominibus'). Again, the writer begins with the plural of authorship ('posuimus'); but even a *schriftstellerisch* plural would naturally be followed by 'offerentes,' not 'offerens'—if this participle

---

[1] Cf. further vii 14, 39; viii 8, 20; ix 30. A few lines on in the prologue of Eg. C. O. we find 'ut...traditionem *exponentibus nobis* custodiant.' I have no doubt that the Greek was ἐκθεμένων ἡμῶν.
[2] Schwartz (*Oriens Christianus*, 1915, n. Ser., 4 B. 2 H. p. 351 ff.) and Dr Frere (*J. T. S.* XVI 330) take 'verticem' to be the 'Hauptsache,' 'the chief matter,' of the tradition, viz. the Christian ministry. Schwartz, however, is partly influenced in this by an interpretation he gives to the preceding sentence—an interpretation which can hardly be upheld [see (d) below].
[3] *Oriens Christianus* (see preceding note).

C. 11

be referred to the author himself, and not (as the context surely requires) to 'Deus.'

The true interpretation of the passage is, I think, to be gathered by comparing passages in the works of Hippolytus.

(α) *In Dan.* lib. iv cc. 36-37 (ed. Bonwetsch)[1]. "Καὶ ἰδοὺ ἀνὴρ εἶς ἐνδεδυμένος βαδδίν" (Dan. x 5). τὸ γὰρ ποικίλον τῆς κλήσεως τῶν χαρισμάτων ἐνδεδυμένος ὁ Χριστὸς ποικίλον χιτῶνα μυστηρίῳ ἐπεδείκνυεν· ὅτι ἐκ διαφόρων χρωμάτων ἦν κατηρτισμένος ὁ ἱερατικὸς χιτὼν εἰς ἔνδειξιν τῶν ποικίλων ἐθνῶν τὴν παρουσίαν Χριστοῦ προσδεχομένων, ἵνα ποικίλοις χαρίσμασιν καταρτισθῆναι δυνηθῶμεν. (c. 37) "Καὶ ἡ ὀσφὺς αὐτοῦ περιεζωμένη ἐν χρυσίῳ Ὠφάζ." τὸ δὲ Ὠφὰζ χρυσίον καθαρὸν σημαίνει...καθαρὰν οὖν ἦν περιεζωμένος περὶ τὴν ὀσφὺν [αὐτοῦ] ζώνην· πάντας γὰρ ἡμᾶς ἤμελλεν ὁ λόγος περὶ τὸ ἑαυτοῦ σῶμα τῇ ἰδίᾳ ἀγάπῃ, ὡς ζώνην σφίγξας, βαστάζειν· τὸ γὰρ σῶμα [αὐτοῦ] τὸ τέλειον αὐτὸς ἦν, ἡμεῖς δὲ αὐτοῦ μέλη, ὡς ἐν τελείῳ σώματι ἡνωμένοι καὶ ὑπ' αὐτοῦ βασταζόμενοι.

(β) *Philos.* x 34. Χριστὸς γάρ ἐστιν ὁ κατὰ πάντων θεός, ὃς τὴν ἁμαρτίαν ἐξ ἀνθρώπων ἀποπλύνειν προσέταξε, νέον τὸν παλαιὸν ἄνθρωπον ἀποτελῶν, εἰκόνα τοῦτον καλέσας ἀπ' ἀρχῆς, διὰ τύπου τὴν εἰς σὲ ἐπιδεικνυμένος στοργήν, οὗ προστάγμασιν ὑπακούσας σεμνοῖς, καὶ ἀγαθοῦ ἀγαθὸς γενόμενος μιμητής, ἔσῃ ὅμοιος ὑπ' αὐτοῦ τιμηθείς. οὐ γὰρ πτωχεύει θεός καὶ σὲ θεὸν ποιήσας εἰς δόξαν αὐτοῦ.

(γ) *Contra haer. Noëti* c. 4. Ἔστι μὲν οὖν σὰρξ ἡ ὑπὸ τοῦ λόγου τοῦ πατρῴου προσενεχθεῖσα δῶρον...πρόδηλον οὖν ὅτι αὐτὸς ἑαυτὸν προσέφερεν τῷ πατρί[2].

(δ) Serm. *in Elcanam et Annam*[3]. Αὐτὸς πρῶτος εἰς οὐρανοὺς ἀναβάς, καὶ τὸν ἄνθρωπον δῶρον θεῷ προσενέγκας.

The incarnate Word, the perfect Man, presents in Himself, as a gift to the Father, man restored to that original image which he had lost: that, I think, is the thought of Hippolytus. And that, I also think, is the thought in the prologue of Eg. C. O.—except that here God is regarded as presenting to Himself the restored image. Passage (α), above, shews us how such thoughts could connect themselves in the mind of Hippolytus with the idea of charismatic gifts. In Christ we are all bound and united to the perfect body of the divine Word, which is clothed in various 'charismata' that we may be equipped with the same. Hence, in offering Himself to the Father, He offers us. According to Eg. C. O., as I read the passage, the presentation to God in Christ of the restored image is viewed as the culmination of the 'charismata' which 'God from the beginning, according to His own purpose, granted to men, presenting to Himself that image which had gone astray[4].'

---

[1] In the Berlin series, *Hippolytus* I, part 1, p. 282.
[2] For this passage in its context see below, p. 164 (α).
[3] *Hip.* I, part 2, p. 122. The fragment is preserved by Theodoret in *Dial.* ii.
[4] The 'imaginem' of the Latin may well stand not for τύπον (as Schwartz will have it), but for εἰκόνα (Gen. i. 26). But if τύπον was the word, it refers to the first man as a type of the perfect Man.

ADDITIONAL NOTES 163

(ii) I turn now from the prologue to the epilogue of Eg. C. O. This may be given in a Greek retranslation made by Schwartz on the basis of the Coptic and a small fragment of the Latin[1].

Ταῦτα συμβουλεύομαι φυλάσσειν πᾶσιν τοῖς εὖ ἐπισταμένοις· πάντων γὰρ ἀκουόντων τὴν ἀποστολικὴν παράδοσιν[2] καὶ φυλασσόντων οὐδεὶς αἱρετικὸς δυνήσεται πλανᾶν οὐδὲ ὅλως ἄνθρωπος. οὕτως γὰρ αὐξάνουσιν αἱ πολλαὶ αἱρέσεις διότι οἱ **προιστάμενοι** οὐ θέλουσιν μαθεῖν τὴν τῶν ἀποστόλων προαίρεσιν, ἀλλὰ κατὰ τὴν ἑαυτῶν ἡδονὴν πράττουσιν ἃ ἂν βούλωνται καὶ οὐχ ἃ πρέπει. εἴτινα παρελίπομεν, ἀγαπητοὶ ἡμῶν, ταῦθ' ὁ θεὸς φανερώσει τοῖς ἀξίοις ὁ **κυβερνῶν τὴν ἐκκλησίαν** ἣ ἂν ἀξία ᾖ ὁρμίσασθαι **εἰς τὸν λιμένα** τῆς ἀναπαύσεως αὐτοῦ[3].

(a) Schwartz (p. 39) cites two passages in which Hippolytus likens the Church to a ship. One is *de Antichr.* c. 59; a remarkable passage containing a detailed comparison of the Church to a ship, in which Christ is called τὸν ἔμπειρον κυβερνήτην, and the cross is referred to as **εἰκὼν σημείου πάθους** Χριστοῦ (with which compare Hauler pp. 118, 121: 'Hoc enim *signum passionis*'). The other passage occurs in Hippolytus's exposition of the Blessings of Moses, edited by Bonwetsch[4]. In the latter of these passages it is said that the Church, attacked by disorders and disturbances of the 'alien spirit of this world,' 'turns to the Lord, as one puts in at a *quiet landing*.' To these passages may be added the two following:

(b) *Philos.* iv 46. καὶ ἀφροσύνην τῶν πειθομένων κατηγορήσαντες **πείσομεν** παλινδρομεῖν ἐπὶ τὸν τῆς ἀληθείας **εὔδιον λιμένα**.

(c) *Ib.* vii 13. Πελάγει κλυδωνιζομένῳ ὑπὸ βίας ἀνέμων ἐοικότα ὁρῶντας τὰ τῶν αἱρετικῶν δόγματα ἐχρῆν τοὺς ἀκροατὰς παραπλεῖν ἐπιζητοῦντας **τὸν εὔδιον λιμένα**...ὃ ποιῆσαι τοῖς ἐντυγχάνουσιν **συμβολὴ** <ἐμή>, κτλ.

In both (b) and (c) Hippolytus likens the faithful Christians to sailors at sea; and he proffers the advice that they should make for the 'quiet harbour.' The harbour is the true teaching, and the heresies are the sea and its dangers. In the epilogue of Eg. C. O. we find the faithful similarly *advised* to escape from the heresies by holding to the 'apostolic tradition'; and shortly after this the Church is figured as a ship steered by God to 'the quiet haven' (Horner). That the dangers of the sea are here again the heresies, is naturally under-

---

[1] *Die pseudoapost. Kirchenord.* p. 39.

[2] The Latin is extant thus far in duplicate: 'Custodiri haec consilium do ab omnibus bene sapientibus. Universis enim audientibus apostolicam tra(ditionem)' (Hauler p. 121); and: 'Quae custodiri moneo ab eis, qui bene sapiunt. Universis enim audientibus apos(tolicam traditionem)' (p. 118, where the passage is out of its place).

[3] Horner translates 'in the quiet haven'; and the translation given in Achelis (*op. cit.* p. 136) has 'im Hafen (λιμήν) der Ruhe.' I should prefer to retranslate ἐπὶ τὸν εὔδιον λιμένα.

[4] In *Texte u. Untersuch.*, n. F., xi 69. This work is preserved only in a Georgian version, from a Russian version of which Bonwetsch gives a German translation.

11—2

stood. And here it may be added that the Greek word συμβουλεύειν (or perhaps συμβουλή or σύμβουλος) is attested by the Coptic version. For the stylistic feature presented by these proffers of personal advice we may compare yet again the following:

(d) *Philos.* x 34. Τοιοῦτος ὁ περὶ τὸ θεῖον ἀληθὴς λόγος, ὦ ἄνθρωποι... οἷς σύμβουλος ἐγὼ γίνομαι...ὅπως προσδραμόντες διδαχθῆτε παρ' ἡμῶν, τίς ὁ ὄντως θεός.

(e) In the same epilogue the word προιστάμενοι (or, it may be, προστάται) is again vouched for by the Coptic. I have noticed several instances in which Hippolytus speaks of heretical leaders as προστάται :—*Philos.* v 6 : Οἱ οὖν ἱερεῖς καὶ προστάται τοῦ δόγματος γεγένηνται πρῶτοι οἱ ἐπικληθέντες Νααασηνοί. Also v 20 : Ταῦτά ἐστιν ἃ λέγουσιν...οἱ προστάται τῶν Σηθιανῶν λόγων. Again, ix 8 : οἱ νῦν προστάται τῆς αἱρέσεως. And ix 10 : Φανερὸν δὲ πᾶσι τοὺς ἀνοήτους Νοητοῦ διαδόχους καὶ τῆς αἱρέσεως προστάτας...ἀναφανδὸν ταὐτὰ ὁμολογεῖν.

(iii) The next passage in Eg. C. O. for comparison with Hippolytus is the opening of the eucharistic prayer. The following is the Latin text :

'Gratias tibi referimus, Deus, per dilectum puerum tuum Iesum Christum, quem in ultimis temporibus misisti nobis salvatorem et redemptorem et angelum voluntatis tuae ; qui est verbum tuum inseparabilem (*sic*), per quem omnia fecisti et bene placitum tibi fuit ; misisti de caelo in matricem virginis, quique in utero habitus incarnatus est et filius tibi ostensus est ex spiritu sancto et virgine natus ; qui voluntatem tuam conplens et populum sanctum tibi adquirens extendit manus, cum pateretur, ut a passione liberaret eos, qui in te crediderunt ; qui cumque traderetur voluntariae passioni, ut mortem solvat et vincula diaboli dirumpat et infernum calcet et iustos inluminet et terminum figat et resurrectionem manifestet, accipiens panem,' etc.

There are several points for consideration in this passage.

According to the Latin, we have in it a statement that the divine Logos was 'shewn to be' God's Son in the incarnation ('filius tibi ostensus est'). This is a feature of the theology of Hippolytus in regard to the Logos. Bardenhewer says of him, in summarizing his teaching on this subject, that he taught that ' only in the incarnation did He [the Word] become the true and perfect Son of the Father.'[1] Whatever may be thought as to the subordinationism which Bardenhewer finds in the writings of Hippolytus, there can be no doubt as to the substantial accuracy of the particular statement just quoted. Compare these passages of Hippolytus :

(a) *Contra haer. Noëti* c. 4. Ἔστι μὲν οὖν σὰρξ ἡ ὑπὸ τοῦ λόγου τοῦ πατρῴου προσενεχθεῖσα δῶρον, ἡ ἐκ πνεύματος καὶ παρθένου, τέλειος υἱὸς θεοῦ ἀποδεδειγμένος. πρόδηλον οὖν ὅτι αὐτὸς ἑαυτὸν προσέφερεν τῷ πατρί· πρὸ δὲ τούτου ἐν οὐρανῷ σὰρξ οὐκ ἦν. τίς οὖν ἦν ἐν οὐρανῷ ἀλλ' ἢ λόγος ἄσαρκος, ἀποσταλεὶς ἵνα δείξῃ αὐτὸν ἐπὶ γῆς ὄντα εἶναι καὶ ἐν οὐρανῷ ; λόγος γὰρ ἦν,

[1] *Patrology* (Engl. trans., 1908) p. 210.

πνεῦμα ἦν, δύναμις ἦν. ὃς τὸ κοινὸν ὄνομα καὶ παρὰ ἀνθρώποις χωρητὸν ἀνελάμβανεν εἰς ἑαυτόν, τοῦτο καλούμενος ἀπ' ἀρχῆς υἱὸς ἀνθρώπου διὰ τὸ μέλλον, καίτοι μήπω ὢν ἄνθρωπος[1]. (b) *Ib.* c. 11. Τὸ δὲ πᾶν πατήρ, ἐξ οὗ δύναμις λόγος. οὗτος δὲ νοῦς, ὃς προβὰς ἐν κόσμῳ ἐδείκνυτο παῖς θεοῦ. (c) *Ib.* c. 15. Ποῖον οὖν υἱὸν ἑαυτοῦ ὁ θεὸς διὰ τῆς σαρκὸς κατέπεμψεν ἀλλ' ἢ τὸν λόγον; ὃν υἱὸν προσηγόρευε διὰ τὸ μέλλειν αὐτὸν γενέσθαι. καὶ τὸ κοινὸν ὄνομα τῆς εἰς ἀνθρώπους φιλοστοργίας ἀναλαμβάνει ὁ υἱὸς καλούμενος. οὔτε γὰρ ἄσαρκος καὶ καθ' ἑαυτὸν ὁ λόγος τέλειος ἦν υἱὸς (καίτοι τέλειος λόγος ὢν μονογενής), οὔθ' ἡ σὰρξ καθ' ἑαυτὴν δίχα τοῦ λόγου ὑποστῆναι ἠδύνατο διὰ τὸ ἐν λόγῳ τὴν σύστασιν ἔχειν. οὕτως οὖν εἰς υἱὸς τέλειος θεοῦ ἐφανερώθη.

We may add yet another passage from the *contra haer. Noëti* in illustration of the general thought and expression of the earlier portion of the passage from the eucharistic prayer:

(d) *Ib.* c. 17. Πιστεύσωμεν οὖν, μακάριοι ἀδελφοί, κατὰ τὴν παράδοσιν τῶν ἀποστόλων[2], ὅτι θεὸς λόγος ἀπ' οὐρανῶν κατῆλθεν εἰς τὴν ἁγίαν παρθένον Μαρίαν, ἵνα σαρκωθεὶς ἐξ αὐτῆς, λαβὼν δὲ καὶ ψυχὴν ἀνθρωπίνην (λογικὴν δὲ λέγω), γεγονὼς πάντα ὅσα ἐστὶν ἄνθρωπος ἐκτὸς ἁμαρτίας, σώσῃ τὸν πεπτωκότα, καὶ ἀφθαρσίαν ἀνθρώποις παράσχῃ τοῖς πιστεύουσιν εἰς τὸ ὄνομα αὐτοῦ. ἐν πᾶσιν οὖν ἀποδέδεικται ἡμῖν τῆς ἀληθείας λόγος, ὅτι εἷς ἐστιν ὁ πατήρ, οὗ πάρεστι λόγος, δι' οὗ τὰ πάντα ἐποίησεν, ὃν ὑστέροις καιροῖς (καθὼς εἴπαμεν ἀνωτέρω) ἀπέστειλεν ὁ πατὴρ πρὸς σωτηρίαν ἀνθρώπων. οὗτος διὰ νόμου καὶ προφητῶν ἐκηρύχθη παρεσόμενος εἰς τὸν κόσμον. καθ' ὃν οὖν τρόπον ἐκηρύχθη, κατὰ τοῦτον καὶ παρὼν ἐφανέρωσεν ἑαυτὸν ἐκ παρθένου καὶ ἁγίου πνεύματος, καινὸς ἄνθρωπος γενόμενος.

There are some further minor conicidences between the prayer and Hippolytus which seem to deserve notice.

(e) The prayer says of the Word: 'per quem (*sic*) omnia fecisti *et bene placitum*[3] *tibi fuit.*' Hippolytus (*Philos.* x 33) says: ὅθεν κελεύοντος πατρὸς γίνεσθαι κόσμον τὸ κατὰ ἓν λόγος ἀπετελεῖτο **ἀρέσκων θεῷ**.

(f) Our Lord's stretching out His hands on the cross ('extendit manus cum pateretur') is an idea met with several times in Hippolytus. In *de Antichr.* c. 61 he thus interprets the 'two wings of the great eagle' (Apoc. xii 14): τουτέστι τὴν εἰς Χριστὸν Ἰησοῦν πίστιν, **ὃς ἐκτείνας τὰς ἁγίας χεῖρας ἐπὶ τῷ ξύλῳ ἥπλωσε** δύο πτέρυγας...προσκαλούμενος πάντας τοὺς εἰς αὐτὸν πιστεύσαντας καὶ σκεπάζων ὡς ὄρνις νεοσσούς[4]. St Jerome (*Ep.* xxxvi 16; ad Damasum) quotes Hippolytus on Genesis thus: 'Pelles, quae eius (Jacob's)

---

[1] The meaning of this will appear more clearly from passage (c) which follows.
[2] Compare the 'apostolica traditio' in the epilogue of Eg. C. O.
[3] This probably refers to 'verbum.' The Latin translator frequently varies the genders of pronouns and adjectives referring to 'verbum' or 'spiritus,' sometimes following the Latin, sometimes the Greek gender.
[4] Ed. Achelis, *Hippolytus* I, part 2, p. 42.

brachiis circumdatae sunt, peccata utriusque sunt plebis, quae Christus *in extensione manuum* cruci secum pariter affixit.' Also in his comments on the Blessings of Jacob and Moses Hippolytus interprets Gen. xxxvii 16, xlix 8 and Isai. ix 6 as foreshewing the outstretched hands of Christ on the cross[1].

(g) In the prayer the Word is called 'angelum voluntatis tuae.' Compare Hippolytus *in Dan.*: ὁ δὲ λόγος ἀκούσας τὴν βουλὴν τοῦ πατρὸς καταβὰς ἀπὸ οὐρανῶν τὸ θέλημα τοῦ πατρὸς τοῖς ἀγγέλοις ἀνήγγειλεν, ὡς λέγει ἡ γραφή· "ἅγιος ἀπὸ οὐρανῶν κατέβη."[2]

(h) It is said in the prayer that one of the ends for which Christ suffered was that He might 'shew forth the resurrection' ('et resurrectionem manifestet'). In *Philos.* x 33 Hippolytus writes: Ἵνα δὲ μὴ ἕτερος παρ' ἡμᾶς νομισθῇ, καὶ κάματον ὑπέμεινε...καὶ πάθει οὐκ ἀντεῖπε, καὶ θανάτῳ ὑπήκουσε, καὶ ἀνάστασιν ἐφανέρωσεν. The source of the idea may be Barnabas v 6.

(iv) Schwartz (*Pseudoapost. Kirchenord.* p. 39) brings from Hippolytus a remarkable verbal parallel to the passage in Eg. C. O. on the milk and honey administered after baptism. The latter passage is as follows:

'lac et melle mixta simul ad plenitudinem promissionis...quam dixit terram fluentem lac et mel, quam et dedit carnem suam Christus, per quam sicut parvuli nutriuntur, qui credunt, *in suavitate verbi amara cordis dulcia efficiens.*'

Hippolytus interprets the promise of 'a land flowing with milk and honey' as signifying the Old Testament and the New; and then he speaks of the honey as 'the sweetness of the Word, by whom the griefs of our souls are made sweet.' The passage occurs in Hippolytus's exposition of the Blessings of Moses, a work preserved only in a Georgian version[3].

With the same passage in Eg. C. O. we must compare a fragment of Hippolytus on Gen. xlix 15 b. He thus comments on the words καὶ τὴν γῆν ὅτι πίων in Jacob's blessing of Issachar: Ὅπερ ἐστὶν ἡ σὰρξ τοῦ κυρίου ἡμῶν ἡ "πίων," τουτέστιν ἡ λιπαρά. αὕτη γὰρ "ἡ ῥέουσα γάλα καὶ μέλι."[4] Here, as also in the Eg. C. O. passage, the flesh of Christ is equated with the land flowing with milk and honey.

(v) The prayer over firstfruits in Eg. C. O. begins thus: 'Gratias tibi agimus, Deus, et offerimus tibi primitivas fructuum, *quos dedisti nobis ad percipiendum,* per verbum tuum enutriens ea (*sic*), iubens terrae omnes fructus adferre *ad laetitiam et nutrimentum hominum*[5] et omnibus animalibus.'

---

[1] Bonwetsch, *Texte u. Untersuch.*, n. F., xi pp. 8, 25, 26 and 65.
[2] Lib. iii c. 9, ed. Bonwetsch p. 140. Cf. *ib.* lib. ii c. 32.
[3] A German translation from a Russian version of this is given by Bonwetsch in *Texte u. Untersuch.*, n. F., xi 67.
[4] *Hippolytus* I, part 2, p. 63 (ed. Achelis).
[5] A. C. viii 40, which embodies portions of this prayer, has εἰς εὐφροσύνην καὶ τροφὴν ἡμετέραν. Cf. Acts xiv 17, ἐμπιπλῶν τροφῆς καὶ εὐφροσύνης τὰς καρδίας ἡμῶν.

In *Philos.* ix 30 Hippolytus states that the Jews perform their worship of God in a careful and reverent manner, καθὼς τοῖς βουλομένοις ῥᾴδιόν ἐστιν ἐντυχοῦσι τῇ περὶ τούτων ἐξαγορευούσῃ βίβλῳ μαθεῖν, ὡς σεμνῶς καὶ ὁσίως τῷ θεῷ ἀπαρχόμενοι τῶν παρ' αὐτοῦ δεδωρημένων εἰς χρῆσιν καὶ ἀπόλαυσιν ἀνθρώπων... ἐλειτούργουν[1].

The last words of this passage recall 1 Tim. vi 17 (παρέχοντι ἡμῖν πάντα πλουσίως **εἰς ἀπόλαυσιν**); whereas the last italicized words in the prayer of Eg. C. O. are evidently reminiscent of Acts xiv 17. It is possible that χρῆσιν stood in the original text of the prayer, since the Coptic reads 'for profit (" Nutzen ": Achelis *Die Can. Hip.* p. 113) and rejoicing and nourishment' (Horner p. 325). But it is not found in the Ethiopic or in A. C. viii 40.

(vi) The reason for praying at the ninth hour is thus given in Eg. C. O. (the beginning of the passage is wanting in the Latin, and so I supply it from the Ethiopic):

(Horner p. 183) 'And at the ninth hour they shall be long in prayer,... that ye may *join in glorifying with the soul of the righteous ones, glorifying the living God*, (Hauler p. 119) qui non mentitur, *qui memor fuit sanctorum suorum et emisit verbum suum inluminantem eos*.'

Again, the following reason is given for praying at midnight (Hauler p. 120):

' Hac igitur hora necessarium est orare; nam et hi, qui tradiderunt nobis, seniores ita nos docuerunt, quia hac hora omnis creatura quiescit ad momentum quoddam, ut laudent dominum; stellas et arbusta et aquas stare in ictu, et omne agmen angelorum ministrat ei, in hac hora *una cum iustorum animabus laudare Deum*.'

In the first of these passages the 'souls of the righteous' are clearly the souls in Hades visited by Christ immediately after His death. In the eucharistic prayer of Eg. C. O. we read similarly (Hauler p. 106-7): 'ut mortem solvat et vincula diaboli dirumpat *et infernum calcet et iustos inluminet*.' But are these the same as the 'souls of the righteous' mentioned in the second passage? It might seem that in the second passage the souls could no longer be thought of as in Hades. Yet it is natural to suppose that the expression 'the souls of the righteous' has the same meaning in both passages; and we know at least that according to the view of Hippolytus all souls, of good and bad alike, remain in Hades till the judgment, in the custody of ἄγγελοι φρουροί[2]. Now, in the second passage the association of the stars, plants and waters with the angels and the 'souls of the righteous' in praising God suggests the Song of the Three

[1] In a fragment on Genesis i 7 (*Hippolytus* I, part 2, p. 52: ed. Achelis) Hippolytus says similarly that a third part of the waters was left below on earth πρὸς χρῆσιν καὶ ἀπόλαυσιν τοῖς ἀνθρώποις.

[2] In the fragment of the treatise Περὶ τῆς τοῦ παντὸς αἰτίας; Lagarde, *Hippol. Roman. quae feruntur omnia graece*, p. 69.

Children. If we turn to Hippolytus's comments on that Song, we find that he explains the πνεύματα καὶ ψυχαὶ δικαίων (Dan. iii 86) as the 'spirits' of the ταρταρούχων ἀγγέλων and the souls of the just *in Hades*. On the assumption, then, that Eg. C. O. was written by Hippolytus we have the required link between the two Eg. C. O. passages under consideration. But there are other points in Hippolytus's comment on the Song which deserve attention, and it must be quoted at some length[1].

"Ἤρξαντο μὲν τὸ πρῶτον ἀπ' αὐτῆς τῆς δόξης τοῦ θεοῦ <καὶ ἐδόξαζον·> ἔπει<τα δὲ "τὰ> ὑπερ<άνω τοῦ οὐρανοῦ," τὰ λεγόμενα ὑπερκόσμ>ια· εἶτα τὸ στερέωμα <σὺν> τοῖς φωστῆρσιν ὠνόμασαν· εἶτα <τὰ> ἐν μέσῳ τῷ στερεώματι· εἶτα πρὸς τὴν γῆν λέγοντες "εὐλογείτω ἡ γῆ τὸν κύριον..."· ἔπειτα "ὅρη καὶ βουνούς"· εἶτα "πάντα τὰ φυόμενα ἐν τῇ γῇ." ἔπειτα μετῆλθον ἐπὶ τὰ ὕδατα, ποταμούς τε καὶ πηγὰς καὶ θαλάσσας· εἶτα "τὰ κινούμενα ἐν τοῖς ὕδασι" "κήτη" τε καὶ ἰχθύας· ἔπειτα "πετεινὰ <τοῦ> οὐρανοῦ" "κτήνη" τε καὶ "θηρία." ἔπειτα μετῆλθον ἐπὶ τοὺς υἱοὺς τῶν ἀνθρώπων κατὰ τάξιν τὸν ὕμνον ἀναφέροντες. ἔπειτα τὰ καταχθόνια ὠνόμασαν "πνεύματα" ταρταρούχων ἀγγέλων καὶ ψυχὰς δικαίων, ἵνα καὶ αὐτοὶ σὺν αὐτοῖς τὸν θεὸν ὑμνήσωσιν.... (c. 30) Εἴπατέ μοι τρεῖς παῖδες...τίς ἦν τέταρτος σὺν ὑμῖν;...τίς ὁ οὕτως εὐτάκτως [ὁ] πᾶσαν κτίσιν διὰ στόματος ὑμῶν διηγησάμενος, ἵνα μηδὲν τῶν ὄντων καὶ γενομένων παραλείπητε; μίαν ὥραν ἐν καμίνῳ ποιήσαντες, τὴν τῆς κτίσεως δημιουργίαν ἐδιδ<άσκεσθε· ὁ> γὰρ λόγος <ἦν σὺν ὑμῖν καὶ> δι' ὑμῶν φθεγγόμενος, ὁ καὶ ἐπιστάμενος τὴν τῆς κτίσεως δημιουργίαν.

According to Hippolytus, then, the 'spirits' and the 'souls of the righteous' are mentioned nearly last in the Song because they are those of angels and men under the earth. And in the second Eg. C. O. passage the souls of the righteous—evidently identical with those whom Christ visited in Hades—are also mentioned last, and in conjunction with the angels. Moreover Hippolytus sees much significance in the order in which the various creatures are bidden to praise God ; and in the Eg. C. O. passage the order stars, plants, waters, angels, souls of the righteous is, so far as it goes, that emphasized by Hippolytus, and, of course, that of the Song.

These parallels are not all of equal force; but their cumulative effect is considerable. On the lowest possible estimate of them they fully suffice for the purpose for which they are adduced : that is, to shew that the evidence for the Hippolytean authorship of Eg. C. O., which was set out in the body of this essay, loses nothing of its force when the language and ideas of Eg. C. O. are compared with those of Hippolytus[2].

[1] *In Dan.* lib. ii, cc. 29, 30 (ed. Bonwetsch p. 98).
[2] To the parallels adduced in this Note must be added the occurrence of the expression 'in sancta ecclesia' in several of the doxologies of Eg. C. O. and in one at the end of the *contra haer. Noët.* (see p. 154 above). We have also seen (at pp. 117 and 158) that Eg. C. O. has certain features which admit of ready explanation only on the view that the document proceeds from Rome: viz. the mention of κέραμοι in connexion with burial, and the allusion to the custom of giving *apophoreta*. I have purposely refrained from basing any argument on the 'western'

VI. Supplementary note on the 'Testament of our Lord'

In discussing the prologue of Eg. C. O. at p. 43 f. above I failed to notice that Test. has a passage which shews a striking coincidence with it. To this passage the Editor has drawn my attention. It occurs in one of the transitional chapters between the apocalypse, with which Test. begins, and the Church Order which the compiler has constructed largely out of Eg. C. O. I translate the Syriac as literally as I can into Latin, which offers here a rather better medium than English.

'Dicetur autem et dabitur[1] eis qui sunt *firmi* et stabiliti et indeclinabiles, qui faciunt mandata mea et *traditionem* hanc, ut *custodientes* sancti et recti et fortes in me *maneant* fugientes a *lapsu* (*shur‘ăthă*) iniquitatis et a morte peccati, *donante* (*kadh mĕshakken*) *eis spiritu sancto gratiam suam ut recte credant*' (Test. i 19).

The italicized words in this passage at once recall the prologue of Eg. C. O. (cf. p. 141 above), in which we find the expressions 'traditionem...custodiant,' 'firmiores maneant,' 'propter eum, qui nuper inventus est...*lapsus* vel error,' and particularly 'praestante sancto spiritu perfectam gratiam eis qui recte credunt.' The passage leaves no doubt in my mind that the author of Test., like the compiler of A. C., had before him a copy of Eg. C. O. which contained the prologue.

Another passage in Test. which appears to be reminiscent of the Eg. C. O. prologue occurs in bk. i ch. 14, as follows:

'*Ad ecclesiam* (cod. B '*ecclesias*') igitur *conversi*, recte disponite[2], bene ordinantes et praecipientes; et omnia in aequitate et sanctitate facientes unicuique secundum quod ipsi utile est loquimini, ut pater vester qui est in caelis glorificetur. Cognoscite quomodo eis persuadeatis, qui captivati sunt ab *errore*, et eis qui mersi sunt *in ignorantia*.'

With the italicized words we may compare 'ad ecclesias perreximus' and 'propter eum, qui nuper inventus est *per ignorantiam* lapsus vel *error*, et hos qui *ignorant*' of the Eg. C. O. prologue.

form of creed in Eg. C. O. Our knowledge of baptismal creeds in use in both East and West, at the date to which I assign our document, is too scanty to furnish satisfactory grounds for comparison. It may be said, however, that the creed in Eg. C. O. is of the type found later in the West, not of that found in the East. With it may be compared two passages in Hippolytus, *contra haer*. *Noët*. cc. 1 and 8.

[1] It is not clear what is the subject of these two verbs, which are 3rd fem. sing. The context suggests that the subject was 'my holy things,' τὰ ἅγιά μου.

[2] The verb is really a present indicative, but is not easy to translate as such. The meaning may be 'you are to set (them) in right order.'

APPENDIX A

Comparative tables of A. C. viii and Ep.

In this Appendix I give two tables.

I. The purpose of the first is to illustrate what was said at p. 37 as to the distribution of the contents of A. C. viii and Ep. among the apostles. The name of an apostle placed in brackets *under* a numeral denoting a chapter of A. C. viii or a section of Ep. indicates that the chapter or section in question, and also those *which follow without names*, are put into the mouth of that apostle. The nature of the contents of the corresponding chapters and sections is indicated on the right-hand side of the page. The chapters and sections are numbered as in Funk's edition (vol. I for A. C., vol. II for Ep.). The sign >< signifies 'different from.'

A. C. viii		Ep.	Contents
1–2	=	1–2	on *charismata*.
3			transitional.
4	=	3	election of bishop.
(Πέτρος)		(Πέτρος)	
5¹⁻⁸	><	4	bishop's ordination prayer.
5⁹⁻¹²			
6			
(Ἀνδρέας)			
7–11		... ...	liturgy.
12			
(Ἰάκωβος τοῦ Ζεβ.)			
13–15			
16¹⁻²	=	5	ordination of presbyter.
(ὁ φιλούμενος ὑπὸ τοῦ κυρίου)		(ὁ φιλούμενος ὑπὸ τοῦ κυρίου)	
16³⁻⁵	=	6	ordination prayer.
17	=	7	ordination of deacon.
(Φίλιππος)		(Φίλιππος)	
18	=	8	ordination prayer.
19	=	9	ordination of deaconess.
(Βαρθολομαῖος)		(Βαρθολομαῖος)	
20	=	10	ordination prayer.
21¹⁻²	=	11	ordination of subdeacon.
(Θωμᾶς)		(Θωμᾶς)	
21³⁻⁴	=	12	ordination prayer.
22¹⁻²	><	13	the reader.
(Ματθαῖος)		(no name)	
22³⁻⁴		... ...	ordination prayer.
23	=	14	confessors.
(Ἰάκωβος ὁ Ἀλφαίου)		(Ἰάκωβος Ἀλφαίου)	

APPENDIX A 171

A. C. viii		Ep.	Contents
24	=	15	virgins.
(ὁ αὐτός)		(ὁ αὐτός)	
25	=	16	widows.
(Λεββαῖος ὁ ἐπικληθεὶς Θαδδαῖος)		(Λεββαῖος ὁ ἐπικληθεὶς Θαδδαῖος)	
26	=	17	exorcists.
(ὁ αὐτός)		(ὁ αὐτός)	
27	=	18	by how many bishops a bishop is ordained.
(Σίμων ὁ Κανανίτης)		(Σίμων ὁ Καναναῖος)	
28	=	19	'on canons.'
(ὁ αὐτός)		(ὁ αὐτός)	
29		... ...	... blessing of water and oil.
(Ματθίας)			
30	=	20	first fruits and tithes.
(ὁ αὐτός)		(ὁ αὐτὸς Σίμων ὁ Καν.)	
31	=	21	'de reliquiis' (eulogiae).
(ὁ αὐτός)		(ὁ αὐτός)	
32	=	22	on ecclesiastical canons.
(Παῦλος)		(Παῦλος)	
33	=	23	rest for servants.
(Παῦλος καὶ Πέτρος)		(Παῦλος καὶ Πέτρος)	
34	=	24	on prayers.
(no name)		(no name)	
35		... ...	... evening service.
(Ἰάκωβος ἀδελφὸς τοῦ Χριστοῦ)			
36–37		... ...	... the same.
38–39		... ...	... morning service.
40		... ...	... blessing of first fruits.
41		... ...	... prayer for departed.
42–43	=	25	memorials for departed.
44	=	26	memorial suppers.
45	=	27	on persecution.
46	=	28	ecclesiastical orders.
(κοινῇ πάντες)		(κοινῇ πάντες)	
47		... ...	... Apostolic Canons.
48		... ...	... Conclusion.

II. In the second table I give references to the sections, pages and lines of Funk's edition for every item in Ep. and the corresponding items in A. C. viii. Beneath each reference I place in brackets the number of lines (for lengthy passages) or words (for shorter pieces) occupied by each of the corresponding items in the two documents. I neglect the general title to A. C. viii and those to the five parts into which Ep. is divided. A number of short sub-titles (or indications of contents) to the various sections of Ep. are printed by Funk as headings above the text, while similar sub-titles which often occur in A. C. viii are printed by him currently with the rest of the text. Where a sub-title in Ep. has something corresponding in A. C. I count it in with the text (as in A. C.); where there is nothing corresponding in A. C. I neglect the sub-title of Ep.

The purpose of this table is to illustrate in a summary way what is said on p. 7 above, viz. that Ep. is not really an 'epitome,' or abbreviated redaction, of A. C. viii, but a series of excerpts, in which the passages extracted are kept almost exactly in their original form and extent. The

172   THE SO-CALLED EGYPTIAN CHURCH ORDER

only passage excerpted from A. C. viii which has been shortened by the 'Epitomist' is the ordination prayer for a presbyter (on which see pp. 50 ff.). The bishop's ordination prayer and the passage on the reader have been shewn to present quite different phenomena from the rest of Ep., and to have been drawn, not from A. C. viii, but directly from Eg. C. O.

As regards A. C., only the alternate pages (those with *even* numbers) are to be counted, since those with *odd* numbers contain Funk's Latin translation.

Ep.		A. C. viii
1–2 p. 72 l. 5–p. 77 l. 12 (172 *lines*)	=	1–2 p. 460 l. 4–p. 470 l. 10 (173 *lines*)
3 p. 77 l. 15–p. 78 l. 21 (29 *lines*)	=	4 p. 470 l. 23–p. 472 l. 27 (29 *lines*)
4 p. 78 l. 23–p. 79 l. 17 (23 *lines*)[1]	><	5^{1-8} p. 474 l. 1–p. 476 l. 16 (41 *lines*)[1]
5 p. 79 ll. 18–22 (34 *words*)	=	16^{1-2} p. 520 l. 31–p. 522 l. 4 (34 *words*)
6 p. 79 l. 24–p. 80 l. 10 (15 *lines*)[2]	=	16^{3-5} p. 522 ll. 4–25 (21 *lines*)[2]
7 p. 80 ll. 11–14 (25 *words*)	=	17 p. 522 ll. 26–29 (26 *words*)
8 p. 80 ll. 16–28 (111 *words*)	=	18 p. 522 l. 29–p. 524 l. 10 (106 *words*)
9 p. 81 ll. 1–5 (26 *words*)	=	19 p. 524 ll. 11–13 (22 *words*)
10 p. 81 ll. 7–18 (114 *words*)	=	20 p. 524 ll. 13–24 (112 *words*)
11 p. 81 ll. 19–21 (18 *words*)	=	21^{1-2} p. 524 l. 25–p. 526 l. 1 (20 *words*)
12 p. 81 l. 23–p. 82 l. 2 (78 *words*)	=	21^{3-4} p. 526 ll. 1–8 (77 *words*)
13 p. 82 ll. 3–5 (12 *words*)[3]	><	22 p. 526 ll. 9–22 ($13\frac{1}{2}$ *lines*)[3]

[1] This is the bishop's ordination prayer.
[2] Presbyter's ordination prayer, shortened in Ep.
[3] This is the passage on the reader.

APPENDIX A

Ep.		A. C. viii
14 p. 82 ll. 6–14 (70 words)	=	23 p. 526 l. 23–p. 528 l. 4 (78 words)
15 p. 82 ll. 15–19 (31 words)	=	24 p. 528 ll. 5–7 (27 words)
16 p. 82 ll. 20–28 (68 words)	=	25 p. 528 ll. 8–15 (65 words)
17 p. 83 ll. 1–7 (50 words)	=	26 p. 528 ll. 16–22 (50 words)
18 p. 83 ll. 10–16 (56 words)	=	27 p. 530 ll. 1–8 (58 words)
19 p. 83 l. 17–p. 84 l. 10 (21 lines)	=	28 p. 530 ll. 9–30 (21 lines)
20 p. 84 ll. 11–17 (54 words)	=	30 p. 532 ll. 15–21 (53 words)
21 p. 84 ll. 18–25 (69 words)	=	31 p. 532 l. 22–p. 534 l. 3 (67 words)
22 p. 85 l. 3–p. 87 l. 14 (53 lines)	=	32 p. 534 l. 4–p. 538 l. 9 (53 lines)
23 p. 87 l. 17–p. 88 l. 18 (22 lines)	=	33 p. 538 l. 10–p. 540 l. 12 (22 lines)
24 p. 88 l. 20–p. 89 l. 20 (26 lines)	=	34 p. 540 l. 13–p. 542 l. 15 (26 lines)
25 p. 90 ll. 2–12 (11 lines)	=	42–43 p. 552 l. 19–p. 554 l. 8 (11 lines)
26 p. 90 l. 14–p. 91 l. 12 (19 lines)	=	44 p. 554 l. 9–p. 556 l. 3 (19 lines)
27 p. 91 ll. 14–20 (54 words)	=	45 p. 556 ll. 4–10 (54 words)
28 p. 92 l. 3–p. 96 l. 9 (100 lines)	=	46 p. 556 l. 11–p. 562 l. 27 (101 lines)

APPENDIX B

A Text of Eg. C. O.

Following a suggestion of the Editor of *Texts and Studies*, I append here a continuous text of the whole of Eg. C. O. For this Hauler's Latin fragments are printed in their entirety, but without his annotations. Their very considerable lacunae are filled up from Mr Horner's translation of the Ethiopic, the most complete of the other versions. Beyond adding a few notes, where this seemed desirable, and substituting a certain number of readings from Mr Horner's collations for those in his text, I have attempted nothing in the way of editing[1]. I keep Hauler's punctuation of the Latin almost unchanged, though in places it might be improved upon.

This *qualecumque subsidium* is intended only to help the reader to follow more easily and conveniently the discussions in the body of the volume, by enabling him to locate in their contexts the passages dealt with. It should be evident that such a text as is here presented cannot dispense the reader from consulting, for the purpose of any serious study of these Church Orders, the editions from which it is taken. Much of the Ethiopic, for instance, and the whole of the Coptic and Arabic versions are unrepresented; yet for any adequate understanding of the text the whole of the Ethiopic and the Coptic, at the least, must constantly be kept in view, especially where the Latin is wanting.

The arabic numerals in the margin refer, when placed opposite the Latin, to the pages of Hauler's edition; when they stand opposite the English, they refer to the pages of Mr Horner's *Statutes of the Apostles*. The roman numerals inserted in square brackets in the Latin portions are those attached by Hauler to the pages of the MS which contain the fragments published by him. According to Hauler the MS has a number of blank, or nearly blank, spaces which once contained short sectional headings in red ink. Wherever a space of this kind is indicated in his edition I place an asterisk (*) before the words following the space.

---

[1] Such substitutions have been made only where the weight of the manuscript authority and the intrinsic character of the readings thereby supported seemed decisive.

APPENDIX B 175

THE SO-CALLED
EGYPTIAN CHURCH ORDER

p. 101 [LXVII] *Ea quidem quae uerba fuerunt digne posuimus de donationibus, quanta quidem Deus a principio secundum propriam uoluntatem praestitit hominibus offerens sibi eam imaginem, quae [LXVIII] aberrauerat. Nunc autem ex caritate, quam in omnes sanctos habuit, producti ad uerticem traditionis, quae catecizat, ad ecclesias perreximus, ut hii, qui bene ducti sunt, eam, quae permansit usque nunc, traditionem exponentibus nobis custodiant et agnoscentes fir-
p. 103 miores maneant, propter | eum qui nuper inuentus est per ignorantiam lapsus uel error, et hos qui ignorant, praestante sancto spiritu perfectam gratiam eis qui recte credunt, ut cognoscant, quomodo oportet tradi et custodiri omnia eos, qui ecclesiae praesunt.

*Episcopus ordinetur electus ab omni populo; quique cum nominatus fuerit et placuerit omnibus, conueniet populum una cum praesbyterio et his qui praesentes fuerint episcopi, die dominica. Consentientibus omnibus inponant super eum manus et praesbyterium adstet quiescens. Omnes autem silentium habeant orantes in corde propter descensionem spiritus; ex quibus unus de praesentibus episcopis ab omnibus rogatus, inponens manum ei qui ordinatur episcopus, oret ita dicens :

'Deus et pater domini nostri Iesu Christi, pater misericordiarum et Deus totius consolationis, qui in excelsis habitas et humilia respicis, qui cognoscis omnia antequam nascantur, tu, qui dedisti terminos in ecclesia per uerbum gratiae tuae, praedestinans ex principio genus
p. 105 iustorum Abraham, principes | et sacerdotes constituens et sanctum tuum sine ministerio non derelinquens, ex initio saeculi bene tibi placuit in his, quos ele-[LXIX]gisti, pr⟨a⟩edicari[1]: nunc effunde eam uirtutem, quae a te est, principalis spiritus, quem dedisti dilecto filio tuo Iesu Christo, quod donauit sanctis apostolis, qui constituerunt ecclesiam per singula loca, sanctificationem tuam, in gloriam et laudem indeficientem nomini tuo. Da, cordis cognitor pater, super hunc seruum tuum, quem elegisti ad episcopatum, pascere gregem sanctam tuam et primatum sacerdotii tibi exhibere, sine repraehensione seruientem noctu et die, incessanter repropitiari uultum tuum et offerre dona sancta⟨e⟩ ecclesiae tuae, spiritu[2] primatus sacerdotii habere potestatem dimittere peccata secundum mandatum tuum, dare sortes secundum praeceptum tuum, soluere etiam omnem colligationem secundum

---
[1] The MS has 'elegisti dari.' Probably read 'laudari.' The Ethiopic has 'to be glorified.'
[2] The MS has 'spm.'

176 THE SO-CALLED EGYPTIAN CHURCH ORDER

potestatem, quam dedisti apostolis, placere autem tibi in mansuetudine et mundo corde, offerentem tibi odorem suauitatis per puerum tuum Iesum Christum, per quem tibi gloria et potentia et honor,
p. 106 patri et filio cum spiritu sancto, | et nunc et in saecula saeculorum. Amen.'

Qui cumque factus fuerit episcopus, omnes os offerant pacis, salutantes cum, quia dignus effectus est. Illi uero offerant diacones oblationem, quique inponens manus in eam cum omni praesbyterio dicat gratia[n]s agens : 'Dominus uobiscum'; et omnes dicant : 'Et cum spiritu tuo.' 'Sursum corda.' 'Habemus ad dominum.' 'Gratias agamus domino.' 'Dignum et iustum est.' Et sic iam prosequatur :

'Gratias tibi referimus, Deus, per dilectum puerum tuum Iesum Christum, quem [LXX] in ultimis temporibus misisti nobis saluatorem et redemptorem et angelum uoluntatis tuae ; qui est uerbum tuum inseparabilem (sic), per quem omnia fecisti et bene placitum tibi fuit ; misisti de caelo in matricem uirginis, quique in utero habitus incarnatus est et filius tibi ostensus est ex spiritu sancto et uirgine natus ; qui uoluntatem tuam conplens et populum sanctum tibi adquirens extendit manus, cum pateretur, ut a passione liberaret eos qui in te crediderunt ; qui cumque traderetur uoluntariae passioni, ut mortem
p. 107 soluat et uincula diaboli dirumpat et infernum | calcet et iustos inluminet et terminum figat et resurrectionem manifestet, accipiens panem gratias tibi agens dixit : Accipite, manducate : hoc est corpus meum, quod pro uobis confringetur. Similiter et calicem dicens : Hic est sanguis meus, qui pro uobis effunditur ; quando hoc facitis, meam commemorationem facitis. Memores igitur mortis et resurrectionis eius offerimus tibi panem et calicem gratias tibi agentes, quia nos dignos habuisti adstare coram te et tibi ministrare. Et petimus, ut mittas spiritum tuum sanctum in oblationem sanctae ecclesiae ; in unum congregans des omnibus, qui percipiunt, sanctis in repletionem spiritus sancti ad confirmationem fidei in ueritate, ut te laudemus et glorificemus per puerum tuum Iesum Christum, per quem tibi gloria et honor, patri et filio cum sancto spiritu, in sancta ecclesia tua et nunc et in saecula saeculorum. [LXXI] Amen.'

p. 108   *Si quis oleum offert, secundum panis oblationem et | uini et non ad sermonem dicat, sed simili uirtute gratias referat dicens : 'Ut oleum hoc sanctificans das, Deus, sanitatem utentibus et percipientibus, unde unexisti reges, sacerdotes et profetas, sic et omnibus gustantibus confortationem et sanitatem utentibus illud praebeat.'

*Similiter, si quis caseum et oliuas offeret, ita dicat : 'Sanctifica lac hoc, quod quoagulatum est, et nos conquaglans tuae caritati. Fac a tua dulcitudine non recedere fructum etiam hunc oliuae, qui est exemplum tuae pinguidinis, quam de ligno fluisti in uitam eis, qui sperant in te.' In omni uero benedictione dicatur : 'Tibi gloria, patri et filio cum sancto spiritu, in sancta ecclesia et nunc et semper et in omnia saecula saeculorum. ⟨Amen⟩.[1]

p. 141 [*Stat.* 22.] And the people shall say : 'As it was, is and shall be to
(l. 21) generation of generation and to age of age. Amen.'

And the bishop shall say : 'And again we beseech thee, Almighty God, the Father of the Lord and our Saviour Jesus Christ, to grant us to receive with blessing this holy Mystery ; and that he may not condemn any of us, but cause worthiness in all them who take the reception of the holy Mystery, the Body and the Blood of Christ,
p. 142 Almighty Lord, our God.' |

The deacon shall say : 'Pray ye.' [And the bishop shall say] : 'God, almighty, grant to us the reception of thy holy Mystery as our strengthening ; nor condemn any amongst us, but bless all through Christ, through whom to thee with him and with the Holy Spirit be glory and might now and always and for ever and ever. Amen.'

The deacon shall say : 'As ye stand, bow down your heads.'

[The bishop shall say] : 'Eternal God, knower of that which is secret, to thee thy people bowed down their heads, and to thee they bent the hardness of heart and flesh ; look from thy worthy dwelling-place, bless them both men and women, incline thine ear to them and hear their prayer, and strengthen (them) with the might of thy right hand, and protect (them) from evil sickness, be their guardian for both body and soul, increase to them and to us also thy faith and thy fear, through thine only Son, through whom to thee with him and with the Holy Spirit be glory and might now and always and for ever and ever. Amen.'

And the deacon shall say : 'Let us attend.'

And the bishop : 'Holiness to holy ones.'

And the people shall say : 'One holy Father, one holy Son, one is the Holy Spirit.'

The bishop shall say : 'The Lord (be) with you all.'

And the people shall say : 'With thy spirit.'

And then they shall lift up glory ; and the people shall come in

[1] The Ethiopic omits this section on cheese, etc., and after the section on the oil proceeds with the eucharistic service, adding the following prayers, which the Latin omits. There is perhaps nothing in the body of these additional prayers that might not have come from the age of Hippolytus ; but they appear to differ in style and spirit from those which precede, and they have no traceable impression of the language and ideas of Hippolytus. Moreover the doxologies are of a later cast than that at the end of the great eucharistic prayer ; and the dialogues between the prayers are, there is every reason to believe, later interpolations. The whole of this section in the Ethiopic and absent from the Latin is almost certainly no part of the work of Hippolytus.

178   THE SO-CALLED EGYPTIAN CHURCH ORDER

for the salvation of their souls, in order that their sin may be remitted.

The prayer after that they have communicated: 'God, Almighty, the Father of the Lord and our Saviour Jesus Christ, we give thee p. 143 thanks, because thou hast imparted | to us the reception of thy holy Mystery: let it not be for guilt or condemnation, but for the renewal of soul and body and spirit through,' etc.[1]

And the people shall say: 'Amen.'

And the presbyter shall say: 'The Lord be with you all.'

Laying on of hand after they have received: 'Eternal God, almighty, the Father of the Lord and our Saviour Jesus Christ, bless thy servants and thy handmaids, protect and help and prosper (them) by the power of thine angel. Keep and confirm in them thy fear by thy greatness; provide that they shall both think what is thine and believe what is thine and will what is thine; grant to them peace without sin and anger through,' etc.

And the people shall say: 'Amen.'

And the bishop shall say: 'The Lord (be) with you all.'

And the people shall say: 'With thy spirit.'

And the deacon shall say: 'Go forth in peace.'

And after (that) the Ḳeddāsē is finished.

p. 108 *Cum autem praesbyter ordinatur, inponat manum super caput (cont.) eius episcopus contingentibus etiam praesbyteris et dicat secundum ea, quae praedicta sunt, sicut praediximus super episcopum, orans et dicens:

'Deus et pater domini nostri Iesu Christi, respice super seruum tuum istum et inpartire spiritum gratiae et consilii, praesbyteris[2] ut p. 109 adiuuet et gu-|bernet plebem tuam in corde mundo, sicuti respexisti super populum electionis tuae et praecepisti Moysi, ut elegeret praesbyteros, quos replesti de spiritu tuo, quod donasti famulo tuo; et nunc, domine, praesta indeficienter conseruari in nobis spiritum gratiae tuae et dignos effice, [LXXII] ut credentes tibi ministremus in simplicitate cordis laudantes te, per puerum tuum Christum Iesum, per quem tibi gloria et uirtus, patri et filio cum spiritu sancto, in sancta ecclesia et nunc et in saecula saeculorum. Amen.'

*Diaconus uero, cum ordinatur, eligatur secundum ea, quae praedicta sunt, similiter inponens manus episcopus solus, sicuti et praecipimus[3]. In diacono ordinando solus episcopus inponat manus

---

[1] '"Through, etc." means "through thine only Son, through whom to thee with him and with the Holy Spirit be glory and might, now and always and for ever and ever. Amen."' (Horner).

[2] Read (?) 'praesbyterii,' with the Eth. (mss b, e) and Test., and punctuate 'consilii praesbyterii, ut.'

[3] So the MS.

APPENDIX B

propterea, quia non in sacerdotio ordinatur, sed in ministerio episcopi, ut faciat ea, quae ab ipso iubentur; non est enim particeps consilii in clero, sed curas agens et indicans episcopo, quae oportet; non accipiens communem praesbyteri[1] spiritum cum, cuius participes praesbyteri sunt, sed id, quod sub potestate episcopi est creditum.

p. 110 Qua de re episcopus solus diaconum faciat, super praesbyterum | autem etiam praesbyteri superinponant manus propter communem et similem cleri spiritum. Praesbyter enim huius solius habet potestatem, ut accipiat; dare autem non habet potestatem. Quapropter clerum non ordinat; super praesbyteri uero ordinatione consignat episcopo ordinante. Super diaconum autem ita dicat:

'Deus, qui omnia creasti et uerbo perordinasti, pater domini nostri Iesu Christi, quem misisti ministrare tuam uoluntatem et manifestare nobis tuum desiderium, da spiritum sanctum gratiae et sollicitudinis et industriae in hunc seruum tuum, quem elegisti ministrare ecclesiae tuae et offerre[2]

p. 145 in thy holy of holies that which is offered to thee by thine or-
(l. 19) dained Chief Priests to the glory of thy name; thus without blame in pure life having served the degrees of ordination he may obtain the exalted[3] and thy honour[4], and glorify thee, through thy Son Jesus Christ our Lord, through whom to thee with him[5] (be) glory and power and praise with the Holy Spirit now,' etc.

Stat. 25. Concerning those who confessed and were condemned for
p. 146 the name of Christ. If | the confessor has been in the place of punishment, in chains for the name of Christ, they shall not lay hand on him for a ministering, for that is the work of a deacon: but (as for) that of the presbyterate, though he hath the honour of the presbyterate by that which he confessed, (yet) the bishop shall ordain him, having laid his hand upon him. And if the confessor was one who came not before the judges, and if he was not punished with chains, nor was shut up in prison, nor suffered any affliction, but withal was only derided for the name of his Lord, and was condemned to the least punishment, yet he professed all the work of the priesthood which is meet for him, they shall lay hand on him and make him a deacon.

And the bishop shall give thanks as we have already said. And it

---

[1] Read 'praesbyterii' (?).

[2] Here the Latin breaks off; the missing matter is supplied from the Ethiopic.

[3] Horner's text adds 'priesthood,' but the MS evidence is against this.

[4] One MS (c) reads 'in thy counsel' for 'and thy honour'; another (b) omits 'and thy honour.' Test., which is fairly close to Eth. here, seems to give the true sense: 'so that ministering without blame...*he may be counted worthy of this great and exalted office by thy good will*, praising thee continually through,' etc.

[5] Two MSS (b, v) omit 'with him.'

is (not)[1] necessary that we should mention the things which we have already said, that he should recite clearly and carefully, according as it is possible[2] for each to pray. And if there was one who could pray with devotion or use (make) a grand and elevated prayer, it is well[3]; and if he prayed and speaks praise with moderation [i.e.? moderately, sufficiently], no one shall prevent him from praying, who is true in right (faith)[4].

Stat. 26. Concerning the ordination of Widows. If a widow is ordained she shall not be sealed, but be made by the name. And if it was one whose husband died a long time, she shall be ordained. And if it was one whose husband had lately died, she shall not be trusted. But even if she is aged, she shall be tried many days, because lust will contend with those who are ordained to a place[5]. And the widow shall be ordained by word only, and she shall (then) be joined to the rest of the widows; and they shall not lay hand upon her, because she does not offer the sacrifice, nor has she a (sacred) ministry. For the sealing is for the priests because of their ministry, but (the duty) of widows is about prayer, which is the duty of all.

Stat. 27. Concerning the Reader and the Virgins and the Subdeacons, and concerning the grace of healing. To the reader who is ordained the bishop shall deliver the Scripture, and shall not lay hand upon him. As for the virgin also, he shall not lay hand on a virgin; but it is with her heart alone that she became a virgin. As for the subdeacons, he shall not lay hand upon a subdeacon, but he shall make (mention) over them of the name that they may minister to the deacons. As for the grace of healing, if some one says, 'I have acquired the grace of healing and prophecy,' they shall not lay hand upon him until his deed make evident that he is trustworthy.

Stat. 28. Concerning new persons who wish to be baptised, and concerning the occupations which they ought to leave off. New persons who are to be baptised[6] in order that they may hear the word, shall be brought to the teachers before all the people come in; and they shall ask them for what reason they sought the Faith. And they who brought

---

[1] So the Coptic (οὐ πάντως): see on this p. 65 above.

[2] So one MS (v) and Copt. ('according to the ability of each one'); text 'proper.'

[3] So one MS (c) and Copt. ('then it is good'); text, without sense, 'and he himself being good.'

[4] On the whole of this paragraph see pp. 65 ff.; it is evidently very corrupt in Eth.

[5] See on this p. 67 above. The Coptic has the right sense: 'For often the passions even grow old with him who gives place for them in himself.'

[6] Copt. 'who shall be brought in to the new faith.' There is no question of baptism in these sections, which deal with conditions for the catechumenate only.

them shall be witness as to whether they are able to hear (the word). And they shall examine them concerning their life, as to what they are; if they have a wife; or, if he was a slave, if his master allowed him to hear; and if his master was not witness for him, he shall go away: and if his master was an idolater, and they know not if there was permission of his master[1], that there be not scandal. And if he was a man who had a wife, or a woman who had a husband, they shall know if the man lives with his wife, and the wife with her husband. And if it was a man who did not live with a wife, he shall be instructed not to be a fornicator, but to marry according to law or to remain so. And if it was a man who had a devil, then he shall not hear the word of instruction.

Concerning the occupations of those whom they bring to exhortation[2]. If there was a pander, he shall be rejected. And if there was one who makes an image or a picture, they shall teach him that he should not make an image; and if he will not give up he shall be rejected. And if it was one who caused to go to the Circus, let him leave off or be rejected. And if it was one who teaches children the work of this world, then it is good if he leave off; yet if there is no other occupation by which he may live, he shall be excused. And let him who causes to go to idolatrous sacrifices leave off or be rejected.

And if there was one who hunts or teaches hunting, or who teaches fighting, or war, or | a driver of horses, let him leave off or be rejected. And if it was a priest of the gods, let him leave off or be rejected. A soldier of the prince they shall not receive; if he was condemned to kill, he shall not do (it); and if he does not leave off he shall be rejected.

Stat. 29. Concerning other persons. Either he who is a soldier among the believers, or a star-gazer or magician and the like[3], and a magistrate with the sword or a chief of prefects, and he who is clad in red[4], let him leave off or be rejected. And a catechumen or believer, if they wish to be a soldier, shall be rejected, because it is far from God. An adulteress, or a man without pity, or a man who does that which is not proper to be mentioned, shall be rejected, because they are alien

---

[1] 'and they...his master': so three MSS (b, d, e); but there are variants which shew that the reading is precarious.

[2] The reading is doubtful.

[3] 'Either...the like': the Coptic omits this; and in the Eth. it anticipates what is said just after.

[4] So Copt.: 'who is clad in purple.' C. H. has a curious perversion of this (can. xiii § 73): 'Omnis autem homo qui ad gradum praefecturae vel praecedentiae vel potestatis elevatus, *ornamento iustitiae quod est secundum evangelium non induitur*, hic a grege segregetur, neve episcopus coram illo oret.' Riedel renders 'ornamento iustitiae' by 'unarmedness' ('Waffenlosigkeit'). Here C. H. contemplates the case of *Christian* prefects, or the like, an idea foreign to the context.

and unclean, and it is not fitting to bring them to be ranked in the congregation of the Faithful. A star-gazer and a diviner by the sun, or soothsayer, or interpreter of dreams, or seducer of the people, or who sells clothes for forearms[1], or a maker of potions, let him leave off or be rejected.

Stat. 30. Concerning Concubines. If there is anything which we have omitted, decide as is proper[2]. The concubine of a man, if she was a servant, and if she has brought up her children, and if she did not come near another man beside him, they shall receive her, but if there was another man, she shall be rejected. And a man who has a concubine, | let him desist or marry according to law; and if he is not willing, let him be rejected. And if there is aught that we have omitted, decide as is proper, because we all have the Spirit of God.

Stat. 31. Concerning the time during which they shall hear instruction after (they have left off their) occupations. The catechumens shall remain three years hearing the word of instruction: yet if he was a good scholar and one who knows good conduct, no length of time need be required of him, but the conduct alone shall decide for him.

Stat. 32. Concerning the prayer of him who hears instruction, and his kiss. When the teacher has finished the admonition the catechumens shall pray alone, apart from the believers. And the women shall stand in (one) place in the church; and the women believers shall pray alone and the women catechumens. And if the prayer is finished, the catechumens shall not kiss with the believers, because their kiss is not yet pure. And the believers shall kiss one another; man shall kiss man and woman shall kiss woman, and males shall not kiss females. And all the women shall have their heads veiled with a pallium or with a mantle, and not with sindon only, because this is not what is allowed to them[3].

Stat. 33. Concerning the laying hand upon the catechumen. And after the prayer, when the teacher has laid his hand upon the catechumen he shall pray, and dismiss them. And if it was one belonging to the | church who teaches, or a layman, he shall do likewise. And if a catechumen was arrested for the name of our Lord Jesus Christ, he shall not be doubtful about the testimony (which he gives); because if they overpower and injure and kill him before he receives baptism for the forgiveness of his sin, he shall be justified; because he was baptised in his own blood.

Stat. 34. Concerning him who is baptised. When one has been chosen or who is ready for baptism, they shall examine their life; if

---

[1] Two MSS (a, b) read 'for lascivious ornament.'
[2] This clause is out of place, coming again at the end of the paragraph.
[3] The Coptic has: 'for this is not a veil' ($κάλυμμα$).

APPENDIX B   183

they lived in the fear of God before they are baptised, if they honoured the widow, or if they visited the sick, or if they did all good, and if there is witness in their favour from those who bring them; and if they have done thus they shall hear the Gospel from the time that they were set apart, and[1] they shall lay hand upon them every day and instruct them[2]. And when the day draws near on which they shall be baptised, the bishop binds every one of them by oath[3], that he may know if they are pure. And if one was found that was not pure, they shall put him aside by himself; for he has not hearkened to the word of instruction with faith; because it is not proper to baptise (*lit.* do to) an utter alien[?][4]. And they shall instruct those who shall be baptised that they should wash and be exorcised on the fifth day of the week; and if there was a menstruous woman among them, she shall be put aside, that she may be baptised on another day. And those who desire to be baptised shall fast on Friday, and the bishop shall |

p. 152 assemble all those who shall be baptised on the sabbath into one place, and shall command all of them (to make) prayer and prostration[5]; and when he has laid his hand upon them, let him exorcise every unclean spirit that he may flee away from them and not enter into them again. And when he has finished his exorcising, he shall breathe upon them, and they shall read to them and exhort them. And they who shall be baptised shall not bring with them any ornament of gold, nor ring nor gem of any kind; but every one of them shall give thanks[6], and it is fitting for them whom it beseems to bring their oblations also at the time.

Stat. 35. Concerning the order of Baptism, and the profession of the Faith, and the confession of sin at baptism, and the Oblation; and concerning the milk and honey. At the time of cock-crow they shall first pray over the water[7]. And it shall be either such as flows into the tank[8] of baptism or is caused to flow down upon it[9]. And it shall

[1] The Coptic takes 'from the time...apart' with what follows, omitting the 'and.' This seems preferable.

[2] Coptic 'in exorcising them.'   [3] Copt. 'let the bishop exorcise them.'

[4] Copt.: 'for it is never possible for the alien to be concealed.'

[5] Cf. Tertullian *de Bapt.* c. 20: 'Ingressuros baptismum orationibus crebris, ieiuniis et geniculationibus et pervigiliis orare oportet.'

[6] The Coptic shews that this is a misunderstanding; it has: 'Moreover let not those who will be baptised bring any other vessel except only that which each one will bring for the Eucharist: for it is right for him who is worthy to bring his oblation then.'

[7] Cf. St Cyprian *Ep.* LXX (Hartel p. 767): 'oportet vero mundari et sanctificari aquam prius a sacerdote.'

[8] The Coptic has the Greek word κολυμβήθρα.

[9] Copt. and Arab. are similar. C. H. and Test. compared together suggest that the oriental versions of Eg. C. O. represent a text that has been somewhat glossed. C. H. c. xix (Riedel): 'At cock-crow let them cause

be thus unless there is a scarcity of water; but if there is a scarcity they shall carry water to the tank, having drawn (it from a well). And they shall put off their garments and be baptised naked. And they shall baptise the little children first; and if they can speak for themselves, let them speak. But if they cannot, their parents shall answer the word instead of them, or one of their relatives. And afterwards they shall baptise the grown-up men. And afterwards all the women shall loose their hair; and they shall be forbidden to wear their ornaments and their gold; and none shall go | down having anything alien with them into the water. And whenever they baptise, the bishop shall give thanks over the oil which is in a vessel, and it is named mystic oil[1]; and he shall take other oil and exorcise in it, and it is named oil that has been exorcised from every unclean spirit. And there shall be a deacon who will carry the oil in which (Satan) was exorcised, and he shall stand on the left of the presbyter; and another deacon shall take the mystic oil, and shall stand on his right. And let the presbyter, having taken every one of those who shall be baptised, bid them renounce and say: 'I renounce thee, Satan, and all thine angels and all thine unclean work.' And when he has professed this, he shall anoint him with the oil which he made pure from all evil, saying: 'All unclean spirits shall depart from him.' Thus he shall deliver (him) to the bishop, naked, or to the presbyter—to him who stands at the water of baptism. Let the deacon go down with him to the water, and he shall say and instruct him: 'I believe in one God the Father almighty, and in his only Son Jesus Christ, ⌜our Lord and Saviour,⌝ and the Holy Spirit, ⌜giver of life to all creation, the Trinity equal in Godhead, one Lord, and one Kingdom and one Faith⌝ and one Baptism, in the holy Church ⌜Catholic, and life eternal.⌝ Amen.'[2]

p. 153

them to *go to the water* of a *clean running* ('brausenden' = ζέων?) stream that has been prepared beforehand by the hallowing.' Test. ii 8: 'Let them be baptized thus, *coming to the water*: now let that water be *pure and flowing*.' The use of Eg. C. O. in this chapter of Test. is in other respects clear and unmistakable; so that Test. may well give us here the true reading of Eg. C. O., or something nearer to it than is preserved in the oriental versions. The mention of the baptismal 'tank' may be a later addition.

[1] Copt., doubtless correctly, 'the oil of thanksgiving' (εὐχαριστία). Cf. Cyprian Ep. LXX (Hartel p. 768): 'porro autem eucharistia est unde baptizati unguntur oleum in altari sanctificatum.'

[2] The words which I have included in ⌜ ⌝ may safely be regarded as no part of the original work. We should probably also omit the comma after 'Baptism.' It is possible that the three oriental versions go back on a text which was here defective, and which accidentally omitted the first clause of the interrogatory Creed which follows; this I supply conjecturally from C. H. xix, which (as also Test.) seems to me to be here based on a sound text of Eg. C. O.

APPENDIX B   185

⟨Tunc descendat in aquas, presbyter autem manum suam capiti eius imponat cumque interroget his uerbis: 'Credisne in Deum patrem omnipotentem?'⟩[1] And he who shall be baptised shall say again thus: 'Yea, I believe.'
And thus he shall baptise him and lay his hand upon him, and upon him who answers for him.   (Hauler p. 110 cont.)...[LXXIII] manum habens in caput eius inpositam baptizet semel. Et postea dicat: 'Credis in Christum Iesum, filium Dei, qui natus est de spiritu sancto ex Maria uirgine et crucifixus sub Pontio Pilato et mortuus est et sepultus et resurrexit die tertia uiuus a mortuis[2] et ascendit in caelis et sedit ad dexteram patris uenturus iudicare uiuos et mortuos?' Et cum ille dixerit: 'Credo,' iterum baptizetur. Et iterum dicat: 'Credis in spiritu sancto et sanctam ecclesiam et carnis resur-|rectionem?' Dicat ergo, qui baptizatur: 'Credo.' Et sic tertia uice baptizetur. Et postea cum ascenderit, ungueatur a praesbytero de illo oleo, quod sanctificatum est, dicente: 'Ungueo te oleo sancto in nomine Iesu Christi.' Et ita singuli detergentes se iam induantur et postea in ecclesia ingrediantur. Episcopus uero manum illis inponens inuocet dicens: 'Domine Deus, qui dignos fecisti eos remissionem mereri peccatorum per lauacrum regenerationis spiritus sancti, inmitte in eos tuam gratiam, ut tibi seruiant secundum uoluntatem tuam; quoniam tibi est gloria, patri et filio cum spiritu sancto, in sancta ecclesia et nunc et in saecula saeculorum. Amen.' Postea oleum sanctificatum infunde⟨n⟩s de manu et inponens in capite dicat: 'Ungueo te sancto oleo in domino patre omnipotente et Christo Iesu et spiritu sancto.' Et consignans in frontem offerat osculum et dicat: 'Dominus tecum.' Et ille, qui signatus est, dicat: 'Et cum spiritu tuo.' Ita singulis faciat. Et postea iam simul cum omni populo orent, [LXXIV] non primum orantes cum fidelibus, nisi omnia haec fuerint consecuti. Et cum | orauerint, de ore pacem offerant.

Et tunc iam offeratur oblatio a diaconibus episcopo et gratias agat panem quidem in exemplum, quod dicit Gr⟨a⟩ecus antitypum, corporis Christi; calicem uino mixtum propter antitypum, quod dicit Graecus similitudinem, sanguinis, quod effusum est pro omnibus, qui crediderunt in eum; lac et melle mixta simul ad plenitudinem promissionis, quae ad patres fuit, quam dixit terram fluentem lac et mel, quam et dedit carnem suam Christus, per quam sicut paruuli nutriuntur, qui credunt,

---

[1] Test. (ii 8) has similarly: 'But when he who is being baptized goeth *down into the water, let him* that baptizeth him *say, putting his hands on him*, thus: "*Dost thou believe in God the Father Almighty?*" Let him that is being baptized say: "I believe." Let him immediately baptize him once. Let the priest also say,' etc. C. H. continues: 'Baptizandus respondet: "Ego credo." Tum prima vice immergitur aquae, dum (ille) manum capiti eius *impositam relinquit*' (cf. Eg. C. O. Lat. above).

[2] So Test.: 'alive from the dead.'

in suauitate uerbi amara cordis dulcia efficiens; aquam uero in oblationem in indicium lauacri, ut et interior homo, quod est animale, similia consequa[n]tur sicut et corpus. De uniuersis uero his rationem reddat episcopus eis, qui percipiunt; frangens autem panem singulas partes porrigens dicat: 'Panis caelestis in Christo Iesu.' Qui autem accipit, respondeat: 'Amen.' Praesbyteri uero si non fuerint sufficientes, teneant calices et diacones et cum honestate adstent et cum
p. 113 moderatione: primus, qui | tenet aquam, secundus, qui lac, tertius, qui uinum. Et gustent, qui percipient, de singulis ter dicente eo, qui dat: 'In Deo Patre omnipotenti.' Dicat autem, qui accipit: 'Amen.' 'Et domino Iesu Christo et spiritu sancto et sancta ecclesia.' Et dicat: 'Amen.' Ita singulis fiat. Cum uero haec fuerint, festinet unusquisque operam bonam facere[1]

p. 156 (to do good works) which please God, going in the right way and
(l. 16) united to the Church, performing this instruction, and progressing in the service of God. This we have taught you to be said openly concerning baptism and the ordinance of the Oblation; and behold, we have finished the instruction which we give you concerning the resurrection of the body, and the rest as it was written[2]. And if there is anything else which is right to be told, then the bishop shall tell it to those who are communicated. And they shall accept (it), and none shall know it except the believers, but only after they have first communicated. This is the holy blessing[3] which Yuhannes speaks
p. 157 of, that there was | written upon it a new name (which) no one knows except him who receives the blessing.

And on the sabbath and on the first day of the week the bishop, if it be possible, with his own hand himself shall deliver to all the people while the deacons break the bread. And the presbyters also shall break the delivered bread. And whenever the deacon approaches

[1] Here the Latin breaks off.

[2] The Coptic has this allusion to a teaching on the Resurrection thus: 'Now we have delivered these things to you in brief concerning the holy Baptism and the holy Oblation, since they have already instructed you concerning the resurrection of the flesh, and all other things according as it is written.' Comparing the Ethiopic and Coptic of this passage, I am inclined to think that we have here a reference to some earlier treatise on the Resurrection. There is nothing in Eg. C. O. itself to satisfy the allusion, nor could it well have contained originally anything in the nature of a discussion of the Resurrection. It may be recalled that St Jerome (de Viris illustribus, c. lxi) mentions amongst other works of Hippolytus which he had seen one de Resurrectione, and the statue catalogue mentions a work Περὶ θεοῦ καὶ σαρκὸς ἀναστάσεως.

[3] Horner says in a note: 'Corrupt reading of the unpointed Arabic, which really reads "ticket," referring to Revelation ii 17.' The Coptic has 'white stone' (ψῆφος).

APPENDIX B 187

the presbyter, he shall hold out his robe, and the presbyter himself shall take and deliver to the people with his hand. And on other days they shall give (it) according to the command of the bishop[1].

Stat. 36. Concerning Widows and Virgins, and at what time the bishop should fast. And they shall do as we have often said. The widows and virgins shall fast, and pray in the church. And the presbyters and the deacons shall fast at any time they will. And likewise shall the people fast. And the bishop ought not to fast, except at the time when all the people fast; because if they bring that which is proper to bring into the church, and no (one) can be refused; and (the man) having broken his own bread, he shall taste and eat with the other believers who are with him, who shall receive from the hand of the bishop a piece of delivered bread before they partake. It is Eulogia—everyone shall receive the bread which has been offered. For this is bread of blessing, and not the Oblation as of the Body of our Lord.

p. 158   *Stat.* 37. Concerning the time at which it is seemly | to eat. It is not proper for the catechumens to eat with the believers[2].

Before they taste and drink anything whatsoever, it is proper for them to take the cup and give thanks over it, and (then) drink and eat, for then they are pure. To the catechumens let them give the bread of blessing and the cup.

Concerning the impropriety of the catechumens sitting down with the believers at the table of the Lord.

(Hauler p. 113 cont.) [LXXV] qui praesentes estis, et ita acpulamini.

Catecuminis uero panis exorcizatus detur et calicem singuli offerant.

* Catecuminus in cena dominica non concumbat. Per omnem uero oblationem memor sit qui offert[3] eius, qui illum uocauit; propterea enim depraecatus est, ut ingrediatur sub tecto eius.

* Edentes uero et bibentes cum honestate id agite et non ad ebrietatem et non ut aliquis inrideat, aut tristetur qui uocat uos in uestra p. 114 inquietudine, | sed ut oret, ut dignus efficiatur, ut ingrediantur sancti ad eum. 'Uos enim,' inquit, 'estis sal terrae.' Si communiter uero omnibus oblatum fuerit, quod dicitur Graece apoforetum, accipite ab

---

[1] This paragraph ('And on the sabbath...the bishop') is not found in the Coptic or Arabic, and so is peculiar to Eth. But it is clear that the compiler of C. H. had it in his copy of Eg. C. O., since can. xxx § 214—xxxi § 216 presents an unmistakable parallel to it.

[2] This sentence is out of place, and should come after the heading (just below) as to the catechumens—'Concerning the impropriety,' etc.

[3] Eth. and Copt. 'who eats,' i.e. ὁ προσφερόμενος, not ὁ προσφέρων (cf. Schwartz *op. cit.* p. 40 n. 1).

188 THE SO-CALLED EGYPTIAN CHURCH ORDER

eo ; si autem ut omnes gustent, sufficienter gustate, ut et superet et quibuscumque uoluerit, qui uocauit uos, mittat tamquam de reliquiis sanctorum et gaudeat in fiducia. Gustantes autem cum silentio percipiant, qui uocati sunt, non contendentes uerbis, sed qu(a)e hortatus fuerit episcopus et, si interrogauerit aliquit, respondeatur illi ; et cum dixerit episcopus uerbum, omnis cum modestia laudans eum taceat, quandiu iterum interroget. Etiamsi absque episcopo in cena adfuerint fideles, praesente presbytero aut diacono similiter honeste percipiant. Festinet autem omnis siue a praesbytero siue a diacone accipere benedictionem [= εὐλογίαν ?] de manu. Similiter et catecuminus exorcizatum id ipsut accipiat. Si laici fuerint [LXXVI] in unum, cum moderatione agant. Laicus enim benedictionem facere non potes.

*Unusquisque in nomine domini edat. Hoc enim Deo placet, ut aemulatores etiam aput gentes | simus, omnes similes et sobrii.

p. 115

p. 159
(l. 19)
Concerning[1] the gift to the sick. The deacon in time of adversity shall give the sealing to the sick with diligence. If there is no presbyter to give that which is distributed, as much as ought to be received, (the deacon) shall give thanks and shall take count there of them who take (it) away, that they minister with care and give the Eulogia. If there is any who takes it away, let him bear it to the widows and the sick. And[2] let him who is occupied with the church take (it) away. And if he did not take it away, the next day, having added of that which was with him, he shall take it away. For it remained with him as bread of the poor.

Concerning[3] the bringing in of lamps at the supper of the congregation. When the evening has come, the bishop being there, the deacon shall bring in a lamp, and standing in the midst of the faithful, being about to give thanks, the bishop shall first give the salutation, |

p. 160 saying : 'The Lord (be) with you.' And the people also shall say : 'With thy spirit.' 'Let us give thanks to the Lord.' And they shall say : 'Right and just, both greatness and exaltation with glory are due to him.' And he shall not say : 'Lift up your hearts,' because that shall be said at the Oblation. And he prays thus, saying : 'We give thee thanks, God, through thy Son Jesus Christ our Lord, because thou hast enlightened us by the revealing of the incorruptible light; we having therefore finished the length of a day and having come

---

[1] The paragraph which follows is peculiar to Eth. It is not merely absent in the Latin but (in this position at least) definitely omitted, as also in the Coptic and Arabic. But it has parallels in C. H. (can. xxxii §§ 159ᵇ-163) and Test. (ii 11).

[2] The words 'And let...bread of the poor' will not be found in Horner's translation p. 159 l. 26. They were accidentally omitted there, and are supplied in the Collations (p. 384).

[3] This passage on the evening lamp is again peculiar to the Ethiopic. But there are parallels in C. H., Test. and A. C. viii (see above, pp. 112 ff.).

APPENDIX B

to the beginning of the night, and having been satiated with the light of the day, which thou hast created for our satisfaction, and now since we have not been deficient of the light of the evening by thy grace, we sanctify thee and we glorify thee through thy Son Jesus Christ our Lord, through whom to thee (be) glory and might and honour with the Holy Spirit now,' etc. And they shall say: 'Amen.' And having risen up therefore after supper, the children having prayed, they shall say the psalms, and the virgins[1]: and afterwards the deacon holding the mingled cup of the Presphora, shall say the psalm from that which is written Hālē luyā, [and] after that the presbyter has commanded: 'And likewise from those psalms[2].' And afterwards the bishop having offered the cup, as is proper for the cup, he shall say the psalm Hālē luyā; and all of them as he recites the psalms shall say Hālē luyā, which is to say: 'We praise him who is God[3]: glorified and praised is he who founded all the world

p. 161 with one word.' And likewise, the psalm having been | completed, he shall give thanks over the cup, and shall give of the fragments to all the faithful. And as they are eating their supper, those who are the believers shall take a little bread from the hand of the bishop before they partake of their own bread, for it is eulogia and not eucharist as the Body of our Lord[4].

p. 115 * Uiduas, si quando quis uult, ut aepulentur, iam maturas aetate
(cont.) dimittat eas ante uesperam. Si autem non potest propter clerum, quem sortitus est, escas et uinum dans eis dimittat illas et aput semet ipsas, quomodo illis placet, de re sumescant.

---

[1] Most of the MSS (b, c, d, e, v) have this curious order; but one of them (b) has 'of the virgins.' Is the word 'virgins' a corruption of something else? Test. has here: 'And let the little boys say spiritual psalms and hymns of praise by the light of the lamp' (ii 11).

[2] There seems to be some confusion here.

[3] A couple of MSS (a, d) add 'most high.'

[4] After this Eth. repeats a passage which has already occurred in a position corresponding to that of Lat., Copt. and Arab. It is as follows: '[And when the bishop speaks let every one be silent. And if the bishop is not present they shall receive the bread of blessing from the presbyter or from the deacon;] and when the bishop speaks let all be silent, nor shall one answer another, for the bishop shall ask them. And if the bishop is not (there), but only the faithful, at the meal, they shall take the Eulogia from the hand of the presbyter, and if the presbyter is not there, they shall take from the hand of the deacon; and the catechumens also shall take the bread, a mystic portion. And if there are laymen only they shall eat quietly: and for the laymen it is not proper that they should make the Eulogia' (for this in the Latin see Hauler p. 114; and for the other text of Eth., Horner p. 158 (fin.) to p. 159 l. 11). There is considerable difference in the text of the two pieces in Eth.

*Fructus natos primum quam incipiant eos omnes festinent offerre episcopo; qui autem offerit, benedicat et nominet eum, qui optulit, dicens: 'Gratias tibi agimus, Deus, et offerimus tibi primitiuas fructuum, quos dedisti nobis ad percipiendum, per uerbum tuum enutriens ea, iubens terrae omnes fructus adferre ad laetitiam et nutrimentum hominum et omnibus animalibus. Super his omnibus laudamus te, Deus, et in omnibus, quibus nos iuuasti, adornans nobis omnem creaturam uariis fructibus per puerum tuum Iesum Christum, dominum nostrum, per quem tibi gloria in saecula saeculorum. Amen.'

*Benedicuntur quidem fructus, id est uua, ficus, mala grania, oliua, pyrus, malum, sycaminum, Persicum, cera-|seum, amygdalum, Damascena, non pepon, non melopepon, non cucumeres, non cepa, non aleus nec aliut de aliis oleribus. Sed et aliquotiens et flores offeruntur.

[LXXVII] *Offeratur ergo rosa et lilium, et alia uero non. In omnibus autem, quae percipiuntur, sancto Deo gratias agant in gloriam eius percipientes.

*Nemo in Pascha, antequam oblatio fiat[1], percipiat. Nam qui ita agit, non illi inputatur ieiunium. Si quis autem in utero habet et aegrotat, et non potest duas dies ieiunari, in sabbato ieiunet propter necessitatem, contenens panem et aquam. Si quis uero in nauigio uel in aliqua necessitate constitutus ignorauit diem, hic cum didicerit hoc, post quinquagesimam reddat ieiunium. Typus enim transiit, quapropter secundo mense cessauit, et debet quis facere ieiunium, cum ueritatem didicerit.

*Diaconus uero unusquisque cum subdiaconibus ad episcopum obseruent; suggeretur etiam illi, qui infirmantur, ut, si placuerit episcopo, uisitet eos. Ualde enim oblectatur infirmus, cum memor eius fuerit prin-|ceps sacerdotum.

*Fideles uero mox, cum expergefacti fuerint et surrexerint, antequam operae suae contingant, orent Deum et sic iam ad opus suum properent. Si qua autem per uerbum catecizatio fit, praeponat hoc, ut pergat et audiat uerbum Dei ad confortationem animae suae; festinet autem et ad ecclesiam, ubi floret spiritus.

*Omnis autem fidelis festinet, antequam aliquid aliut gustet, eucharistiam percipere. Si enim ex fide percipit, etiamsi mortale quodcumque [LXXVIII] ⟨d⟩atum illi fuerit, post hoc non potest eum nocere.

*Omnis autem festinet, ut non infidelis gustet de eucharistia aut ne sorix aut animal aliud aut, ne quid cadeat et pereat de eo. Corpus enim est Christi edendum credentibus et non contemnendum.

[1] Copt. (and Eth. similarly) 'before the hour in which it is right *to eat.*' This suggests that the Latin translator has again treated προσφέρεσθαι as προσφέρειν (see above, p. 187 n. 3). The Greek may have been πρὶν ἢ δεῖν προσφέρεσθαι.

*⟨Calicem⟩ in nomine enim Dei benedicens accepisti quasi antitypum sanguinis Christi. Quapropter nolito effundere, ut non spiritus
p. 118 alienus uelut te contemnente illut delingat[1]: reus eris | sanguinis, tamquam qui spernit prae[pu]tium, quod conparatus est[2].

p. 181 *Stat.* 46. Concerning the Deacons and Presbyters, that they should assemble every day where the bishop is. Deacons therefore and presbyters shall assemble in the place where the bishop is, and he shall command them to go with him. And the deacons and presbyters shall not neglect to assemble every day, unless sickness prevents them. And having assembled together they shall instruct the churches; and when they have prayed they shall turn each to their own work.

Stat. 47. Concerning the grave. No man shall compel by his command to bury a man in a grave which is made for all the poor; but they shall give wages to the hired man who digs, and to him who guards that place, and to him who has care of those things[3]. And the bishop shall sustain him with what they offer to the churches. |

p. 182 *Stat.* 48. Concerning the times at which it is seemly to pray, and to hear instruction; and the sealing the forehead with the cross. All believing men and women, having risen at dawn, before they do any work, should wash their hands and pray to God; and then turn to their works: and if they tell them where is the word of instruction, everyone shall choose to go thither to the place of instruction: and he shall know this in his heart, and consider that that which he heard, it is God who speaks by the mouth of him who instructs, and it is he who dwells in the church, and he shall cause to pass away from him all wickedness in the day; and it shall be reckoned great loss to him who fears God, if he goes not to where is the place of instruction, and especially for him who can read. And if there is an instructor he shall not defer (from going) to the church and the place where is the instruction. Then indeed to him who speaks shall be given the word which he speaks. This is profit for everyone, (viz.) what he shall hear; and thou shalt hear that which thou thoughtest not there, and thou shalt profit by that which the Holy Spirit gave to thee by him who instructs: and thus thy faith shall become firm because of what thou hearest. And further, they shall tell thee in that place what it is proper for thee to do in thy house: and therefore all men shall hasten to go to the church and to the place wherein the Holy Spirit rises (like the sun).

[1] Hauler suggests that the words 'Deus enim tibi irascetur et tu' have fallen out after 'delingat.' He cites the Coptic: 'lest God be angry with thee, seeing that (ὡς) thou hast despised and become guilty,' etc.

[2] Read 'pretium quo conparatus est.' Copt.: 'in despising the price with which thou hast been bought.' The rest of p. 118 in Hauler is occupied by a piece of text which comes again, in its proper place, later (LXXX, Hauler p. 121). The two texts are printed below (p. 193) in parallel columns.

[3] Eth. is here corrupt. On the Coptic see above, p. 116 ff.

And if there is a day on which there is no instruction, every one shall stay in his house, and shall take the holy Scripture and read as well as he can, for it is good.

p. 183   And if thou wast in thy house, pray at the third hour | and glorify God : and if thou wast in another place, and if that hour has come, pray in thy heart to God ; because in that hour they stripped Christ and nailed him to the cross : and therefore the ancient law commanded to give the bread which they offer at the third hour, as a type of the holy Body and Blood of Christ ; and they sacrificed the lamb which was a type of the perfect Lamb, for Christ is the Shepherd, and he is the Bread which came down from heaven. And pray at the sixth hour ; for at that (hour) was the hanging of Christ upon the wood, and the day was divided and darkness came : and they shall pray at that hour a strong prayer ; and they shall be like the word which he prayed, and made all the world darkness : and the catechumens shall make a great prayer. And at the ninth hour he [? ye] shall be long in prayer with glorifying, that ye may join in glorifying with the soul of the righteous ones, glorifying the living

p. 119   [LXXIX] Deum, qui non mentitur, qui memor fuit sanctorum suorum et emisit uerbum suum inluminantem eos. Illa ergo hora in latere Christus punctus aquam et sanguem effudit et reliquum temporis diei inluminans ad uesperam deduxit. Unde incipiens dormire principium alterius diei faciens imaginem resurrectionis conpleuit. Ora etiam, antequam corpus cubili requiescat. Circa mediam uero noctem exurgens laua manus aqua et ora. Si autem et coniunx tua praesens est, utrique simul orate ; sin uero necdum est fidelis, in alio cubiculo secedens ora et iterum ad cubilem tuum reuertere. Noli autem piger esse ad orandum. Qui in nuptias conligatus est, non est inquinatus[1] ; qui enim loti sunt, non habent necessitatem lauandi iterum, quia mundi sunt. Per consignationem cum udo flatu et per manum spm[2] amplectens corpus tuum usque ad pedes sanctificatum est. Donum enim

p. 120 spiritus et infusio lauacri, sicuti | ex fonte corde credente cum offertur, sanctificat eum qui credidit. Hac igitur hora necessarium est orare ; nam et hi, qui tradiderunt nobis, seniores ita nos docuerunt, quia hac ⟨h⟩ora omnis creatura quiescit ad momentum quoddam, ut laudent dominum ; stellas et arbusta et aquas stare in ictu, et omne agmen angelorum ministrat ei, in hac ⟨h⟩ora una cum iustorum animabus laudare Deum. Quapropter debent hii, qui credunt, festinare hac ⟨h⟩ora orare. Testimonium etiam habens huic rei dominus ita ait : 'Ecce clamor fac-[LXXX]tus est circa mediam noctem dicentium : Ecce sponsus

---

[1] Schwartz (*loc. cit.*) corrects by the Coptic : 'Noli...orandum qui in nuptias conligatus es[t] : non es[t] inquinatus, qui enim,' etc.

[2] Schwartz expands 'sputum,' with the oriental versions (*op. cit.* p. 37 n. 2).

APPENDIX B 193

uenit, surgite ad occursum eius,' et infert dicens: 'Propterea uigilate; nescitis enim, qua hora uenit.' Et circa galli cantum exurgens, similiter; illa enim hora gallo cantante fili Istrahel Christum negauerunt, quem nos per fidem cognouimus, sub spe luminis aeterni in resurrectione mortuorum spectantes diem in hac. Itaque[1], omnes fideles agentes et memoriam eorum facientes et inuicem docentes et catecu-

p. 121 minos prouocantes neque temptari neque perire po-|teritis, cum semper Christum in memoriam habetis.

Semper autem imitare cum honestate consignare tibi frontem. Hoc enim signum passionis aduersum diabolum manifestum et conprobatum est, si ex fide itaque facis, non ut hominibus appareas, sed per scientiam tamquam scutum offerens; nam aduersarius, cum uidit uirtutem, quae ex corde est, ut homo similitudinem uerbi in manifesto deformatam ostendat, infugiatur non sputante sed flante sp⟨irit⟩u i⟨n⟩[3] te. Quod deformans Moyses in ouem Paschae, quae occidebatur, sanguem asparsit in limine et postes uncxit, designabat eam, quae nunc in nobis est fides, quae in perfecta oue est. Frontem uero et oculos per manum consignantes declinemus eum, qui exterminare temptat. Haec itaque si cum gratia et fide recta accipiuntur, praesta⟨n⟩t aedificationem in ecclesia et uitam aeternam credentibus. Custodiri haec consilium do ab omnibus bene sapientibus. Uniuersis enim audientibus apostolicam tra⟨ditionem⟩...	[*Semper[2] tempta modeste consignare tibi frontem. Hoc enim signum passionis aduersum diabolum ostenditur, si ex ⟨f⟩ide faciat quis, ut non hominibus placens, ⟨s⟩ed per scientiam sicut loricam offerens; siquidem aduersarius uidens uirtutem spiritus ex corde in similitudine lauacri in manifestum deformatam tremens effugatur, te non illum cedente, sed inspirante. Hoc ipsut erat, de quod (sic) in typo Moyses in oue, quae per Pascha immolabatur, sanguem asparsit in limine et duos postes unguens significat eam, quae nunc in nobis est, fidem in perfecta oue. Frontem et oculos per manum consignantes declinemus ab eo, qui exterminare temptat. Haec itaque cum gratia et fide recta gloriosae[4] cum audiantur, aedificationem praestant ecclesiae et uitam aeternam credentibus. Quae custodiri moneo ab eis, qui bene sapiunt. Uniuersis enim audientibus apos]

p. 185 (l. 26) (He who keeps the teaching of the Apostles) will not be hindered by any heretics. Those are the perverse who went astray and corrupted

---

[1] Schwartz (p. 37 n. 2) would read 'diem. Haec itaque.'
[2] This is the duplicate text which occurs out of place at Hauler p. 118 [LXXVIII].
[3] So Hauler; but his annotation shews that these two (?) words are almost entirely illegible. He supplies also '⟨te⟩' after 'sputante.'
[4] See above, p. 105 n. 2.

C. 13

p. 186 the teaching of the Apostles. And if men come from them [?]. | And thus many heretics increased, because they who listened to them are not willing to learn the commandment of the Apostles, but do only their own will, that which they chose; and it was that which was suiting their heart[1]. And if there was anything that we have diminished [=omitted?], brethren, God will reveal (it) to those who are worthy, while he steers the holy Church into quiet and a harbour.

[1] The Coptic has this more intelligibly thus: 'For if all should follow the tradition (παράδοσις) of the Apostles, these things which they have heard, and keep them, no heretics will prevail to lead them astray, nor any man at all. For thus the numerous heresies increased, because that they who were leaders would not learn the purpose (προαίρεσις) of the Apostles; but according to their own pleasures do what they like, not what is proper.' See p. 146 above.

INDEX

[*This Index is intended merely to supplement the Table of Contents.*]

Apophoreta; the giving of, a Roman custom, 158–159
Apostolic Constitutions (=A.C.), 8–9; contain interpolated form of prayer for ordination of bishop, 28–33; bk. viii based on Eg. C. O., 34, 54; bk. viii, ch. 1–2, 42, 43, 137, 140, 143, 147–148; bk. viii, ch. 3, omitted in but presupposed by Ep., 42–44; bk. viii, ch. 3 based on prologue of Eg. C. O., 43–44, 140–143; on ordination of reader, 46–48; contain interpolated form of prayer for ordination of presbyter, 51–52; prescribe both *Quadragesima* and Holy Week fast, 74; on the evening service, 113, 115; form of doxology in, 32, 153–154
Apostolic Tradition, Hippolytus's work on; identified by Achelis with C. H., 136–137; to be identified with Eg. C. O., 144–149
Athanasius; Ps.-Ath., *de Virginitate*, 32, 156–157 (on hours of prayer); *see* Canons

Baptismal features in C. H., 129; b. creed, 168 n. 2, 184, 185; b. water, 183 n. 9
Barnabas, Epistle of, 88–89, 166
Basil, St, 80, 109, 115; *see* Canons

Canons of Athanasius, 118–119
Canons of Basil, 82
Canons of Hippolytus (=C. H.), 2, 6, 9, 11 (etc.); supposed interpolations in, 60–62, 67–70, 72–73, 83, 114; not directly related to A. C. or Test., 36; in relation to Eg. C. O., 55–134; a late and unskilful redaction of Eg. C. O., 59, 132–134
Catacombs, 118–119
Cemetery, 116–117
Church; 'in Holy Ch.' (in doxology), 94, 154. [To the reference to Hippolytus, at p. 154, add one to the doxology of the first of the two prayers erroneously ascribed to St Cyprian: Hartel, Appendix, p. 146.]
Clement of Alexandria; on 'milk and honey,' 87–88; as to administering a cup of water to newly baptized, 91
Cock-crow; *see* Prayer
Communion (Holy); fasting C., 67–71; private C. at home, 79–81; formulae for administering, 78, 93–94; *see* Eucharist, Reservation
Constitutiones per Hippolytum; *see* 'Epitome'
Creed, baptismal, 168; in Eg. C. O. lacks first clause, 184, 185
Cross, sign of the; curious manner of making, 94, 99, 104–106; hands outstretched upon the cross, 165–166; *see* Plough
Cyprian, St, 80, 81, 105, 106, 183, 184

Demons; puffed away or expelled with breath, 105–106; early ideas concerning, 106
Descensus; *see* Hades

Didascalia, 149; on fixing time of Easter fast, 76–77; on ceremonial washings, 104

Dionysius of Alexandria; on the Easter fast, 75, 103

Doxology, 32, 153–154

East; turning to the E. at baptism, 129

Edification; passages in C. H. expressing the idea of, 56–59, 60 n. 1

Egyptian Church Order (=Eg. C. O.), 2–6; direct source of A. C., 34–35, 54; direct source of Test., 35–37; direct source of bishop's ordination prayer in Ep., 45, 54; direct source of ordinance as to reader in Ep., 49–50, 54; direct source of C. H., 59–63, 133; contains all that is shared by any two of the other Orders, 34 (cf. 26); identified with 'Αποστολικὴ παράδοσις of Hippolytus, 144–149

Epilogue to Eg. C. O., 145–146, 163–164

'Epitome' of A. C. viii (=Ep.), otherwise called *Constitutiones per Hippolytum*, 6, 7, 8, 9; an excerpt from A. C. viii in its present form, 7 (see also Appendix A); not excerpted from earlier form of A. C. viii, 39–40; not a first draft of A. C. viii, 41–46; prayer for ordination of bishop in, identical with that in Eg. C. O., 21–26; this prayer derived immediately from Eg. C. O., 45, 54; section on reader in, derived immediately from Eg. C. O., 46–50; name of Hippolytus attached to, 7, 50 n. 2, 135–140, 144, 147; some Ep. readings in bishop's ordination prayer, 150–154

Ethiopic version of Eg. C. O., 2, 4–5; passages peculiar to the, 36, 73, 112

Fasting; on Wednesday and Friday, 68, 73; in *Quadragesima*, 74–75; of widows, virgins, clergy, laity, bishop, 71–72; f. communion, 68–71; f. in Holy Week, 73–77; date of H. Week fast fixed by Jewish Passover, 75–77

Firstfruits; prayer over, 119–121, 167

Genuflexion of catechumens, 183

Hades; descent to, 107–108; angels in charge of, 167–168; souls of righteous in, 107–108, 167–168

Hermas, 64, 159

Hippolytus; his name attached to Ep., 7, 50, 135–140, 144, 147; his name attached to C. H., 7, 137–138, 144; his name originally in title of Eg. C. O., 136–138, 144, 147; H. the author of Eg. C. O., 144–149; parallels to Eg. C. O. in writings of, 160–168; *see* Canons

Interpolations, supposed in Eg. C. O., 111, 119, 155; see *Canons of Hippolytus*

Irenaeus, 87, 88

Jerome, St, 91, 92, 186

Lamp, service of the evening, 111–116

Latin version of Eg. C. O., 2–6

Lent; *see* Fasting

Logos, the; 'shewn' to be Son of God, 164–165

'Lost Church Order'; hypothesis of a, 2, 10, 33–34, 148

Milk and honey, administered to newly baptized, 87–94; forbidden to be placed on altar, 92–93

Minucius Felix, 24, 106

Monasticism, 127–128

Order, Church; *see* Egyptian, Lost, Roman

Origen, 80, 106

'Plough of the cross,' 24

Prayer; eucharistic p. in Eg. C. O. presents parallels to teaching and ideas of Hippolytus, 164–166. Ordination p. for bishop, 12–21 (synoptic table of texts); form of identical in Eg. C. O. and Ep., 21–26; this form interpolated in A. C., 26–33; the p. in C. H. contains interpolation embodying favourite idea of compiler, 56–59. Ordination p. for presbyter presents different problem from that

INDEX 197

for bishop, 50-52. Ordination p. for
deacon in C. H. shews marks of compiler's hand, 56-59. P. over firstfruits
in C. H. has marks of contact with
liturgy of St Mark, 120-121. Hours
of p., 96-111. Midnight p.; tradition
connected therewith, 108, 167. P. at
cock-crow connected in Eg. C. O.
with idea of resurrection, 102-103;
this a Roman feature, 103. Hours
of p. in Ps.-Athanasius *de Virginitate*,
156-157
Prologue, *or* preface, to Eg. C. O., 4,
43-44, 140-144; its style that of
Hippolytus, 160-161; its interpretation, 161-162

Quadragesima; *see* Fasting

Reservation of Eucharist; private, 79-80
Ritual, in C. H., 81-83
'Roman Church Order,' 2, 3

Saturnalia; giving of *apophoreta* at the,
158

Schwartz, E., vi, 35, 45, 49, 50, 62, 66,
71, 98, 99, 111, 119, 133, 142, 144,
148, 152, 153, 155, 158, 161, 163, 166,
187, 192, 193
Solomon, *Odes of*, 93, 107
Statutes of the Apostles, vii, 2

Teachers, lay, 64
Tertullian, 24 n. 1, 80, 81, 90, 104,
105, 107, 109, 117, 183
Testament of our Lord (=Test.), 6, 9,
11 (etc.); its relation to the other
Orders, 35-37; on service of evening
lamp, 112-114; possible connexion
of Test. with Ps.-Athanasius *de
Virginitate*, 157; echoes of the
Eg. C. O. prologue in, 169

Veil, of the church sanctuary, 83, 131
Vestments, 82, 132

Water, cup of, administered after
baptism, 90-92
Washing hands before prayer, 104
West; turning to w. at baptism, 129

ERRATUM

Page 163 (c) *for* συμβολή *read* συμβουλή

www.ingramcontent.com/pod-product-compliance
Lightning Source LLC
Chambersburg PA
CBHW070327230426
43663CB00011B/2238